Out FRONT!

British Motocross Champions
1960 - 1974

Ian Berry

Foreword by Jeff Smith, MBE

Panther Publishing

Published by Panther Publishing Ltd in 2011
Panther Publishing Ltd
10 Lime Avenue
High Wycombe
Buckinghamshire HP11 1DP
www.panther-publishing.com

© Ian Berry

The rights of the author have been asserted in accordance with the Copyright Designs and Patents Act 1988

Cover Picture
In the twilight of his motocross career, two-time World Champion Jeff Smith is pictured at the 500 British Grand Prix at Farleigh Castle in July, 1967, where he finished 3rd overall. (Photo by Cecil Bailey, supplied by Nick Haskell)

All rights reserved, no part of this publication may be reproduced, stored in a retrieval system or transmitted, in any form or by any means, electronic or mechanical, including photocopying, digital copying, and recording without the prior permission of the publisher and/or the copyright owner.

ISBN 978-0-9564975-3-6

Dedication

I would like to dedicate this book to my father, Roy Berry, as without his interest in motorcycle sport I am sure this book could not have been written. He got me hooked on scrambling and it was he who introduced me to the pleasures of off-road riding, when he built up my very first bike, a 197cc Villiers-engined Bantam. I spent many happy hours in his company at both trials and scrambles in East Anglia during the 1960s and '70s and it's a period of my life that I look back on with great affection.

Acknowledgements

Firstly, I have to thank Dave Bickers, Jeff Smith, Arthur Lampkin, Fred Mayes, Alan Clough, John Banks, Tony Davis for his comments on his brother Malcolm, Bryan Wade, Bryan Goss, Andy Roberton and Vic Allan. They gave me their time, showed me great courtesy and it was a real pleasure for me to meet them. Their memories and insights help to bring the book to life and I cannot thank them enough.

A special word of thanks also goes out to the photographers who supplied the magnificent images portrayed in the book. I would especially like to thank Malcolm Carling, Ray Daniel, Nick Haskell, (who supplied the photographs taken by Cecil Bailey), and Brian Holder, who supplied the bulk of the photographs. Your time and effort are greatly appreciated. Thanks are also due to Bill Brooker, who supplied some photographs, Bob Light, who supplied the Bill Cole photographs, Dave Kindred and Maurice Rowe. The captions to the photos identify the photographer or source either directly by name, or to save repetition, by their initials. Thus

BC	Bill Cole	MC	Malcolm Carling
BH	Brian Holder	MR	Maurice Rowe
CB	Cecil Bailey	NH	Nick Haskell
DK	Dave Kindred	RD	Ray Daniel
IB	Ian Berry		

Thanks are also due to Richard Rosenthal, the former EMAP archivist, who was very helpful and encouraging when I first started work on the project, as was Brian Crichton, the former editor of the Classic Bike. More recently Jacqui Harris, the archivist at Bauer Media, provided invaluable help and I am indebted to her for her patience and diligence.

I would also like to thank Rollo Turner at Panther Publishing for giving me the opportunity to publish this work. Throughout the project he has given me unwavering support and encouragement and I am greatly indebted to him.

Finally, I would like to thank my wife, Xana, my children, Thomas and Lauryn, and the rest of my family for showing so much support over the years and for the sacrifices they have made in order for me to be able to complete this book. Thank you.

Ian Berry

About the Photographers

Cecil Bailey (1918-2008)

Cecil Bailey was born in Liverpool but moved to Southampton at the age of three. As a school leaver, he was employed at the Supermarine works in Southampton and before turning to photography he was a talented all-round motorcyclist, trying his hand at hill climbs, trials, grass track and scrambles. His skills were put to good use during the war, when he served as a despatch rider.

He returned to motor cycle sport after the war and soon won a factory ride with BSA, competing in both grass track and scrambles events. In 1947 he was selected for the British team to contest the inaugural Motocross des Nations in Holland. The same year he started a successful career with Southampton Speedway. He then joined Plymouth in 1950, before retiring from motorcycle sport the following year.

Turning to photography, he initially covered speedway events, before landing a job as a staff photographer for *Motor Cycle News* in 1958, where he stayed for thirty years.

Cecil was an outstanding photographer, covering events across the length and breadth of the British Isles, getting amazing results with his medium format cameras, as the photos on the following pages testify.

I am indebted to motorcycle sport photographer Nick Haskell, for the use of Cecil Bailey's photographs.

Malcolm Carling

Born in Ripon, Yorkshire in 1932, Malcolm Carling moved to Manchester in 1953 on completion of his national service. After attending motorcycle meetings with his father, he started taking photos in the mid-50s, mainly covering scrambling and trials.

In the late 1950s, in company with fellow photographer Harry Stansfield, he launched a ground breaking off-road magazine entitled *Event*. Mainly photographic in content, this potentially brilliant publication ultimately failed when Carling and Stansfield couldn't find a reliable outlet.

In 1961 Malcolm began work with *Motor Cycle News*, covering events throughout the country but especially in the north of England. During the 1960s and '70s he was without doubt one of the leading photographers in the country and later in his career he went on to cover the road race scene for *MCN*, taking in the World Championships.

Ray Daniel

His first whiff of *Castrol R* came as a 4 year-old, when the 1949 ISDT passed through his tiny village, nestled in the Cambrian Mountains in Wales. The whole village turned out on the street cheering on the competitors; the British Trophy Team emerged triumphant, as they would the following year.

Many years later at the nearby Lampeter Scrambles, Ray began taking pictures and eventually his efforts were published in *Motor Cycle News*. He contributed to this weekly on a freelance basis for 25 years, before turning to the road racing World Championships, where he worked for the German language weekly *Motor Sport Aktuell* based in Zurich.

During the 1960s and '70s he travelled all over Britain every weekend, covering the big events as well as making forays to many of the European motocross events. His book of images *Motocross Rich Mixture* (Ariel Publishing 2001), captures the magic of the period.

Brian Holder

Brian Holder was a motorcyclist for many years and, in his own words, a pretty average trials rider. However, in 1961, at the age of 26, he was part of a *Motorcycle Mechanics* team that rode in the Scottish Six day Trial on new works James 250cc trials machines, alongside official works riders. Brian continued riding in trials, but also started taking pictures of trials, scrambles (motocross) and road racing. His pictures appeared in *Motorcycle Sport*, *Motor Cyclist Illustrated* and later in *Motor Cycle News* and various overseas magazines.

It was soon clear that he was a better photographer than trials rider, so he hung up his boots in 1964 to concentrate on motorcycle photography. He eventually became *Motorcycle News'* London-based freelance, covering events in the east and southeast each weekend, and many international road racing, motocross, speedway, trials and sprint events for *MCN* and *Motorcycle Sport*. He is now retired, and is in the process of setting up a digital library of pictures from the 750 events he covered, to meet the demand for pictures from agencies, riders and writers.

Bill Cole (1911-2005)

Bill Cole, a resident of Staunton, Gloucestershire, was a keen motorcyclist and self-taught photographer. In 1946, he bought himself an early Leica IIIc with a f3.5 50mm Elmar lens, which cost the equivalent of three months wages. For the next fifteen seasons he combined the two interests, photographing motor cycle sport wherever it could be found.

His first love was scrambles. He photographed the riders because they were his friends and they welcomed the results, as the pictures were of the highest quality. He travelled to road racing at Eppynt, Aberdare Park and Blandford; to major scrambles at Hawkstone Park, the Experts Grand National at Rollswood, the Sunbeam Point-to-Point and more.

Motor cycling researcher Bob Light is now the custodian of Bill's sporting pictures.

CONTENTS

Foreword by Jeff Smith, MBE	vii
Introduction	viii
The History of Motocross in Britain	1
Overview of the British Motocross Championships 1951-1974	10
Brief History of the European and World Championships	11
Scrambles and Motocross Winners 1951-1974	12
Glossary of Terms	14
Dave Bickers: Full of Eastern Promise	15
Jeff Smith: From Barr Beacon to the Top of the World	43
Arthur Lampkin: Yorkshire's Finest	71
Fred Mayes: Steady Freddie	89
Alan Clough: Good Things Come To Those Who Wait	103
John Banks: The Man Who Would be King	123
Malcolm Davis: Cheltenham Gold	143
Bryan Wade: Born to be Wild	169
Bryan Goss: From Grasstrack Hopeful to Scrambling Champion	195
Andy Roberton: The Little Man with a Big Talent	217
Vic Allan: The Highlander Who Rewrote History	239
The End of an Era	263
Map of Circuits used in the British Championship Rounds	264

A snow flurry at the gates of Buckingham Palace fails to dampen the spirits of Jeff Smith, as he proudly exhibits the MBE he has just received from the Queen Mother. He is pictured with his wife Irene, sister to Johnny Draper, daughter Christine and son James. (Photo supplied by Jeff Smith)

Foreword

by

Jeff Smith, MBE

What a first class account Ian Berry has written of the British Motocross Championship in the 1960s and early '70s. In a lucid and sympathetic hand he draws the characters and action into a spell binding story. Frequent use of quotations from the main players adds immediacy to the text.

These events took place 40 years ago so there is now some perspective. Ian covers a time during which 30 championships, 250 and 500cc, were up for grabs to literally hundreds of fit young men with good quality machines. Yet there are only 11 names covering the British Championships during those years. Clearly there was some dominance! David Bickers and I had long runs and Banks, Wade, Davis and Arthur Lampkin showed their class. What is even more telling to my mind is fate's cruel handling of at least two of our contemporaries. Don Rickman and Vic Eastwood were both superlative riders and fired with determination and ambition, yet the famous fickle finger never pointed to them.

None of us revels in his British Motocross Championships or regrets that we never had one, but for all of us and the many fans there is real pleasure in seeing such an excellent and well researched book bringing back half forgotten memories and a happy time.

During those years I was very focused on winning and was successful in keeping myself isolated from most of my fellow riders and thus avoiding distractions. I have learned more things about my comrades in competition which, because of the busy rush of events, were unknown and to some extent immaterial at the time.

Ian has done a magnificent job of recreating those wonderful days and reconnecting many of us who had drifted apart. I recommend this book to anyone who has the slightest interest in the late days of scrambling and the early days of motocross. It is truly a fine read.

Jeff Smith, MBE
July 2010

Introduction

The original idea for this book came to me back in the old millennium, when my father, in searching for the ideal birthday gift for his errant son, despatched a couple of videos to my home in Portugal. Now, like all dads, me included, he doesn't always get the birthday presents quite right, but on this occasion he really hit the spot! The tapes in question were entitled *Scrambling in the '50s* and *The Roughriders (Also featuring Three in Europe)* and they grabbed and held my attention from the first minute to the last.

Dad and I had passed many a happy hour at scrambles meetings during the 1960s and '70s and after watching the exploits of such legendary scrambles riders as Geoff Ward, Phil Nex, Dave Curtis, John Giles and the Rickman brothers, not to mention the BSA factory team of John Banks, Dave Nicoll and Keith Hickman flying the flag in Europe, the memories came flooding back. As a result I scoured the classic motorcycle mags of the day (pre-internet) in search of books that I could read on the subject, but unfortunately, I drew a blank. So I began to jot down some notes of my own and the project started to take shape and now, after more years than I care to mention, the book is in your hands which gives me immense satisfaction.

My principle objective in writing this book was to paint a picture, not only of the motocross scene in Britain during the 1960s and '70s, but also of the riders who captured the British Championships during this period. In doing so, my task has been made easier by the inclusion of the wonderful photographs that grace the pages of this book and I am greatly indebted to all of the photographers.

I chose to cover the period 1960 to 1974 mainly for logical reasons, though I must admit that, personally, I find it the most interesting era in off-road motorcycling. 1960 ushered in an exciting new decade in the sport and brought with it a new national 250cc championship to add to the 500cc championship which had existed since 1951. As for the cut-off, 1974 seemed a logical point, as we saw the dawning of a new era in 1975 with the introduction of a single category British Championship.

In researching this book it has been my great pleasure to meet, and while away a few priceless hours with, my childhood heroes and I would like to take this opportunity to thank them all for their cooperation and patience, without which the book would have proved impossible to write. Of course they were the stars of the day and they take a starring role on these pages, but I trust you will agree that it is a role that they richly deserve.

In closing, I would just like to add that I hope reading the book will bring you as much pleasure as writing it has for me.

Ian Berry, June 2010

From Little Acorns...
The History of Motocross in Britain

What a wonderfully evocative photo of Britain's first recorded scramble, the 'Southern Scott' which took place on Camberley Heath in 1924. (Photographer unknown)

The Motocross and Supercross (stadium) events taking place globally today are a far cry from the pioneering off-road events held in Britain before the Second World War. At that time machines were standard road going models, with very few, if any, modifications, and competitions tended to be long, single lap affairs with the emphasis on reliability. The first official 'Scramble' was organised by the Camberley Club in Surrey, inspired by the long distance Scott Trial which was run on the wild and windy West Yorkshire moors and is widely recognised as the first off-road competition ever.

In 1914 Alfred Scott, founder of Scott Motorcycles, threw down a challenge to his employees; to ride and navigate their way from the factory in Shipley across the Yorkshire Dales to Bumsall. The outbreak of the First World War curtailed sporting events, but the Scott workers re-established the event themselves from 1919 to 1926 and it was their efforts that so impressed the Camberley Club in Surrey. The first Southern Scott Scramble, took place in 1924 on a demanding course laid out on Camberley Heath, which incorporated two very steep climbs and contained a three-mile straight, where the top riders of the day reputedly hit 65 mph! Competitors had to complete two laps of a thirty plus mile course, one in the morning and the other in the afternoon. Needless to say, the event was very demanding and the consequent drop out rate was very high. Curiously enough the race was won by an AB Sparks, riding what else but a Scott!

Post-war boom

Off-road events grew in popularity and continued to be organised between the wars, with tracks like the Wakes Colne circuit in Essex, where racing continues to this day, being established as early as 1934. But it was in the post-war Britain of the late '40s and early '50s that the sport really began to blossom, when the big motorcycle manufacturers realised that good results in competition motorcycling equated to good publicity and, hence, increased sales. In addition, development on the race tracks inevitably filtered through to the road-going models of the day, which was where the real money was being made.

As a result, the big factories such as Matchless, BSA and Ariel began to develop 'Sports' models, specifically intended for off-road use. However, at this time although scrambling was increasing in popularity, the bulk of off-road competition was still in observed trials. Obviously, when 350 lb motorcycles with very limited suspension were raced on the rough stuff, both rider and machine took a real hammering and whereas a machine intended for trials use could have some weight trimmed off, those which would be raced off-road had to be strong enough to withstand the knocks.

During this period, the leading riders were the likes of Fred Rist, Bill Nicholson, and Ray Scovell, who all rode for the Birmingham Small Arms (BSA) factory, Bob Ray, Harold Lines and Jack Stocker who were Ariel mounted, Jim Alves and Bob Manns on Triumphs, Basil Hall and Eddie Beasant on Matchless, future AMC competitions manager Hugh Viney riding for AJS and a certain young Geoff Duke, on a Norton, who in those days was mixing his road-racing with scrambling. It was this crop of talented riders that formed the nucleus for the British teams that would dominate the early years of the blue riband *Motocross des Nations*, a team event established back in 1947 when it was held at Duinrell, Holland.

By the early '50s, a new generation of riders such as Brian Stonebridge, Les Archer, Johnny Draper, John Avery and Geoff Ward were beginning to make their mark on the scrambling scene and the bikes were also evolving to meet the increasing demands being placed on them by the riders. The use of 'telescopic' forks had become *de rigueur* in competition in the post war years, but it was the addition of 'swinging arm' rear suspension units in the early '50s that transformed off-road racing, as it meant that the machines could cover the ground much quicker, in turn making racing a far more interesting spectacle.

A scrambles championship

It was during this period that the first British Championship, then known as the 'ACU Scrambles Drivers' Star', came into being in 1951, when Ward on his AJS became the first Champion with a clear advantage over Norton mounted Archer, and Stonebridge, who at that stage of his career was riding for Matchless. The following season, 1952, the inaugural British Grand Prix was held at Nympsfield in Gloucestershire. The victor was 23 year-old Stonebridge, followed home by Phil Nex riding for BSA and another emerging talent, Derek Rickman, also on a BSA to complete a one-two-three for Britain.

Despite such success on home soil, most of the British riders initially found it difficult to adjust to the continental motocross style meetings. These differed from scrambles (run on the basis of heats and finals, typically four to six lap 'sprints' lasting about 15 minutes) in that the continental races usually comprised two long races of about 40 minutes which naturally required great stamina. Admittedly, a few riders such as Harold Lines and Basil Hall had been riding for many years on the continent to good effect and in 1952 the reigning British Champion, John Avery, enjoyed some success in the very first European Championship, becoming the first Briton to win a round of the series with victory in Sweden. He went on to finish the season

Bill Nicholson was the archetypal post war off-road factory rider, riding in trials throughout the winter months and scrambling during the summer. He is pictured at the 1948 Gloucester Grand National at Tirley. (BC)

Geoff Ward was the winner of the first ACU Scrambles Drivers' Star in 1951. Here he is pictured racing his factory AJS at the 1951 Inter-Centre Team event at Shotover near Oxford. (BC)

Cheltenham's John Draper was Britain's first European Motocross Champion in 1955. Known for his prowess in wet conditions, here he is pictured ploughing the BSA through the deep sand of the Dutch GP. (Photographer unknown)

in 3rd place, behind the Belgian duo of Victor Leloup on the Belgian FN and Auguste Mingels on a Matchless. Although British riders weren't dominant in those early days of the European Championship, British-built bikes were, with Matchless, BSA and a very potent Norton, in the hands of Les Archer, leading the way.

Britons to the fore in Europe

Archer, who came from a motorcycle racing family (father, Les Snr, was a top road and track racer, whilst his grandfather had been an ace tuner), was one rider who experienced a lengthy learning curve when he started racing on the continent. In his book *Scrambles and Motocross*, written towards the end of his career in 1962, he recalled: *Easter 1952 saw the end of my military service and the start of my Continental racing. In company with Basil Hall, by then a well-known figure on the Continent, I attended two meetings in Belgium and we both returned battered and extremely shaken up. ... Although I had had five years' experience it took another twelve months before I felt at home on the Continental circuits or got accustomed to all the tricks of a clutch start.*

But he did just that, and by 1953 he had beaten the great Mingels at the Luxembourg GP in a race that went all the way to the line. Curiously, it was Mingels who encouraged Archer to have a serious crack at the European title, which he did for the first time in 1955 winning the French and Luxembourg GPs. That season saw BSA's brilliant all-rounder John Draper crowned Britain's first European Champion pipping Sweden's Bill Nilsson by a point, who in turn finished a point ahead of his compatriot Sten Lundin to complete a one-two-three for BSA.

Archer may have been overshadowed by Draper in '55, but the tables were turned the following year when the Aldershot man became the first rider to win the title with the maximum score possible; four wins from the best four rides to count. That particular year, British bikes completed a whitewash, with Draper on his BSA as runner up, Belgium's Nic Jansen riding a Matchless in 3rd and the BSAs of Lundin, Nilsson and Geoff Ward completing the rout.

Ward's dominance ended by Jeff Smith

On the domestic front, Geoff Ward was definitely the man to beat following up on his ACU Star for 1951, with wins in '53 and '54, before a very determined Jeff Smith succeeded him in '55, thereby beginning a very

Les Archer was one of the first British riders to race almost exclusively on the continent. After a three year 'apprenticeship' racing all across Europe he was crowned European Champion in 1956. Here he is pictured racing on home soil in the 1953 Motocross des Nations at Brands Hatch, Kent. (BC)

History of Motocross in Britain

Maurice Rowe's photo catches 20 year-old Jeff Smith on his way to the first of his five 500 British GP wins at Hawkstone Park in July 1955. The same year he won the first of his nine national titles, when he took the ACU Scrambles Drivers' Star.

By the mid '50s the Dot scramblers had become the lightweight two-stroke of choice for aspiring clubmen. Here J Hilton of Wolverhampton, launches the 197 Dot downhill in the support races at the 1955 500 British GP at Hawkstone Park. (MR)

long and successful run of form. Over the coming years Smith would amass no less than nine national titles, with his last championship win coming in 1967. In the late '50s it was Geoff Ward's good friend Dave Curtis on his Matchless, who was Smith's main rival and they enjoyed many memorable battles during this period. Arthur Lampkin, who was one of Smith's closest friends during his long career, also put up a stiff challenge to his supremacy, even though they were teammates at BSA. Indeed only Curtis ('58) and Lampkin ('59) were able to temporarily break the stranglehold he held on the shield, following a lull in racing in 1957 due to petrol rationing as a result of the Suez crisis.

Two-stroke development

But let's backtrack a little here. During the late '40s and early '50s a very talented rider on an unlikely machine was making his presence felt. The rider was Bill Barugh and the bike the diminutive Villiers-powered Dot, the creation of Burnard Scott Wade. Barugh shook the motorcycle world at the 1952 British Grand Prix at Nympsfield, where he thrilled the crowds as he fought tooth and nail with American visitor Bud Ekins on a Matchless, narrowly missing out on fifth place at the finish. Ekins, who was a larger than life character, then reputedly sought out Barugh to ask him, *"What in God's name have you got in that thing?"* In their cavalier fashion, Barugh and teammates Reg Pilling and young Terry Cheshire, enlivened meetings across the length and breadth of the country on their 125 and 200cc models, during the mid '50s.

Meanwhile, Brian Stonebridge had moved from Matchless to BSA in 1954, where his exemplary engineering skills were soon being put to good use. Stonebridge was without doubt one of the greatest ever development riders and he, like Barugh, was soon pitting the 125cc Bantam model against the 350cc machines which at that time were considered 'lightweights'. Indeed, Stonebridge would gladly take on, and frequently beat, all but the best of the 500s.

His ability to get the best out of an underpowered, but vastly lighter two-stroke did not escape the attention of a certain Bertram Greeves, who was pioneering a purpose-built two-stroke scrambler of his own down at Thundersley on the Thames estuary.

The Greeves evolves

In 1957 Stonebridge was invited to join Greeves in a developmental role which marked the start of one of the British motorcycle industry's great success stories. Greeves couldn't have asked for a better development rider and publicity vehicle, as Stonebridge rode their machines throughout the year in trials and scrambles, before taking part in the Swiss round of the new 250cc European Championship. There, in his first ever Grand Prix for Greeves, he rode a 197 model to the runner-up spot behind the full 250 Jawa of Czech ace Jaroslav Cizek, who would go on to become European Champion the following year.

At this time there was a plethora of 'lightweight' British machines emerging, from companies such as Cotton, DMW, Francis-Barnett, James and Norman (invariably powered by the ubiquitous Villiers engines), which with a good rider on board were a match for most of the big four-strokes. This movement effectively marked the beginning of the end for the big British four-strokes. More significantly, in the long run, European manufacturers such as Husqvarna, CZ and Maico were producing 250cc two-strokes of their own which would dominate the early years of the European Championship.

Dave Bickers links up with Stonebridge

In late 1958, the raw, but super-talented Dave Bickers joined Stonebridge at Greeves, their goal being to win the following year's European Championship. Stonebridge continued to race and develop the bike, which by now was a full 250 with a square barrel and head, riding it to a first race win and a creditable second

The immaculate style of Brian Stonebridge, racing the 250cc Greeves at the 250 British GP at Beenham Park, Berkshire, in July 1959. (CB)

overall at the inaugural British GP at Beenham Park. Bickers, who had failed to finish the first race, chased Champion in the making, Cizek, to 2nd in race two. However, during the season Stonebridge, in his search for a more competitive machine, built up a 250 OHC NSU-powered Greeves, which he rode in some of the championship rounds. However, Bert Greeves, whose motto was always 'What the factory tests this year, will be yours to buy and ride next year', was not so keen on the project though he couldn't prevent a John Griffith penned description of the bike appearing in the March 26, 1959 edition of *Motor Cycling*. Griffith noted that, '…during a visit last week to the factory I gathered that quite a lot of 'blind-eyes' have been turned in Stonebridge's competition shop over the past few months!'

Great season for Stonebridge ends tragically

Stonebridge had an excellent season, winning rounds in Switzerland, Belgium and Italy, though there is still some doubt as to whether he had won on the Villiers or the NSU-powered bike. Though it is highly unlikely that the stoically patriotic Greeves would ever have sanctioned a link up with the German company, we will never really know how far the project might have gone. A shoulder injury from the Dutch GP sidelined Stonebridge and before he could return to competition he was tragically killed in a road accident whilst travelling with Bert Greeves.

Four-stroke hybrid

Whilst Greeves were developing their two-stroke lightweight, down on the South coast in New Milton, Hampshire, the Rickman brothers, Derek and Don, who had been factory riders for Royal Enfield and Dot, were working on a project of their own. They felt that the competition machines produced by the leading manufacturers were not developing as rapidly as they should have been and took their lead from what the 'Super Swedes', such as Bill Nilsson and Sten Lundin were doing in the 500cc World Championship. Riding exquisitely prepared bikes, such as the Crescent, Monark and later the Husqvarna, which, to rub salt into the wounds, all made good use of British components, and ably supported by riders such as Lars Gustafsson, Gunnar Johansson and Rolf Tibblin, they had replaced the British riders as the dominant force in motocross.

So, with the help of their mechanic, 'Tiny' Canfield, and encouragement from their benefactor, Harold Wakefield, the Rickmans set about building a more competitive machine. The first bike, which made its debut at Bulbarrow, Dorset in 1959 was on the face of it another TriBSA; a Triumph engine slotted into a BSA Gold Star frame. However, a closer inspection would reveal that they had done everything they could to select the best and the lighest components available. The Rickmans appropriately christened the bike, the *Métisse*, which means mongrel in French, and it was a name that stuck and would go on to sell in great numbers worldwide.

The brothers went on to race and develop the bikes over the coming seasons, with innovative ideas, such as their own oil-in-the-frame chassis made from Reynolds 531 tubing, oil air filters and extensive use of glass fibre for the petrol tank, mudguards and side panels. But ultimately, they were defeated in their aim to mass produce a world-beating British motocross machine by the lethargy of the British motorcycle industry, as despite having discussions with BSA, Triumph and AMC, they never managed to secure a readily available supply of engines.

Four-stroke development; too little too late?

Meanwhile the leading British manufacturers were turning their attention to unit-construction four-stroke engines, where the engine and gearbox came as one, in a lighter, production line friendly package: at least that was the theory. BSA, AMC and Royal Enfield all had unit-construction 250cc four-stroke scramblers by the late 1950s, though only BSA would actively pursue the development of a lightweight four-stroke competition model, which at least explains their reluctance to supply the Rickman brothers with engines. As anyone who raced one of the AMCs in anger would be quick to attest, these machines were bulky, cumbersome, underpowered and overweight. In short, they were not going to give Mr. Greeves, or any of the other manufacturers, too many sleepless nights.

The '60s loom

So, as we approach the period that provides the focus for this book, the sport had become firmly established on the home front, with a national championship and home GPs in both the 500 and 250cc Classes. In addition, Britain had firmly established itself as the leading nation in the sport, with two European Champions, and having won seven of the first ten *Motocross des Nations*.

However, the tide had changed in the late '50s, with Sweden dominating both 250 and 500cc World Championships (Tibblin was 250cc Champion and Lundin won the 500s in 1959) and although British runners remained highly competitive in the GPs during the 1950s, especially those run on home soil, it would be 1960 before Britain would land another European Championship and a further four years before a Briton would be crowned World Champion for the first time. Indeed, as the '60s loomed things looked rather bleak for Great Britain, though on a brighter note, there was a lot of work being done to rectify this situation especially in Birmingham, Southend and New Milton.

The younger of the two Rickman brothers, Don, races the innovative 500 Triumph Métisse Mk 2 at the trade supported event at Shrubland Park in August 1961. (MR)

Taking Shape – The ACU establishes regional 'Centres'

In the early years of off-road motorcycle competition, clubs began to spring up nationwide, organising events on a grassroots basis. But as the popularity of, initially, trials and grasstrack grew, the Auto-Cycle Union (ACU) decided that it would be more advantageous to divide the country into local areas, which would administrate events in their own region. As such twenty 'Centres' were formed. These were: Cheshire, Cornwall, Eastern, East Midland, East South Wales, East Yorkshire, Isle of Man, Midland, Mid-Wales, North Eastern, Northern, North Western, South Eastern, Southern, South Midland, South Western, Wessex, Western, West South Wales and Yorkshire.

Within each of these centres affiliated clubs promoted meetings following the guidelines of the ACU, which in the early days was located at 83 Pall Mall, London, SW1.

Centre Championships

In the scrambles and motocross branch of off-road sport, each centre ran its own championships in tandem with the ACU Drivers' Stars and latterly the British Championships, though these were far from having a standard format. For example, the Midland Centre Championship tended to be a single race held at the autumn meeting at Hawkstone Park and was open to non-residents. The 1966 Midland Championship illustrates this well, with Suffolk man John Banks the winner, followed by Vic Eastwood, from Kent, and Alan Clough, from Cheshire.

Contrast this with, the 1965 Eastern Centre Championships. These were held at Bentley, near Ipswich in August, organised by the Essex and Suffolk Border Club and with four different categories up for grabs. Greeves employee John Pease was the Up-to-200cc Champion, with Dennis Howard also on a Greeves taking the 225-250cc Class. Jim Aim on his splendid 650cc Orcadian (TriBSA) took the 300-650 cc cup and the Sidecar Class was won by Bob Norman (650cc 'EGB' – he was sponsored by the Eastern Gas Board) with Brian Reid in the chair. In this case, all of the solo winners were resident in the Centre, though Norman lived in Bushey, but as a member of the Eastern Sporting Sidecar Association (ESSA), he qualified to race in the championships.

However, by the early 1970s many of the Centre Championships were run over the course of the season, with rounds being strategically placed in the calendar to avoid clashes with the British Championships.

I remember attending a Castle MCC event at Blackheath, Colchester in March 1970, which staged the opening rounds of the Eastern Centre 300-400cc Class and the Sidecar Championships. In addition to this class, there were also 250cc, and 410-750cc Classes which were run on different days.

At the close of the 1970 season, Pease had added another championship in the 250cc Class, whilst Norman Messenger, from Clacton, on his 360 CZ went on to win the 300-400cc Class, despite taking a heavy fall in the opening round. Brian Atkinson on his Kirby BSA won the 410-750cc Class and the Sidecar Class was taken by the Cooper brothers, Paul and John riding a 650 Triumph Wasp. Again, with the exception of the Coopers, who hailed from Basingbourne, Hants but raced with the Diss club, all the winners were Eastern Centre residents.

The Inter-Centre Team Scramble

Once a year, typically in early October, the ACU ran the Inter-Centre Team Scramble. In 1962 it was held at Matchams Park near Ringwood, Hants and it was the 'home' riders from the Southern Centre who carried away the spoils of victory. That particular year there were two team races with 12 centres deploying four-man teams to compete for the prize, the Daily Herald Trophy. Dave Bickers and Don Rickman were the individual stars of the day with a win and a 2nd spot each. With Derek Rickman, Ken Heanes and Ivor England offering solid support, Don Rickman led the Southern Centre to victory.

Overview of the British Motocross Championships 1951- 1975

1951   **The ACU (Auto-Cycle Union) introduces the Scrambles Drivers' Star**

Initially there were 12 rounds with a rider's best eight results counting towards the title. However, an overly complicated points system was employed, where points were allotted to both 350 and 500cc races at selected meetings

AJS' Geoff Ward wins the inaugural contest, outpointing Les Archer (Norton) and Brian Stonebridge (Matchless)

Ward would go on to win the 'Star' three-times in the first four years

1960   **250cc Scrambles Drivers' Star introduced**

This class was introduced in response (albeit tardy) to the growing number of enthusiasts racing 'lightweight' machines, frequently powered by the seemingly ubiquitous 125, 197 and 250cc Villiers engines

By now the Star series consist of five rounds per category held over the course of the season with separate rounds for both 250 and 500cc classes. Points are awarded to the first six riders home:

Place	Points
1st	8
2nd	6
3rd	4
4th	3
5th	2
6th	1

Dave Bickers (Greeves) wins the first 250 'Star', whilst Jeff Smith (BSA) is victorious in the 500cc class, establishing an order that was rarely threatened for the next 5 years

1966   **The ACU Stars become the British Motocross Championships**

Little else changes

Freddie Mayes (Greeves) and Dave Bickers (CZ) are the first official 'British Champions', 250 and 500cc respectively

1968   **Format changes to two races per round of 30 mins + 2 laps**

Unlike the Grand Prix meetings, where to score points riders have to finish both legs, points are awarded in both races

Malcolm Davis (AJS) takes the 250cc class and John Banks (BSA) wins the 500cc class

1973   **A 125cc British Championship is added**

The 125cc Championship is run on the same lines as the established classes. The rounds are often held in conjunction with 250, 500 or even the Sidecar Championships

Bryan Wade (Husqvarna) wins the first 125 Championship, thereby becoming the only rider during the era to win all three classes

1975   **The championships are completely revamped**

A single British Motocross Championship for the nation's top 35 riders with a Support series run in tandem is introduced. At the season's close riders will be relegated and promoted between the two series.

Vic Allan (Bultaco), who won both the 250 and 500cc classes in 1974, wins the inaugural Championship

Brief History of the European and World Championships

1952 FIM launches the European Moto-Cross Championship

FIM (Fédération Internationale Motorcycliste) is the governing body in international motorcycle sport. Run initially over six rounds with a rider's best four finishes to count, points were awarded from 1st to 6th places:

Place	Points	Place	Points
1st	8	4th	3
2nd	6	5th	2
3rd	4	6th	1

Brian Stonebridge racing a Matchless wins the inaugural British 500cc GP (Open to machines up to 500cc. Bill Barugh on a 197cc Dot finished 6th) at Nympsfield, Gloucestershire

Victor Leloup from Belgium riding an FN is the first European Champion; BSA's John Avery is the best Briton, in 3rd place

1953 Championship extended to eight rounds

1955 Two-leg GP format pioneered

At the British GP at Hawkstone Park in July, won by 20 year-old Jeff Smith, the organising Salop club pioneers the two-leg GP format, with riders having to finish both races to be eligible for points

John Draper riding his factory BSA is Britain's first European Champion

1956 Maximum score achieved

Aldershot's Les Archer riding a Norton hybrid becomes the first rider to win the European Championship with the maximum score

1957 The FIM introduces the 500cc World Championship

There are nine rounds with a rider's best five results to count

Bill Nilsson (Sweden) racing his AJS based Crescent special is the first World Champion, whilst Jeff Smith is the highest placed home rider, taking his second British GP on his way to 4th overall

1958 The FIM Coupe d'Europe or 250cc European Championship is held for the first time

It's an arduous series with 12 rounds and a riders best seven results to determine the outcome. Czechoslovakia's Jaromir Cizek racing a Jawa is crowned Champion

The same rider wins Britain's first 250cc GP held at Beenham Park, Berkshire in June, edging out Stonebridge who is now racing for Greeves

1960 Britain's Dave Bickers, also racing a Greeves, is crowned 250 European Champion

1961 Bickers retains his European title

The first rider since the great Auguste Mingels (500cc) to win back-to-back European titles

1962 The 250 World Championship is born

The series has an unprecedented 15 rounds, with a riders best seven results to count

Sweden's Torsten Hallman racing a Husqvarna beats Britain's BSA teammates Jeff Smith and Arthur Lampkin to the title

1964 Jeff Smith becomes World Champion

Racing in the 500cc series with a maximum score of 56 points

1965 Smith retains his title

This time he falls two points shy of the maximum score

Scrambles and Motocross Winners 1951-1974

ACU Scramble Drivers' Star Winners 1951-59 (500cc)

1951	1	Geoff Ward	AJS
	2	Les Archer	Norton
	3	Brian Stonebridge	Matchless
1952	1	John Avery	BSA
	2	Reg Pilling	AJS
	3	Les Archer	Norton
1953	1	Geoff Ward	BSA
	2	David Tye	BSA
	3	John Avery	BSA
1954	1	Geoff Ward	AJS
	2	Phil Nex	BSA
	3	David Tye	BSA
1955	1	Jeff Smith	BSA
	2	Terry Cheshire	BSA
	3	Dave Curtis	Matchless

1956	1	Jeff Smith	BSA
	2	Dave Curtis	Matchless
	3	Terry Cheshire	BSA
1957	*Not run due to Suez Crisis*		
1958	1	Dave Curtis	Matchless
	2	Don Rickman	BSA
	3=	Jeff Smith	BSA
	3=	Arthur Lampkin	BSA
1959	1	Arthur Lampkin	BSA
	2	Don Rickman	BSA & Métisse
	3=	John Draper	BSA
	3=	Derek Rickman	BSA & Métisse

ACU Scramble Drivers' Star Winners 1960-65

250cc

1960	1	Dave Bickers	Greeves
	2	Alan Clough	Dot
	3	Joe Johnson	Greeves
1961	1	Arthur Lampkin	BSA
	2	Dave Bickers	Greeves
	3	Pat Lamper	Dot
1962	1	Dave Bickers	Greeves
	2	John Griffiths	Dot
	3	Alan Clough	Dot
1963	1	Dave Bickers	Greeves
	2	Bryan Goss	Greeves
	3	Norman Crooks	Dot
1964	1	Dave Bickers	Greeves
	2	Alan Clough	Greeves
	3	Ernie Greer	Dot
1965	1	Dave Bickers	Greeves
	2	Bryan Goss	Husqvarna
	3=	Alan Clough	Greeves
	3=	Freddie Mayes	Greeves

500cc

1960	1	Jeff Smith	BSA
	2=	Don Rickman	Metisse
	2=	John Burton	BSA
1961	1	Jeff Smith	BSA
	2	Dave Curtis	Matchless
	3	Arthur Lampkin	BSA
1962	1	Jeff Smith	BSA
	2	John Burton	BSA
	3	John Harris	BSA
1963	1	Jeff Smith	BSA
	2	Vic Eastwood	Matchless
	3	John Burton	BSA
1964	1	Jeff Smith	BSA
	2	Vic Eastwood	Matchless
	3	Chris Horsfield	Matchless
1965	1	Jeff Smith	BSA
	2=	Vic Eastwood	BSA
	2=	Dave Bickers	Greeves

British Motocross Champions 1966-74

250cc

Year	Pos	Rider	Bike
1966	1	Freddie Mayes	Greeves
	2	Dave Bickers	CZ
	3	Alan Clough	Greeves
1967	1	Alan Clough	Husqvarna
	2=	Dave Bickers	CZ
	2=	Freddie Mayes	Norton Villiers
1968	1	Malcolm Davis	AJS
	2	Don Rickman	Bultaco Metisse
	3	Andy Roberton	Husqvarna
1969	1	Bryan Wade	Greeves
	2	Malcolm Davis	AJS & CZ
	3	Bryan Goss	Husqvarna
1970	1	Malcolm Davis	AJS
	2	Andy Roberton	AJS
	3	Jeff Smith	BSA
1971	1	Bryan Wade	Husqvarna
	2	Malcolm Davis	Bultaco
	3	Vic Allan	Bultaco
1972	1	Andy Roberton	Husqvarna
	2	Vic Allan	Bultaco
	3	Bryan Wade	Husqvarna
1973	1	Malcolm Davis	Bultaco
	2	Andy Roberton	Husqvarna
	3	Vic Allan	Bultaco
1974	1	Vic Allan	Bultaco
	2	Malcolm Davis	Bultaco
	3	Ivan Miller	Bultaco

500cc

Year	Pos	Rider	Bike
1966	1	Dave Bickers	CZ
	2	Vic Eastwood	BSA
	3	Jeff Smith	BSA
1967	1	Jeff Smith	BSA
	2=	Alan Clough	Husqvarna
	2=	Vic Eastwood	BSA
1968	1	John Banks	BSA
	2	Vic Eastwood	Husqvarna
	3	Dave Nicoll	BSA
1969	1	John Banks	BSA
	2	Vic Allan	Greeves
	3	Keith Hickman	BSA
1970	1	Bryan Goss	Husqvarna
	2	Vic Allan	Greeves
	3	Keith Hickman	BSA
1971	1	John Banks	BSA & Husqvarna
	2	Bryan Wade	Husqvarna
	3	Andy Roberton	BSA & Husqvarna
1972	1	Bryan Wade	Husqvarna
	2	Andy Roberton	Husqvarna
	3	John Banks	CZ
1973	1	John Banks	Cheney BSA
	2	Bryan Wade	Husqvarna
	3	Vic Eastwood	Maico
1974	1	Vic Allan	Bultaco
	2	Vic Eastwood	Maico
	3	Andy Roberton	Husqvarna

125cc (introduced 1973)

Year	Pos	Rider	Bike
1973	1	Bryan Wade	Husqvarna
	2	Malcolm Davis	Bultaco
	3	Roger Harvey	Yamaha
1974	1	Bryan Wade	Suzuki
	2	Graham Noyce	Maico
	3	Terry Dyer	Suzuki

Most wins 500cc

Rider	Wins	Years
Jeff Smith	9	1955, 56, 60, 61, 62, 63, 64, 65, 67
John Banks	4	1968, 69, 71, 73
Geoff Ward	3	1951, 53, 54
Vic Allan	1	1974
John Avery	1	1952
Dave Bickers	1	1966
Dave Curtis	1	1958
Bryan Goss	1	1970
Arthur Lampkin	1	1959
Bryan Wade	1	1972

Most wins 250cc

Rider	Wins	Years
Dave Bickers	5	1960, 62, 63, 64, 65
Malcolm Davis	3	1968, 70, 73
Bryan Wade	2	1969, 71
Vic Allan	1	1974
Alan Clough	1	1967
Arthur Lampkin	1	1961
Freddie Mayes	1	1966
Andy Roberton	1	1972

Glossary of Terms

Scramble The name given to an off-road race, usually taking place on a circuit set in rolling countryside. With the introduction of the term 'motocross' (see below) it came to be defined as a meeting with short races, the heats, and a longer final.

Motocross (MX) influenced by the race meetings taking place in continental Europe, many clubs introduced motocross-style meetings, with two, or sometimes three, longer 'legs' (typically 45 mins for a two-leg or 30 mins for a three-leg event). Points were awarded to riders, with victory going to the best overall performer.

125 motorcycle with engine capacity up to 125cc

250 motorcycle with engine capacity up to 250cc

350 a motorcycle with engine capacity up to 350cc

500 a motorcycle with engine capacity up to 500cc

750 a motorcycle with engine capacity up to 750cc

Grand National (GN) a prestigious race which would have given its name to the meeting, for example the Cleveland Grand National, though there would also be other, less important races in the programme.

Grand International (GI) a title bestowed on a few Grand National meetings as the popularity of the sport increased, eg the Hants Grand National became the Hants Grand International in 1967.

ACU Scrambles Drivers' Star (ACU Star) - this was the forerunner of the British Championship. A 500 Star was introduced in 1951 with a 250 class following in 1960. (See p10)

British Championships 250 and 500 were introduced in 1966, with the 125 class added in 1973. (See also p10)

Grand Prix (GP) an event counting towards the European or World Championships. Unlike road racing this usually consisted of two legs and until 1973 riders had to finish both legs to get an overall position and qualify for points.

European Championship initially (1952 – 1956) for machines up to 500cc, then for up to 250cc (1958-1961). The 250 Championship was also known as the **Coupe d'Europe**.

World Championship the 500 Championship was introduced in 1957 and in 1962 the 250 Championship was added.

Motocross des Nations (MDN) a highly prestigious competition contested annually by teams representing their nation, the first event being held in 1947.

Trophée des Nations (TDN) a similar event to the MDN, but restricted to machines up to 250cc, it was introduced in 1961.

ACU (Auto-Cycle Union) the governing body of sporting motorcycle events in the UK, it was founded in 1903.

FIM (Féderation International de Motocyclisme) the governing body of international sporting motorcycle events, it was founded in Paris in 1904.

Scottish Six Day Trial (SSDT and the **Scottish)** the premier event in the trials-riding calendar, it is contested over six days and takes place in the Scottish Highlands in springtime.

Scott Trial (the **Scott**) widely recognised as the world's toughest one-day trial, the first event took place in Shipley, Yorkshire in 1914 and served as inspiration for the world's first scramble, the Southern Scott (see p 1) It is still run today and riders accrue points on time as well as observation, the fastest rider setting 'Standard time'.

TV Scrambles Televised meetings first emerged in the late '50s, chiefly on the ITV stations. But they reached their height of popularity in the '60s when the **BBC** introduced the **Grandstand Trophy Series**. These meetings were televised over the winter months and broadcast live on Saturday afternoons. The 10-15 minute races were often run in atrocious conditions when most other sports were cancelled. In the mid-60s **ITV** also launched its own series which was shown on its **World of Sport** programme.

Dave Bickers

Full of Eastern Promise

Photo BH

Dave Bickers was quite simply one of the most determined and courageous riders ever to compete in the sport of motocross. With outrageous amounts of flair and natural ability, he rapidly graduated from centre novice to the very pinnacle of success as 250cc European Champion. In an incredibly successful career spanning three decades, this quietly spoken, modest man from the depths of rural Suffolk amassed six British Championship titles between 1960 and 1966, not to mention two coveted European 250 crowns in 1960 and 1961.

Dave Bickers was born into a farming community in the sleepy Suffolk village of Coddenham, on January 17th 1938, and he has lived in the same village ever since. His father, Geoffrey, ran a coach business there that had been established by Dave's grandfather, a farming man, at the turn of the century. Until recently the original site of the business served as home to Bickers' highly successful TV and Film stunt business, 'Bickers Action', a venture that brought Dave a lot of pleasure after he retired from racing.

Dave's interest in scrambling dates back to the days when he would jump on his push bike and cycle the short distance to Shrubland Park to watch the aces of the day competing. But his love of motorcycles goes back even further as he explained. *I was given an old Norton that didn't have a piston or barrel, but as this was during war time there was no chance of replacing them.* However the enterprising youngster didn't let such mere details spoil his fun. *I'd push it up to the top of a hill and then freewheel down again. It took about 15 minutes to push the damn thing up and less than a minute to get back down!*

At Shrubland Park, he would thrill to the racing that featured the likes of local hero Geoff Revett, John Avery, the visiting American Bud Ekins, Basil Hall, Johnny Draper, Dave Curtis and especially Brian Stonebridge, who, he told me, *Just made it all look so easy.*

Dave recalls the following incident whilst spectating at Shrubland Park which rather frightened him. *Phil Nex crashed in a section they called the Snake Pit and broke his leg. He lay there with his leg all bent up on the ground and said, 'Oh dear, that's another six weeks I've got to have off'.* Frightened he may have been, but even a disturbing event such as this couldn't dampen the Bickers' spirit, he was raring to start racing.

Where there's a will ...

Inspired by the exploits of these great riders, Dave saved his pennies so that he could purchase his first competition motorcycle, a 197cc Villiers-powered Dot. The bike cost him £138 new, Dave having taken up the option of a swinging arm rear suspension. *Dad lent me the extra few quid to get the swinging arm and it was well worth it.*

1954/55

Our hero raced for the first time at an Ipswich MC & CC promotion at Burstall in Suffolk, on Easter Monday 1954, which Dave remembers well. *I won my heat and finished second in the final. My first lesson was not to follow anyone too closely in the mud. I'd only ever ridden alone before and there was a lot of deep mud there. I'd get up too close behind someone and I'd get absolutely plastered.* He paused for a moment and then added. D-O-T. *'Devoid of trouble', but it wasn't!*

Within a month of his first meeting he had been upgraded to Senior status and proceeded to try a variety of bikes including a 350 Jawa and a 350 BSA Gold Star, which he ran on dope. Following this initial success, he rode locally for a few years gaining both experience and confidence racing against such Eastern Centre stalwarts as Geoff Revett and Jack Hubbard.

Early success reaps rewards

1956-58

Bickers' rapid progress soon caught the attention of Burnard Scott Wade, who ran the Dot factory in Manchester, and he offered him his first 'works' bike in 1956. Bickers took to the Dot and was soon challenging the country's leading 'lightweight' exponents, including the great Brian Stonebridge, who had moved from BSA to Greeves. Using his natural gifts to the full, Dave surprised a lot of people when he pushed Stonebridge all the way in a meeting at Hadleigh, Essex, in 1957, not least of all those from the nearby Thundersley factory who couldn't have failed to have been impressed, as Bickers recounts. *He (Stonebridge) was the Greeves number one, and next thing I know, I get a phone call from them. Would I go down to the factory and have a word with them. They gave me a frame, because they wanted to fit my Dot engine in one of their frames, because they thought I had a special engine.*

At this time Dave was still only 19 years old and a full 'works' Greeves soon followed, though as Bickers himself recently confirmed for me, there was never a contract with Greeves *per se*, but with Shell who sponsored the factory's efforts. However, under the watchful eye of Greeves' Derry Preston Cobb and with help and advice from his mentor, Stonebridge, he started to make an impression on the national scene in 1958, winning the 'lightweight' events at the Hants Grand National (GN), the Costwold Scramble and the Shrubland Park meeting and adding the Senior race at the Cotswold Scramble on his 500 BSA Gold Star for good measure.

However, a more significant result was to come in June, when Bickers took runner-up spot in front of a crowd of 30,000 in the second leg of his, and Britain's,

Geoffrey Bickers tops up the Greeves at the family coach business in Coddenham, Suffolk. (Photo supplied by Dave Bickers)

first 250 Grand Prix (GP) at Beenham Park, Berkshire. He finished behind overall winner Cizek, but ahead of fellow Greeves mounted Stonebridge and Brian Leask, a clear pointer to what lay ahead. Greeves' investment in the young East Anglian was beginning to pay dividends.

Two for the road

The following year, 1959, Bickers got to travel to the GPs in the company of Stonebridge, gaining invaluable experience from Greeves' Number One, who was accustomed to travelling on the Continent, but he freely admits that at the time he took a lot of it for granted. Former *Motor Cycle News (MCN)* reporter,

Mick Woollett, was privileged enough to accompany them to the Dutch GP that year and remembers him as being very much in the shadow of Stonebridge. "He was very quiet, though he was just a lad at the time." Ironically, the trip to Holland was a 'bad day at the office' for the Greeves teamsters, as Stonebridge crashed on the first lap and Bickers, who was following close behind, failed to avoid a fallen machine in the *melée* and was also eliminated.

For Stonebridge, the title challenge ended prematurely as a result of a shoulder injury he picked up in the spill in Holland, and though no one knew it at the time, his life would also be cut tragically short in the autumn of the same year. Whilst returning from a visit to the Hepolite piston factory with Bert Greeves, Stonebridge was fatally injured when Greeves' car was involved in an accident on the A1. Bickers recalls, *It was a terrible loss. We all expected Brian to be the European Champion.*

1960

Against all odds

With Stonebridge gone, Bickers had to assume the mantle of Greeves' Number One for 1960 and in his first season in this role he won both the inaugural British 250 Championship (at that time the ACU Scrambles Drivers' Star) and the European 250 Championship. However, if it was a resoundingly successful maiden voyage, it wasn't all plain sailing as Dave explained. *I was so green. I used to go everywhere with him* (Stonebridge) *and when he wasn't there I was lost. I went out to Switzerland for the first GP and went to Geneva, because I thought that was where the track was. That was where you sent the entry and I didn't even realise Geneva was a city! I couldn't find a track anywhere! I eventually found it (Payerne) and I won the GP,* he modestly added. Just like that, in his first full season of GPs!

In addition to navigational problems, Dave had to fend off the attentions of two of Britain and Europe's leading riders, in the shape of Jeff Smith and Arthur Lampkin, in pursuit of a European title. Greeves' push for the European title had coincided with that of BSA, as the Small Heath factory sent their star riders out on the European circus, armed with their new C15 models. What did Dave remember of those halcyon days? *Well, there were always two of them against me, so sometimes I pushed a bit too hard. In Markelo in Holland, I took off from a jump at the same time as Smithy, but I*

Old friends. Dave Bickers (left) catches up with Arthur Lampkin at Farleigh Castle, October 1999. (IB)

hit it all wrong and I flew through the air backwards and landed facing the wrong way! (Luckily, for him, he was racing in sand!) *I kicked the bike over and it restarted, so I carried on. But I remember thinking, 'I'll kill myself in a minute!'*

I wondered what it was like travelling around Europe with BSAs 'dynamic duo'; was it true that Dave used to tease Arthur about his Yorkshire accent? *Yeah, I did a bit of that. Smithy could get a bit nasty to people, but he (Lampkin) wouldn't. Though he'd knock you arse over head perhaps!* Dave added with a wry grin. *Jeff took it so seriously. I was just there to have a go and see what happened but to him it was a little more important. He's a good mate these days though, and he's more relaxed now.*

European and domestic glory

Things went from strength to strength for the young pretender in his assault on the European title in 1960. He was victorious in four GPs, the opener in Switzerland, mid-season in Poland, the deciding round in Sweden and the final one in West Germany, to win the title from his compatriot, Smith, with a 13-point cushion, whilst Czech rider Miroslav Soucek (ESO) just edged out Lampkin for 3rd place. Although he had won the championship, Bickers was disappointed not to have put the icing on the cake with a win in the home GP in his own back yard at Shrubland Park. That particular honour fell to Smith, though following mechanical problems in the first leg Bickers controlled the second race to show what could have and, for the partisan Suffolk crowd, what should have been.

Talking to Bickers, I wondered how difficult it had been setting off to conquer Europe as an inexperienced 22 year-old. *I won the first European title easily, and I mean easily. In some ways it was easier than racing in the Eastern Centre.* This could be perceived as sounding a bit arrogant, though this was not the case as Dave went on to explain. *I was with better blokes, they all knew what they were doing but the longer races suited me because they'd all get knackered and I didn't for some reason.*

Unlike his friend and rival, Jeff Smith, Bickers never did any special physical training and as he told me he could never work out quite where his stamina came from. *I never used to eat meat, just egg and chips or fish and chips. Everybody else had special stuff, but I just never seemed to get tired.*

There is no question that Bickers' efforts on the Essex-built two-stroke, reaped the benefit of the tremendous research and development work done by Stonebridge. But with his success in Europe, sales for the MCS 'Bickers Replica' bike went through the roof and although it paled into comparison with his European success, Bickers' victory in the inaugural 250 ACU Star competition in 1960 helped further the bike's popularity. After being approached by several local riders who wanted to buy a Greeves, Bickers, set himself up in business with a little shop on the side of the family home in Coddenham. This was the beginning of a very successful business venture that would shortly move to new premises in Ipswich as demand for bikes grew.

A bridge too far

Bickers eased to a comfortable victory in the season-long ACU Star series, finishing 20 points clear of Dot's Alan Clough, with fellow Greeves rider Joe Johnson filling 3rd place. But there was one trophy that eluded Dave that season, one which he truly regretted, the Brian Stonebridge Memorial at Hawkstone Park. Maybe the occasion just got to him too much, but it was a very subdued Bickers who rode that day, though fittingly it was another ex-teammate and friend of Stonebridge, Dave Curtis, who lifted the trophy at the afternoon's close to the applause of the 80,000 plus spectators who had turned out to pay tribute to Brian's popularity. The respect he commanded amongst the riders was evident too, with the event heavily over-subscribed and one of Stonebridge's closest rivals in Europe, the great Auguste Mingels, competing on a borrowed Greeves, whilst former rival Geoff Ward came out of retirement for the day to honour his much lamented friend.

Defending the titles

Following such success in 1960, all eyes were on Bickers as the 1961 season got underway and he didn't disappoint. He emerged victorious from a typically muddy TV scramble at Hambleton, Yorkshire in January, where he held off the entire BSA works team of Smith, Lampkin and John Burton to take the GN race.

This early-season success serves as a good indication of his form and when the GP season got underway in Belgium in April, Bickers was on top of his game, opening the defence of his title in perfect style by winning both races, though Lampkin, who finished 2nd in the first leg, may well have sneaked the overall had the BSA's frame not snapped in half, midway through the second leg.

Wins followed in France, Poland and Luxembourg, before a run of three GPs without adding to his points tally (Finland, Italy and West Germany) saw him relinquish the championship lead to Lampkin and Smith, so that when the GP circus headed to Shrubland Park in July, the title battle was very finely balanced. The day's racing was dominated by the struggle between the two riders who would emerge as the main title protagonists, Dave Bickers and Arthur Lampkin, though with 'home advantage', Bickers was always favourite to come out on top. This was indeed the outcome, with Bickers eventually winning both legs quite comfortably from the tough Yorkshireman.

Bickers on his way to his first 250 British GP victory, at Shrubland Park in July 1961. (MR)

Bickers racing a stone's throw away from his Coddenham home at Shrubland Park in August 1961. Here he is pictured on his way to victory in the 250 ACU Star race. (MR)

Following the disappointment of not winning the 1960 British Grand Prix in front of his legions of loyal followers, Bickers was relieved to have put things right. When I asked him about that particular victory, he modestly told me, *Yes, it was always nice to win at home.* This was the first of three home GP wins, with victories at Glastonbury the following year and then again at the same venue in 1965, and the locals that swelled the ranks of the crowd naturally loved it.

Lampkin continued to push Dave for the whole campaign, winning three GPs over the season and it was very satisfying for Bickers to defeat the BSAs of Smith and Lampkin. On the way to the 1961 title he won seven of the thirteen rounds and he cites winning the GP in Sweden, where he clinched his second title, as a career highlight. It had come down to a two-horse race, between Bickers and Lampkin and Dave remembers lapping Jeff Smith (how many riders can recall doing that?) on the last lap.

Although Bickers had retained his European crown with great aplomb, he would yield his ACU Star to arch rival Lampkin before the season's close. The gritty Yorkshireman had had a fantastic season, winning three GPs and putting together a very consistent string of results in the domestic competition to edge out Bickers (See p73 and 75). Despite winning the opening round at Hatherton Hall in May, the third round at Shrubland Park and the final round at the Wessex Scramble at Glastonbury in September, Bickers still fell 8 points shy of his rival's points tally.

A change of focus

Bickers was the 'King of Europe', but two long seasons of racing right across the continent had taken their toll. In November 1961, the *MCN* ran a headline stating: *'ENOUGH' SAYS BICKERS*. In the accompanying article Bickers stressed that he was looking forward to a season racing on British tracks and devoting more

1962

time to running his burgeoning motorcycle business and cited the expense of riding the series and also the travelling as the main reasons why he would not be competing in Europe in 1962, despite the series taking on full 'World' Championship status.

However, talking to Dave recently he insists that it was never his decision to stay at home in '62. *I'd won the European title twice, then Greeves said, 'We've done that, we'd better concentrate on England now'. I stopped in England for a year and in that time the Europeans got much better and I didn't.*

Regardless of whose decision it was, Bickers did not disappoint Greeves or the many spectators who thronged to see him race week in and week out, taking the 1962 250 ACU Star, his second, at a canter from the Dots of John Griffiths and Alan Clough. Wins in the Star series that year included round two at Hatherton Hall, Nantwich, where he was too good for Lampkin and Griffiths and at Cuerden Park in October, where he wrapped up the title when his nearest rival, Griffiths, suffered an engine blow up on the Dot.

With the pressures of regular Grand Prix racing off him, Dave really enjoyed himself competing on the domestic scene. His career as a works rider had taken off so suddenly, and with such success that he had never really had a chance to pause and take stock of where his career had taken him. Dave had never set out with the objective of becoming the world's leading 250 rider; circumstances, huge amounts of talent and determination, and a fair share of good luck had sent him off on that path. So at the age of 24, having done everything there was to do in the smaller category, Dave decided that he would like to have some fun mixing it with the 'Big Boys' on a 500.

The Matchless experience

With the blessings of the Greeves management, Dave approached Hugh Viney at AMC and was entrusted with an ex-Dave Curtis Matchless, as Bickers explained. *I rode it in England and actually won one or two events on it, like the Cumberland Grand National.* What he fails to mention is that he actually finished 5th overall in the British Grand Prix that year, and was second Briton home, after Don Rickman who finished 3rd, at Hawkstone Park, one of the toughest testing grounds for man and machine anywhere. *It went like hell and I was going well enough to get selected to ride in the Motocross des Nations (MDN). AMC were happy and said, 'Bring it back and we'll tune it up for you'.*

Despite Dave's protests that the bike was going just fine, the factory insisted, so Dave took a trip down to Plumstead. *In the race in Switzerland it was as slow as hell. I couldn't understand why, but, it was pretty useless!* It wasn't a happy team debut for Dave, as the British trailed in behind the Swedes, but at least ahead of their other great rivals, Belgium.

Back in Britain, Dave gave the Matchless another outing at Hawkstone Park, where he met up with the bike's previous rider, Dave Curtis, and all was revealed. Bickers recalls a conversation between the two of them going something like this: *I told him, "This don't go very well", and he said, "No, the 500s never did go very well!"* Unbeknown to Bickers, he'd previously been riding a 600 model! *I was totally innocent, and that's why the factory took it back, to swap the motors.*

Bickers' performances on the Matchless, be it a 500 or a 600 should not be underestimated though, as apart from the motor there wasn't anything very special about the bike. It was still weighing in at over 300 lbs, much heavier than the rival Gold Stars, and was far inferior to the bikes that Chris Horsfield, Vic Eastwood and Dave Nicoll would soon be riding. Had it ever been in doubt, Dave had proven that he was a force to be reckoned with whatever he might be mounted on.

What a pity, however, that he never got to go head to head with Husqvarna's Torsten Hallman in Europe in 1962, that really would have been something to see! However, a taster of what might have been was served up at the British GP, held at Glastonbury for the first time that year (well before the legendary rock festivals), when the European Champion beat the World Champion elect in both legs, prompting him to declare: "Dave Bickers is the best scrambles rider in the world!"

A tale of two bikes

1963

When he did return to racing in Europe, in 1963, Alan Clough had joined Greeves and Bickers soon struck up a good relationship with the amiable Mancunian. For Clough, it was a great experience. Bickers had inspired him in his early days and he now found himself as his travelling companion. "David was a great fellow to travel with and we had a lot of fun. He was a great thinker, I suppose a little shy at times, but he was very good with the fans and fellow riders and he always had time for others. Another thing I remember about David was that he was always listening to his favourite radio station, Radio Luxembourg, 208, on a little transistor radio."

There's no mistaking the style. Malcolm Carling captures Bickers on his way to another home GP win, this time at Glastonbury in 1962.

In 1963, disconsolate with Greeves, Bickers bought himself a 250 Husqvarna. In the BBC Grandstand Trophy he was virtually unbeatable; here he is pictured posting another win at Hankom Bottom in December 1963. (CB)

After a dream start to his campaign when he won the season opener in Barcelona, Spain, Bickers went through the most difficult period in his career as he struggled to find form. *I went back to the GPs and I couldn't win as easily then. Joel (Robert) and Torsten Hallman were winning everything. I found it very hard, if Robert wasn't there then Hallman was. It would be an easy day if they both weren't there, but I suppose they'd said the same about me before.*

What he modestly forgets to mention, however, is that in the year he was absent from the GPs the competition continued to steadily develop their bikes, whilst Greeves took a gamble by agreeing to use the new Villiers 'Starmaker' engine for their 1963 model. History shows that this was the biggest mistake the Greeves concern ever made. This was the Wolverhampton factory's first attempt at a purpose-built, single-cylinder, two-stroke competition engine and impressive as it may have looked on paper, the new engine was simply not up to the task.

Following the initial glory of a winning debut in Spain and a runner-up spot for teammate Clough, at the second round in Italy, the points dried up and Bickers would add just four points from the next nine rounds. For Dave, things had reached a crisis point and on his way back from the Finnish GP he made the decision to stop off at the Husqvarna factory in Sweden, where he bought himself a 250.

Alan Clough takes up the story. "Although we did really well in England, we didn't have the bikes for the GPs and David was fed up and that's when he bought the Husky. (Husqvarna) He wanted to put the engine in a Greeves frame and paint it blue, but Mr Cobb didn't like the idea! So he rode it that winter and won everything. We couldn't get near him!"

A Greeves publicity shot of Bickers posing with the new 'Challenger' in 1964. (Photo supplied by Bill Brooker)

Clough's words say it all. On the Husqvarna, Bickers form dramatically improved. Dave had also been struggling in the ACU Star events, but on the Swedish bike at Shrubland Park on August Bank Holiday Monday, he returned to his winning ways taking the 250 Star race from Arthur Lampkin and rising star, and near neighbour, John Banks, though series leader Bryan Goss was absent having picked up an injury the previous day. In the GN race, Bickers borrowed Jeff Smith's 350 BSA and had some fun battling with Dave Nicoll on his factory Matchless, eventually finishing in 6th place. Later in the month he won both legs of the 250 Experts GN held on a new circuit at Larkstone, Warwickshire, on what was entered as a 'Bickers Special' – basically the Husqvarna fitted with Greeves forks.

Around this time, Bickers' name was being linked with a move to CZ to spearhead their attempt on the 250 World Championship and he travelled out to the factory to try the bike in company with John Banks. However, he decided to stick with the Husky until he received a better offer, though he had now re-fitted it with the original forks.

In September that year, he claimed a trophy he had been waiting four long years to win, the Brian Stonebridge Memorial at Hawkstone Park. Bickers was in a race of his own, as he pulverised the opposition to finish over a minute ahead of Dot's John Griffiths and Jeff Smith and having lapped everyone down to 8th place in just eight laps! The form continued a week later at Boltby, where a win in the 250 Star race saw him right back in the title hunt and he went on to comfortably take his third ACU Star from Goss and the surprise package from Dot, Norman Crooks.

Bickers the TV star

But it was over the winter of 1963/4 that Bickers really came into his own. After several years of televising the odd scramble in the 'off season' winter months, the BBC decided to stage the Grandstand Trophy Series for the first time that winter, and Bickers was virtually invincible. Given the treacherous conditions in which the riders were obliged to compete, his record was nothing short of sensational. He set the tone in the first meeting at Hawkstone Park in

October, where he eased to victory in front of Griffiths and Chris Horsfield on the Starmaker-James and from there on he dictated the show. He went on to win at Farleigh Castle, Winchester and Newport before a slip in the last round of the year at Naish Hill saw his only defeat of the series as he finished 4th behind Lampkin, Goss and Clough. But as our intrepid heroes raced into 1964, it was business as usual for Bickers, who demolished the opposition with three consecutive wins at Tweseldown, Clifton and Builth Wells putting himself in an unassailable position.

Returning to the topic of Bickers uncertain future, there was growing speculation at the close of the 1963 season as to what bike he would ride in the coming year. In October 63, *MCN's* Chris Carter informed readers *'THEY'RE ALL AFTER DAVE!'* In his report, Carter stated that Husqvarna, CZ and Bultaco were all pursuing Bickers' signature for 1964. However, Greeves had been burning the midnight oil, putting together a bike that they hoped would prompt the prodigal son to return to the fold.

Competition Chief Bill Brooker remembers very well the efforts Greeves made. "At that time Dave was unhappy with the Greeves and he thought there was too much opposition from Husqvarna and CZ. Greeves were really frightened they'd lose him and I remember going over to Coddenham with a modified bike for him to try out."

Enter the Challenger

The new bike, which would be marketed as the Challenger, obviously met with Bickers' approval, as in the February 12th edition of *MCN* the front page headline ended all speculation. *'BICKERS IS BACK'* it declared, with a photo of Dave astride the all-new 'Challenger', complete with Greeves' first in-house engine, shaking hands with Bert Greeves, while Derry Preston Cobb and Bill Brooker looked on. It was also announced that John Griffiths would join Greeves and would be a travelling partner for Dave on the European circus.

Bickers gave the all-new bike a sensational winning debut in the Grandstand Trophy series at Westleton in his native Suffolk, as he beat fellow Suffolk boy Banks, to the line and a week later he notched another win ahead of similarly mounted Alan Clough at the final round of the series at Cuerden Park. Bickers took the series on 79 points from Clough on 49, and Goss who faded away to third after an impressive run of form in late 1963.

This was the first of five Grandstand trophies that Bickers would claim, including a unique double on a CZ in 1966/67, making him by far and away the most successful TV scrambler of his generation. Although he and Jeff Smith dominated the early days of the Grandstand Trophy series in their respective classes, arguably the most entertaining races were the Invitation races which pitted Bickers on his lighter 250 against the more powerful 420 and 440 BSA's of Jeff Smith.

Top entertainment

The BBC acknowledged the magnitude of those battles, when they included a race from Canada Heights in February 1965 in their retrospective '100 Great Sporting Moments' series. Bickers rocketed into the lead from the start and proceeded to speed away from the rest of the field. But Smith, with typically dogged determination, gradually reeled Bickers in lap after lap and looked smooth and focused as he caught his rival going into the last lap. At this stage the result seemed to be a forgone conclusion, though Bickers had other ideas. The pair passed and re-passed each other on that turbulent final lap, but Smith appeared to have the race won as he led into the final bend. However, Bickers took an extraordinary line through the bend, appearing to just wind the throttle round to the stop, came around Smith and took the chequered flag all crossed up to win by the smallest of margins. This was live TV racing at its best and the world's finest film directors could not have matched the celluloid drama.

Reflecting on his days with Greeves, Bickers told me, *They were ever so good initially, but you had to be very gentle with them* (one wonders whether he was referring to the bikes or the management!). This was a sentiment echoed by fellow Greeves GP runners, Arthur Browning, Vic Allan and Bryan Wade. Continuing his appraisal of the Greeves, Bickers told me, *If you rode it flat-out you broke it. You had to ride it bearing in mind that you had to keep it running. It was always the gearbox that gave you trouble.*

This reminded me of an account I'd read many years earlier, of Bickers' titanic struggle with CZ mounted Joel Robert in the 1964 British GP, the year it was held at Cadwell Park. *Oh yes, that was on the Challenger. I'd pass him lap by lap, only for him to re-pass me every time up the hill, the thing was stuck in third gear. For the record, in an incredible show of*

Cecil Bailey caught Bickers racing the Challenger in fair weather at the 1964 Hants Grand National ...

determination Dave won the first leg and may well have secured a fourth home GP win, had it not been for the gear selection problem.

Simply the best

Bickers regards Robert as the most talented bike rider he ever met. *He was fantastic. The best rider I've ever seen. He could do things the rest of us only dreamt of. We'd try to do it but he'd do it every time. He was a bit hectic to be around though and you never knew what would happen next!* Dave reflected for a moment before adding, *Not a bad old boy!*

Whilst on the topic of riders I asked him about his rivals for the British Championships. *Gossy was always good in Britain. Horsfield was good when he was on form, but he didn't keep the form. Alan Clough was a bit of a thorn in my side at Greeves, 'cause you didn't want to get beat by someone from your own team, so I had to beat him.*

Clough was the one I had to watch out for at Greeves, but Badger (Goss) was better when he went onto the Husky. A lot of riders would have a go from time to time, but Badger and Cloughie were good all the time.

Bring on the 360s

1965 was a pivotal year in the career of Dave Bickers. The '65 Greeves Challenger was certainly an improvement on the previous years' bike and Bickers rode it to three GP victories; in the opening round in Spain, in Belgium in late April, where he won both races, and then in his, and Greeves', last 250 GP win on home soil at Glastonbury. However, over the season it proved to be too unreliable and uncompetitive, with Dave only managing 5th place in the championship.

However, as Greeves still didn't have a 'big' bike for Bickers to ride, he took up the offer to race a 360 CZ in selected events that season, kicking off with a

1965

... and foul, at the BBC Grandstand meeting at Leighton, in November 1964.

sensational 3rd overall, behind World Champions Joel Robert and Jeff Smith, in the international season-opener at St. Anthonis in Holland, where he steadily improved all afternoon to take the third and final leg. Then back on home soil he took the big CZ up to North Yorkshire where he eased his way to a winning debut in the 500 ACU Star race at the Cumberland GN, beating Alan Lampkin and Jerry Scott.

For the bulk of the season he alternated between the Greeves and the CZ taking the last of his five 250 ACU Stars, with wins at the Hants GN, the Cambridge GN and the Cotswold Scramble and was good enough to finish equal 2nd with Vic Eastwood, just six points adrift of Smith in the 500 ACU Star series.

However, from August onwards Bickers was using the new 360cc MX4 Greeves, taking his first race win at the Experts GN at Larkstone, Although broken piston rings in race two denied Bickers and Greeves a winning debut, Alan Lampkin, who won race two, took the prestigious trophy home to Yorkshire. Bickers followed this up with a brace of wins on the 360 at the Lancashire GN meeting, including victory in the 'M6' race (named after the motorway which dissected Cuerden Park), after holding off three factory 440 BSAs, in the hands of the Lampkin brothers and John Banks.

A good day's work

Shrubland Park in late August was the scene of one of Bickers' best days ever, as he won all four finals, the only rider ever to do so. First on the programme was the 250 race, where Bryan Goss proved to be no match for Bickers and had to work hard to fend off a fast finishing Alan Clough. His second win came in the Shrubland GN, though he had to work a little harder for this one. The works BSAs of Arthur Lampkin and Jeff Smith were off to flying starts and when Lampkin was sidelined, Smith

Malcolm Carling caught Bickers kicking up the dust on the prototype 360 Greeves in 1965.

seemed to be on his way to a comfortable victory. But Bickers, on the new 360 Greeves reeled him in after just two laps and following a brief tussle, the dispute was settled in the local man's favour. Race win number three came in the Junior race where Goss set the initial pace, but having been passed by Bickers on lap two, he crashed exiting the bombhole. With the pressure off, Bickers romped away to victory ahead of Clough, with Freddie Mayes completing a Greeves one-two-three. Win number four was probably the sweetest of all, as Bickers brought BSA's dominance of the Senior race to an end, Smith and Lampkin having won the five previous Seniors between them. This time round it was Lampkin, who always went well at Shrubland Park, who got another great start, but Bickers, back on the 360, took up the challenge and was determined to take an historic fourth win. He even dropped the bike briefly, but had enough in store to edge out his old rival, whilst Smith rode in to finish in 3rd place. What made the victories even sweeter for Dave, was the fact that this would be the very last meeting to be held on this famous track, as the land had been sold off to build a health centre.

As the autumn of 1965 passed into winter, Bickers' supremacy on a 250 came under attack from the talented Chris Horsfield, who hailed from the quaintly named village of Hampton Lucy, in Warwickshire. Horsfield, who had poached the 500 Grandstand Trophy from Jeff Smith the previous season on a factory Matchless, was now campaigning a super-fast CZ in the hope of adding a 250 trophy to his cabinet. At Cadders Hill, Lyng, for round two of the Grandstand Trophy series with the nation looking on, Bickers tasted defeat at the hands of Horsfield and two weeks later at Belmont near Durham, he suffered the ignominy of being beaten by both Horsfield and Goss, who had returned to Greeves. Having struggled against Goss on the Husky, he was now having to contend with Horsfield on the CZ. Writing in the *MCN*, Chris Carter observed that *'Horsfield and his CZ are the biggest shake-up British scrambling has had in months. He went on to proffer that ... though he (Bickers) leads at the moment only a major disaster looks as if it could stop Chris from taking his crown.'* Food for thought!

Czech mate

With the New Year looming, speculation was rife about Bickers' future and as 1966 dawned, the man himself announced that he would be riding either a Bultaco or a CZ in the coming season. His news came within hours of being beaten, for the third time in succession, by the Horsfield-CZ combination in the BBC meeting at Caerleon, the midlander also taking the lead in the series. Bickers also expressed a desire to contest the 500 World Championship, which hinted he was swaying towards CZ, who already had a very potent 360 bike ready to go.

By the next round at Nantwich, Bickers was out on a CZ of his own, winning the 250 race to retake the lead and although there were a few hiccups along the way he clinched his third consecutive Grandstand Trophy at Brill, Buckinghamshire, in early March, beating Horsfield in the deciding race, though the TV pundits had to be informed of the outcome following an untimely break in transmission!

A phenomenal season

When I first interviewed Dave Bickers, I told him how I'd first seen him race at Hintlesham Park near Ipswich, in the summer of 1967 to which he responded, *I was past my best by then*. Who am I to argue with such a great rider? But there can be little doubt that he was still very close to his best after making the switch to CZ in 1966.

Following an unofficial ride on a 250 CZ borrowed from mechanic Zdenek Polanka at the BBC TV International team meeting at Clifton, where he took on World Champions Joel Robert on a 360 CZ and Jeff Smith on his trusty 440 BSA, to finish 3rd overall, Bickers' results speak for themselves:

- At St. Anthonis, Holland, in March, he wins two of the three motos, taking 4th overall behind winner Robert, Rolf Tibblin and Smith.
- Later that month he wins the first ever 500 British Championship round at Hawkstone Park.
- At the Hants GN he wins both legs of the motocross style GN race and takes the first ever round of the 250 British Championship.
- Takes five wins at the Maybug Scramble at Farleigh Castle, including round three of the 500 British Championship.
- Wins three races at Wakes Colne, in July, including the fourth round of the 250 British Championship.
- Takes a clean sweep at the Thirsk International in mid-September, where he wins both legs of the 250 motocross and metes out the same punishment in the 500s.
- Wipes the floor with the opposition at the Scramble of the Year at Brands Hatch, winning both legs of the

motocross style event, and adding the 500 and 750 International races for good measure.

- As the BBC Grandstand series returns to the screens he opens with a 250-750 double at Caerleon.
- Follows this with the same result at Dodington Park and Hawkstone Park!
- Wins the 250 race at Tweseldown, on Christmas Eve and the 250 race at East Meon on New Year's Eve, to finish the year unbeaten in the 250 series.

With such a run of success, he comfortably won the 500 British Championship, finished a close runner-up to Freddie Mayes in the 250 Championship (see pp95-96) and paved the way for his historic 250-750 double triumph in the Grandstand Trophy series. He also took a good shot at the 500 World Championship, with podium finishes in Austria (3rd), Czechoslovakia (2nd) and Holland (2nd) for 5th in the championship at his first attempt.

Typical of Bickers' dominant form that year was his performance at the prestigious Hants GN at Matchams Park, Hampshire, in April. Bickers' hectic race schedule began with the first leg of the 'Hants', which he led at a canter from start to finish. He then switched to his 250 and went straight out for the championship race where he chased Malcolm Davis for four laps, until the Bultaco rider's plug whiskered. From there on in he rode unchallenged to the chequered flag after the only other rider who looked even capable of mounting a challenge, fellow CZ mounted Chris Horsfield, retired with a broken exhaust. Then it was the second leg of the main event where Jeff Smith, on his `Titan´ BSA, featuring many ultra-lightweight titanium parts, gave chase to Bickers. However, he was never headed as he relentlessly stretched a five second gap from lap one, to 11 seconds at the flag with no sign of tiring! As MCN reporter Gavin Tripp succinctly put it, *'First for one and a half hours and 39 times over* (laps), *that's Dave Bickers' story of Friday's Hants GN.'*

Tellingly, Bickers' form on the 360 was even better than it was on the 250 and the jewel in his crown that season, was definitely the 500 British Championship success. Bickers had nothing to prove on a 250 and he had won countless races pitting his Greeves against the might of the BSA and Matchless factory teams in unlimited races, though he'd never had the chance to go for victory in the larger capacity class before. But now, armed with the big two-stroke, there was nothing to stop him.

Out front! At the 1966 Hants Grand National Bickers was peerless, here he is pressing on hard on the 360 twin-port CZ. (CB)

With mud flying everywhere, Bickers motors on to clinch the 500 British Championship at Cadwell Park in October 1966. (RD)

Bickers grabs Smith's title

As the newly titled 500 'British Championship' got underway at Hawkstone Park, flagged off by American singing star Roy Orbison, Bickers set the tone for the season taking an immediate lead and simply riding away from a classy field that included Hawkstone supremo Jeff Smith, Artur Lampkin, John Banks and Vic Eastwood, who finished in that order. But he was out of luck at the second round at the Cambridge GN at Elsworth, where he went out whilst leading with water, and there was plenty of it, in the electrics.

But he bounced back at Farleigh Castle, where he was in sensational form at the Maybug Scramble, winning no less than five races. In the third round of the championship his task was eased by the absence of Smith, who had opted to race in an international in Belgium, though it was the BSA team who took the challenge to Bickers, with new boy Jerry Scott leading at the start from Eastwood whilst Bickers and fellow East Anglian, Banks, gave chase. After two laps Bickers eased past Scott and although Eastwood followed suit next time round, he could make no impression on Bickers who went on to win by 17 seconds.

At the Cleveland GN in July, he set himself up for the title, after finishing 2nd to Smith, to lead Eastwood, who finished 3rd, by four points and Smith by eight. The final round was at Cadwell Park in Lincolnshire, in mid-October, and the organisers laid out a good old-fashioned undulating scramble course which zig-zagged its way across the more familiar road race circuit. When the championship race got underway, Bickers soon established himself as the leader, though Eastwood tenaciously hung on to his back wheel and took the lead on the third lap. For the remaining 12 laps Bickers was happy to sit behind Eastwood, safe in the knowledge that if he finished second he would be Champion. Eastwood won the race but Bickers was the Champion, and he celebrated in style by taking the Lincolnshire GN from Eastwood and Alan Lampkin, flying through the field and picking off riders lap by lap after landing on his ear on the first lap.

Dave Bickers

Sound business

With such success, you don't have to be a genius to see why CZ sales in Britain went through the roof! At that time everybody wanted a CZ, not least of all in Bickers' native Eastern Centre. Local ace, and long time Bickers admirer, Norman Messenger, who had previously ridden Greeves like his idol, was one such example. "When Dave went over to CZs, I soon made the same move. He supplied the bikes and supported me for several years. For about 18 months I had a really good winning spell on the 250. That bike was so light and quick off the mark, and by the time the big four-strokes were into their stride, I'd be away. Gone!"

Dave started 1967 as he had finished the previous year, winning on the box. The first Grandstand Trophy event of the year was at Cuerden Park and Bickers emerged victorious in the 250 event, to notch win number six. Then at Naish Hill, Wiltshire, in early February, Bickers was finally beaten in a televised 250 race when he tangled with another rider in the first corner and his bike was in no state to continue. However, in the 750 race he took three points, which were enough to see him crowned Champion, though he trailed in a distant 5th behind race winner Eastwood, Wade, Banks and Smith, but ahead of the only man who could have caught him, Greeves' new sensation, Arthur Browning from Birmingham.

A good indication of Bickers' form at this time can be taken from his performance in the Grandstand Trophy meeting at Hankom Bottom, Winchester, in March, where he won all four of his races. His main challenger on the day was Bryan Goss (see p208) who pushed him all the way in the 250 and 750 races. Arguably, though, Bickers' best performance on the day was in the Handicap race. He started last of the 37 riders and in less than 14 minutes he had passed all of the others to win from Clough, Lampkin, Hickman, Smith and Randy Owen. To cap things off, he took the Invitation race which Smith led until the closing stages when Bickers passed the leading three! At the flag, it was Bickers, from Smith, Clough, Don Rickman,

1967

With shadows lengthening, Bickers closes down Jeff Smith at Hankom Bottom in March 1967. (BH)

Horsfield and Derek Rickman – with none of the 'Brat Pack' (Browning, Davis, Wade, Roberton, etc) in sight!

Two weeks later the TV cameras were at Builth Wells for the final round of the 1966/67 Grandstand Trophy series, where Bickers sealed the 250 series with a win, though he was pushed all the way by the in-form Alan Clough, with Greeves riders Wade, Browning, Horsfield and Scotsman, Vic Allan filling the other point scoring places.

Mixed fortunes

Though Bickers had made history by winning both of the Grandstand Trophies in 1967, he experienced highs and lows over the season, losing his 500 title to a resurgent Jeff Smith and falling short in his effort to retain the 250 Championship. However, it must be remembered that Dave was travelling to and fro across Europe from April to August, racking up somewhere in the region of 35,000 miles in his trusty Mercedes on the 500 World Championship trail in addition to riding a full programme of meetings at home.

He would record just one win in each of the 250 and 500 series, with victory in the 500 Championship coming in the third round at Dodington Park in April and closer to home at Hintlesham Park near Ipswich in the fourth round of the 250s.

At Dodington Park on the new 400 CZ racing in tricky conditions he won the hard way, coming through the field from seventh place on the first lap. In doing so he passed Wade, Arthur Lampkin, Don Rickman, Smith and Browning, before trading places twice with Eastwood on the final lap for good measure! One notable absentee was previous leader Clough, who was away contesting the 250 Belgian GP. As a result, Bickers and Eastwood moved ahead and were tied for the lead in the title hunt. In imperious form, Bickers went on to win the 1,000 cc Invitation, ahead of the factory BSAs of Eastwood and Smith and the Wessex Senior race from the 'two Arthurs', Lampkin and Browning.

The man who once described Bickers as, "the best scrambles rider in the world", Torsten Hallman, comes under pressure from the man himself, at the inaugural Hants Grand International in April 1967. (RD)

Above, few riders could match Bickers for determination. Here he leads his Suffolk neighbour John Banks at the 1967 500 Austrian GP at Sittendorf. (BH)

Below, Bickers racks up some more flying hours at Farleigh Castle! The occasion, the 500 British GP in July 1967 where he finished as runner-up to his teammate Paul Friedrichs. (MC)

Above, before the racing begins, top ACU official Harold Taylor, far right, presents Bickers and Jeff Smith to local dignitaries at the 1967 500 British GP. (MC)

Below, Bickers leads Smith on his way to victory in the 1967 500 British Championship round at Dodington Park. (RD)

Dave Bickers

Always ready to muck in, Bickers is part of an Ipswich Triangle Club work party, as they forge a path through the grounds of their new scrambles venue at Hintlesham Park. (DK)

First sighting

It was in August 1967 that I had the opportunity to see Bickers in action for the first time. Having moved from Sussex to Suffolk in the winter of 1966, my father, who had taken me to my first ever scramble the previous spring, took me along to the National Hintlesham Festival Scramble, at Hintlesham Hall, a few miles from our new home. Coincidentally, it was just a few miles from Bickers' Suffolk home and furthermore it served as the Ipswich Club's replacement for Shrubland Park, the use of which they had sadly lost two years earlier. On a beautiful summer's day, the large crowd was treated to a fantastic day's racing and although not totally dominant, as he had been in the last event at Shrubland Park, Bickers won the races that mattered most, the 250 British Championship round and the Shrubland Trophy.

In the championship race he blew everyone off, winning from Malcolm Davis on his Bultaco and Husqvarna's Alan Clough, who in finishing 3rd clinched the title. Bryan Wade and John Banks each had a win in the Senior and Hintlesham GN races respectively and Davis got the better of Bickers in the Lightweight race. But for most of the crowd, myself included, the highlight was the Shrubland Trophy where Bickers on his 360 CZ was just too strong for Davis. My fondest ever Bickers memory was when he celebrated his win with a hugely exuberant wheelie for about 100m to the finishing line. It was simply spectacular and the partisan local crowd just lapped it up.

Bickers rediscovers his form on the GP stage

Putting his disappointing form in the British Championships aside, Bickers won his first 500 GP at the second round at Hedemora, Sweden in May. In the first leg he battled through the field after a poor start to finish 2nd behind local hero, Christer Hammergren, but ahead of title-topping Gunnar Draugs. They were followed in turn by Friedrichs, Smith and Gunnar Johansson. Second time out and Bickers made no mistake, gating well and rushing off to lead from Smith. After 13 laps at the front, Bickers, knowing the GP was

A picture of concentration. Photographer Dave Kindred catches Bickers on his way to victory in the Shrubland Trophy race at Hintlesham Park, August 1967.

his, sportingly moved over to allow Smith through and into 3rd overall.

Later the same season he picked up what would turn out to be his final GP win, number 18, at Ettelbruck, Luxembourg, in August, when a first lap crash in race one eliminated championship leader Friedrichs and Smith. Smith's disappointment aside, the first race was great for the British contingent, with Eastwood flying to victory ahead of Bickers, Banks 4th and privateer Keith Hickman, on his Cheney Victor, taking an excellent 6th place. In race two Bickers rode a calculated race, content just to follow fellow CZ riders Friedrichs and De Coster, who were out of the overall reckoning, to take top honours. Hammergren was the runner-up, whilst Banks gained his first 500 World Championship points with 3rd overall.

Swiss shenanigans

The following week the GP circus moved on to Wohlen for the Swiss GP, where a final showdown between Smith and Bickers was keenly anticipated. However, as Dave came in from practice the engine of the big CZ nipped up, meaning he would have to use his spare bike in the race. At the time a mad keen 15 year-old Bickers fan observed this and inadvertently let slip what had happened within earshot of Jeff Smith. Legend has it that Smith then told David that as this contravened the rules at that time, should David beat him in the GP he would feel duty bound to report the digression to the FIM committee! The teenager in question was Stuart Nunn, who went on to become a top moto cross rider in his own right, racing for the Bickers' stable for 10 years. So there were clearly no hard feelings!

As it turned out neither Smith nor Bickers finished the GP and after a long and eventful season, Friedrichs was officially crowned Champion for the second time and Bickers finished 3rd in the series just three points shy of Smith's total, but ahead of fellow CZ riders Vlastimil Valek, Roger DeCoster and Gunnar Draugs. Not bad for someone who was, by his own admission, 'past his best'!

At Markelo, Holland in September, the British team of Bickers, Eastwood, Hickman, Lampkin and Smith won the MDN, the fifth straight win for Britain, where Vic Eastwood was the star of the show being the overall winner after finishing 3rd in race one and winning the second leg, whilst the team rallied behind him with Bickers and Smith finishing 4th and 5th overall. Though he didn't do any winning, Bickers was instrumental in making sure that the silverware stayed in Britain. At the beginning of the second race his CZ mysteriously stopped when the air vent to the petrol tank became blocked. Having resolved the problem, he returned to the fray in thirty seventh position, but his resolve never wavered as he set about recovering as many positions as he could. By the flag he had made up 30 positions to finish 7th thereby guaranteeing victory in this prestigious event for another year.

By invitation only

Dave Bickers was the first British rider to be invited to ride in the Inter-Am series in the USA, organised by the then Husqvarna importer, Edison Dye. Bickers flew to the USA in company with Torsten Hallman, Joel Robert, Roger DeCoster, Arne Kring and Ake Johnson and in late October 1967 he won the first meeting of the inaugural Inter-Am series, at Pepperell, Boston, Massachusetts. He kicked off his campaign with a storming overall win finishing 3rd, 1st and 2nd in the three leg motocross, to edge out fellow CZ riders Robert and DeCoster. Their Husqvarna rivals took a real pasting, though they were all riding standard bikes as their factory machines were still in a dock in New York. The Rickman brothers also participated in the meeting on borrowed Triumph Métisses, on their way home from a promotional tour of California.

Though not very impressed by the tracks at that time, Bickers really enjoyed the whole experience and whilst there, he was treated like a movie star and got to meet people such as fellow speed merchant and Formula 1 star Dan Gurney.

Winding down Bickers' style

In 1968 when he would turn 30 years old, Bickers decided that he would take one last shot at the 250 World Championship. At that time, Dave was also concentrating on building up his motorcycle business that was going from strength to strength and was a notable absentee from both the British Championships and the BBC meetings.

Though the World Championship campaign was not a huge success, Bickers did manage to get four podium spots over the season. In the opening GP in Spain, he boosted his confidence in the second leg finishing 3rd ahead of Joel Robert, to take 3rd overall behind

1968

Bickers enjoying a canter on the injured Joel Robert's factory CZ at the 1969 250 British GP at Dodington Park. (BH)

reigning Champion Torsten Hallman and Robert. Then in Luxembourg in May, the podium looked the same, as Bickers edged out fellow Brit, Malcolm Davis. But he was unlucky not to finish higher on the podium with 2nd to Hallman in race one and 3rd to Robert and Hallman next time out for his best ride of the season.

The third podium came at the Russian GP in June, where Hallman and home rider Karel Konecny did the winning, with Hallman edging out the Russian for the overall result. Then in August, Bickers entertained the home crowd at Dodington Park, getting the better of Greeves' Bryan Wade for 3rd overall after finishing 3rd in race one and following that up with 4th in the second race, whilst Robert wooed the crowd with a fabulous display of riding to win both races.

In 1969 Dave focussed almost exclusively on the 250 British Championship and in a closely run contest that went all the way down to the wire he came pretty close to sneaking another title. Malcolm Davis who had been dominant the previous year started the season well before falling out with the AJS management and no single rider stamped their authority on the series, which was lead in turn by Davis, Vic Allan, Alan Clough and Bryan Wade, who would eventually prevail.

Bickers rode consistently and picked up points at each of the five rounds, his best performance being 3rd overall behind fellow 'veterans' Clough and Smith at Nantwich in late March. And after finishing in the points at both races in the penultimate round at the Cotswold Scramble at Nympsfield he was lying sixth in the points classification, but was just eight points adrift of leader Wade, with sixteen up for grabs in the final round at Tirley. However, he didn't have one of his best days, though again he was good enough to score in both races and moved up to finish 5th for the season.

There were still some good days though, such as at Farleigh Castle where he turned back the clock and beat long term adversaries and fellow CZ riders Davis

Still giving it 100%! Bickers represents Britain in the 1969 Motocross des Nations at Farleigh Castle. (BH)

and Mayes to win the 250 Maybug trophy, using all his race guile to pass Davis, who had joined CZ after being sacked by AJS, on the last lap when he was slowed by a backmarker.

Life in the old dog yet

But the highlight of Bickers' season came in the 250 GP at Dodington Park in late June, when Bickers came within a whisker of winning what would have been his fourth home GP. On a works CZ loaned to him by Joel Robert, who was sitting out the GP with an injury, he raced to 4th in race one behind Geboers, Jiri Stodulka and Goss and admitted at the end that *I went around at my own speed without going hard. World Championship points mean nothing to me now."*

However, when the second race got underway, with the fans urging him on, all the old fire returned to his racing. First he found himself in a race with Geboers, passing the Belgian to take the lead and then he came under pressure from Arthur Browning, who rode the best race of his life. Having passed Geboers, Arthur chased down Bickers and passed him briefly for the lead. Then, for a fleeting moment, the impossible seemed to have occurred, as veteran Suzuki rider Olle Pettersson forced his way past Geboers and Bickers was, to coin a modern term, the virtual GP winner! Sadly it didn't last, as Geboers overpowered Pettersson in the closing laps and despite pipping Browning at the post for the race win, Bickers was 2nd overall. But what a performance he had turned in, leaving the 15,000 strong crowd with a memory to cherish.

Racing for the sheer fun of it

Although he quit the GP scene, Dave rode on for many seasons, gracing tracks nationwide with his inimitable style and determination, initially on CZs and latterly on Suzukis. He also tried his hand with sidecars again, having played around with a Greeves outfit in the early '60s. This time he had an interesting oversized CCM-engined outfit, which was followed by a full blown 850cc Norton. Dave remembers his three-wheeled exploits with a lot of affection. *Oh I loved that! It was great fun. The only problem was that I kept losing Peter* (Smith, his 'passenger') *he just couldn't stay in the chair!*

It must have taken a very brave man to climb into a sidecar outfit with Bickers. East Anglian folklore has it that at one event, Smith, shaken by the experience of a first race outing with our hero, went AWOL between races. Eastern Centre aficionado, race commentator and lifelong Bickers fan, Charlie Ralph, takes up the story. "I remember Peter Smith riding sidecar with Bickers at Gt Cornard. He hid up before the start of the second race as a joke, finally appearing just before the off." Apparently after finishing the first race, Smith allegedly proclaimed in his broad Suffolk accent, "I ain't goin' out there n'more!" and promptly disappeared. "What he did," added Ralph, "was to hole up in his brother Colin's burger van and Dave couldn't find him anywhere!"

He also enjoyed racing out on the continent again, in company with his good friend and top Eastern Centre expert Chris Ginn. *We were on guaranteed start money over there. You'd get enough to get you there and back even if you finished last. I made more money racing in French International meetings than I did riding all the GPs! The tracks suited me too as they were fast and smooth, with big jumps.* However, one thing he didn't appreciate about racing over there was the fact that so many riders were billed as 'European Champions'. *There were an awful lot of 'European Champions' racing out there!*

Andy Lee, who had come up against Bickers racing in the Eastern Centre in the late '50s and was known on the continent as the 'King of France', welcomed an opportunity to renew his rivalry with Bickers twenty years on. "Yes, I raced against him in France, when he was winding down and that was so much fun. He's got a tremendous sense of humour and he's just so optimistic about everything and it was just such a pleasure to spend some time in his company."

Bickers Action

When he eventually hung up his boots, Dave made a big career change, as he entered the film stunt business. This came about when Dave visited long-time friend Bud Ekins, at his California home. Ekins had famously become involved in the stunt business when he performed the stunt jump for Steve McQueen in *The Great Escape* and inspired by what his old friend was doing, Dave decided to set up his own business, based, not in Tinseltown, but in Coddenham, of course! He ran the business himself in the early days, before handing over the reins to his son, Paul, and daughter, Andrea. The business, 'Bickers Action' has been a tremendous success and has brought Dave a lot of pleasure over the years.

Today, Dave seems to favour more sedate forms of transport, including vintage tractors and buses which he likes to restore himself, and they give him as much pleasure as his old bikes do. He still enjoys tinkering with bikes though and amonst a large collection he has an interesting vintage FN sidecar outfit. He still attends the occasional Pre-65 Motocross meeting and is guest of honour at an annual reunion of the Ipswich Motorcycle Club, where he gets together with old friends and rivals for an evening of nostalgia.

Bickers seems very happy living in the same village in which he was born and when I last visited him in August 2009, he was preparing a Matchless sidecar outfit for a trip to Ireland. Every year Dave, his wife Silvia, Jeff Smith and his wife Irene, take in a motorcycle rally in Ireland, having a blast on their sidecar outfits and enjoying the countryside and each others' company. He remains to this day an unassuming character who enjoys the simple pleasures in life.

Jeff Smith

From Barr Beacon to the Top of the World

Photo MC

In a career that other riders can merely dream of, Jeff Smith won innumerable national trials, took the prestigious Scottish Six Day Trial, was the winner of the British Experts trial on three occasions, twice captured the ACU Trials Star and claimed eight gold medals in the International Six Day Trial, the first at just 17 years old. He also won 29 GPs, represented Britain in the Trophée des Nations and Motocross des Nations on numerous occasions, took nine British Championships between 1955 and 1967 and was 500cc World Champion in 1964 and '65. In my mind there is no rider who can come close to his record, he is, quite simply, the best off road rider this country has ever produced.

Jeff Smith was born on October 14th 1934 in Colne, Lancashire, but just two years later, his father, in search of work, moved the family south. They first lived in Dunstable, Bedfordshire, before settling in Birmingham. There, Jeff, who was a bright boy, was awarded his Oxford School Certificate at 15, before becoming a General Engineering Apprentice at BSA in Small Heath.

As a young man, his passions were playing football, he was a useful centre-half, and motorcycles. Jeff's father, James, better known to his friends as Vin (short for Vincent), had been a keen trials rider with the Pendle Forest MCC and continued to compete in trials with the West Bromwich MCC up to the outbreak of the Second World War, when he retired his bronze head 250 Royal Enfield to the garden shed.

Happy days

After the war Smith Snr returned to his favourite pastime frequently accompanied by young Jeff, who still cherishes happy memories of those halcyon days. *There was a pillion seat on the machine on which he rode to events and often he took me with him. One morning I remember we had got up at 5am because of the distance to a trial. It was a frosty morning, we both wore balaclavas and goggles and the warmest clothing we had. There was no such thing as Barbour suits in those days, so it was fireman's boots for my father and wellies for me. Oil skins and gauntlets covered the rest of us. When we got to the pub for the start I was amazed to see that my father's face and moustache were covered in ice, as we had ridden through a lot of mist on the way. After a bacon sandwich and a cup of tea he was ready to ride the trial and I was ready to help with the observing.*

Naturally, young Jeff was chomping at the bit to get riding himself and in 1949 Smith Snr bought himself a new 500 'T' Norton and a competition 125 BSA Bantam for his son. *I began practicing every available day at the Barr Beacon sand quarry. I would often be there until dark and then use 'bobby dodgers' (rudimentary lights) to make the 3-mile trip home.* Though he didn't know it at the time, all those hours spent practising in the sand would stand him in good stead many years later, as he was always very comfortable racing on the sandy circuits on the European motocross scene.

Instant success

However, at the time he simply wanted to improve his trials riding technique and it would appear that he did just that, as he won the very first trial he took part in, run by the local club in the Barr Beacon quarry. This was in 1949, and many of the club members including ace sidecar road racer, Bill Boddice, couldn't believe it. *Of course I knew every possible section combination because of my practice schedule riding the Bantam.*

1949/50

In the 1950 season he rode most of the Midland Centre trials, picking up plenty of awards along the way. By this time, Smith Jnr was beginning to get the upper hand over his father which hastened his retirement at the end of the season. *My father decided to retire and put all the competition spirit he had into supporting me on the Norton.*

Factory interest

1951

Things really started to take off for the intrepid youngster in 1951, by which time he was working at BSA as an apprentice. A succession of trophies for premier awards found their way into the Smith household, including his first win in a national trial, the Lomax, which he won as a 16 year-old, and a 3rd place finish in the British Experts Trial. Such success didn't go unnoticed by the leading factories and Smith was soon offered rides by Douglas, AJS and Triumph before he received the promise of a works bike from Norton for the following season.

Indeed for a brief spell he was loaned a factory AJS courtesy of the AMC Competition Chief, Hugh Viney. *The 500 AJS was sent for me to try late in 1951 and it came by train to New Street Station in Birmingham. I rode it in two Midland Centre group trials, winning one of them, but when Viney heard I didn't ride it the third weekend, he sent me a letter which simply read, 'Return machine immediately'. So it went back to London in the Guards van of the next train!*

However, before the year was out Jeff had had his first taste of the ISDT (International Six Day Trial) riding a 500 Norton Dominator twin, on loan from the Bracebridge Street works, in Varese, Italy in September. *I rode the bike from Birmingham to Italy following dutifully and slowly behind my father's Morris. When I arrived there, I changed the rear tyre and chain, rode in the event and then rode back to Birmingham where I was happily relieved of having to follow the Morris! My father bought me a Barbour suit for the event and I still have the jacket, which is in good condition and remains waterproof to this day.* What Smith neglects to mention here, is that the week was a huge success and despite his lack of experience the precocious 16 year-old won the first of eight gold medals he would win in this annual event. Jeff recently pointed out to me that he didn't win his first gold legitimately. *I was not 17 until October and since it was necessary to be 17 to have an FIM licence, it follows that some deception took place!*

Returning to Jeff's other sporting passion during his youth, football, he was playing in a local league and drawing some attention from his local club, West Bromwich Albion, when he got quite badly injured in a game. Step up Mrs. Smith, who told her son in no uncertain terms. "That's the end of football. You're going to concentrate on motorcycling from now on, where any injuries will be your fault - not someone else's!"

Jeff's first off-road heroes were the dominant trials riders of the day, BSA's Bill Nicholson and AMC's Hugh Viney. But he was also a keen road race fan and well remembers a trip to the Isle of Man he made with fellow BSA apprentices, where he caught his first glimpse of another of his idols, Geoff Duke. *He was first on the road because he had won the Senior the year before. It was exciting to hear his Norton labouring towards our vantage point at Ballaugh Bridge, but when he came into view the spectacle and speed were incredible.*

Norton factory rider

When he went to Norton, in 1952, he got to meet his hero Duke, who was a keen off-road rider too and they frequently practiced together. He also got to know trials riders John Draper (who would become his brother-in-law), Rex Young and Ted Breffit and Ted Ogden, who rode a Norton in scrambles.

The friendship with Draper grew as they frequently travelled together and stayed in the same hotels, though there were no expense accounts in those days. *We lived at the same hotels often the whole team in one room, so we got to know each other very well.* It would appear that Jeff was never short of confidence, even in those early days. *I was very much the junior member of the team and I may have been somewhat cocky because they nicknamed me the 'Horrid Kid'.*

A successful move to BSA

However, Jeff's time on Nortons was short lived, as by the end of the 1952 season, he, in company with Draper, Young and his other teammates, found themselves without a ride as Norton disbanded their off-road competition team. Jeff's father mentioned this to BSA's Competition Shop Manager, Bert Perrigo, over a beer one evening and a deal was hastily brokered. *Bert said that he could supply a 500cc works trials machine for £100 and that if I acquitted myself well enough, he would consider refunding the money and putting me on the BSA team with bonuses for success and expenses. Within three months, I had won three nationals and had done sufficiently well to be leading the ACU Trials Star competition. Bert was as good as his word and I became a works rider and began travelling to events with Bill Nicholson.*

Once at BSA in 1953, Jeff's goal was simple. *I wanted to be the best trials rider I could be.* As Smith told me, three men at BSA helped him in achieving this goal; *Perrigo, who was instrumental in helping me succeed in the early days and always showed an interest in what I was doing; Nicholson, who I practiced and travelled with and was a great mentor to me and David Tye, who also taught me a lot.*

With such support, Smith took the trials world by storm winning the ACU Trials Drivers' Star (the forerunner of the British Championship) in 1953 and repeating the feat in 1954. *I had no inclination to go scrambling seriously at that time, it was only after those years that I began to take an interest in scrambling. My earliest motocross hero was John Draper who was a superlative rider in the wet and sometimes surprisingly fast in dry conditions. I often practiced trials and motocross on the Draper farm in Prestbury, near Cheltenham, and learned a great deal from John.*

By 1954 whilst still focusing on trials and retaining the ACU Trials Drivers' Star and winning the Scott Trial, arguably the world's toughest one-day trial, Smith was also trying his hand in a few trade supported scrambles, winning the coveted Experts GN at Rollswood Farm near Redditch and the last Lancashire GN to be staged at, as Smith put it, the 'terrifying' Holcombe Moor. He also found time to take in three European Motocross GPs, winning in Holland and finishing 2nd in France and Belgium to finish 3rd in the European Championship. *I won the Dutch GP when, during the final race, the skies opened up and it rained hard making the track a trials rider's paradise. In retrospect, if, instead of concentrating on trials that year, I had put more effort into motocross, I might well have been European Champion at 19.*

With such prodigious success, it was no great surprise when he was awarded the 1954 Pinhard Prize. This highly prestigious award, named after the founder of the Sunbeam Motor Cycle Club, was awarded

Smith pilots the BSA Gold Star downhill on his way to victory in the 1959 500 British GP at Hawkstone Park. (BC)

annually to (in the words of the Sunbeam Club) 'the young motorcyclist (under 21 years) from an ACU affiliated club, who is adjudged to have made the most meritorious achievement in motorcycle sport in the preceding year'.

1955-59 **Early goals**

However, even as a raw 19 year-old, Smith had very clear objectives in mind. *In my early days there were no World Championships in trails or motocross. So my ambitions were to win the British Trials Championship, the British Scrambles Championship and the European Motocross Championship.*

Within a year he had attained two of the three, as he won the first, of his record nine British Motocross titles, when he took the ACU Scramble Drivers' Star, from fellow BSA man Terry Cheshire and his closest rival during his early motocross days, Bicester farm manager and Matchless works rider, Dave Curtis.

Smith told me that despite such phenomenal success in the early years it was difficult for him to fully focus on his goals. *Becoming 500 European Champion was a definite ambition as early as 1954 when I finished in third place. But during the following years, what with military service, getting married and so on, it was difficult to mount a sustained effort.*

Below is a list of Smith's major successes during the years that lead up to the focus of this book, though needless to say, he was picking up trophies virtually every weekend.

- In May 1955, Smith wins the 'big one' in the trials world, the Scottish Six Day Trial
- Two months later he wins his first 500 British GP at Hawkstone Park, winning both legs in a BSA 1-2-3 ahead of Draper and Stonebridge
- In August, Smith is the best individual in the MDN (Motocross des Nations) in Denmark as Sweden win the team event
- Takes his first ACU Scrambles Drivers' Star edging out fellow BSA man Terry Cheshire with Dave Curtis (Matchless) 3rd
- Wins his first British Experts Trial
- In August 1956 he repeats his best individual performance at the MDN at Namur, Belgium, as the British team triumphs for a 5th time
- Retains his ACU Star comfortably beating Curtis and Cheshire
- Repeats his win in the British Experts
- Gains the Army Trials Championship riding the same 350 Matchless he was using in N° 6 Training Battalion in the REME to train officers to ride motorcycles.

- No ACU Star contest in 1957 due to the Suez crisis and resulting petrol rationing, but he takes another win in the Lancashire GN
- Gets married to Irene Draper in early July and the following day he wins his second home GP at Hawkstone Park, again winning both legs ahead of Les Archer (Norton). Goes on to finish 4th in the inaugural 500 World Championship won by Sweden's Bill Nilsson
- Completes a hat-trick of best individual successes in the MDN held on home soil at Brands Hatch in September, with the British team victorious again
- In a quiet year, having ended military service, Smith cedes the 1958 ACU Star to Curtis and is beaten into 3rd place by Don Rickman (BSA)
- Finishes 6th in the World Championship won by Belgian René Baeten
- Wins the 1959 Experts GN at Rollswood Farm but doesn't mount a challenge for the ACU Star, convincingly won by his teammate Arthur Lampkin
- In July he wins his third home GP at Hawkstone Park though this time he only beats his great rival, Curtis, on time after they finish level on points . He goes on to finish 6th in the World Championship for a second successive year as another Swede, Sten Lundin, is Champion
- Is a member of the winning MDN team in Belgium in August
- Wins the Scott trial on the C15 250 BSA, becoming the first winner on a small bike to also set standard time

A visionary accomplice and a new challenge

Another hugely important figure in Smith's march towards a world title was his BSA stablemate, Brian Martin, who would replace Bert Perrigo as the Competition Shop Manager and was keen to develop a lightweight unit construction scrambler. *Brian had already foreseen the advantages of light weight in trials machines and the works trials team had been using C15s for some time with great success. It was a short step to envision that a lightweight motocross machine would be just as rewarding.* With this in mind, Martin prepared a handful of C15 based machines that he, Smith, Lampkin, John Draper and John Harris would try.

In 1960 Smith had a new goal for his season. *That year Arthur Lampkin and I were set the task of attempting to bring home the 250 European Championship. My second place on a rock standard C15 in the British 250 GP at Beenham Park in 1959 had set this plan in motion and for three years Arthur and I crisscrossed Europe repairing delicate machines and chasing the dream we were destined not to achieve.*

1960

At the same time Greeves were gearing up for their own attempt on the European Championship, with their young, as yet uncut diamond, Dave Bickers. As it turned out, the three British riders would dominate the series in a style that drew the respect of motocross fans across the length and breadth of Europe. *Dave Bickers was then, and still is, a great friend. We all three travelled together in the same vehicle quite often and had a great deal of fun on the road. But when we arrived at an event it was serious business and real rivalry.*

Smith's early season form augured well. At the Hants GN, he won the 250 race ahead of Bickers on his Greeves and then edged out Don Rickman on time in the GN event after they had each won a race apiece. But in the GPs it took him some time to find his feet and after a near miss in the fourth round in Czechoslovakia where he was runner-up to the home rider Soucek, it was a bit like waiting for a bus, as two wins came back-to-back at the ninth round in Luxembourg and the tenth in Britain. After two exciting races in Luxembourg, Smith was tied with Bickers, the GP result finally being decided in Smith's favour with a faster aggregate time.

Whilst GP riders today spend their Saturdays walking the course, practicing, getting their carefully controlled nutrition and listening to their favourite music on their iPods, back in July 1960, Smith and several of his contemporaries prepared for the 250 British GP at Shrubland Park, by racing a full day's programme at the Experts GN meeting at Rollswood Farm, some 150 miles away! Jeff finished second to Joe Johnson on a Greeves in the 250 race, but took the 500 race and the GN event too. His form and his luck continued as he won the GP on the Sunday, winning the first leg from Husqvarna's Stig Rickardsson and teammate Lampkin and following local hero Bickers home in the second.

Smith finally had to cede the title to the relentless Bickers, but only after the East Anglian man had won

Early days on the 250 C15. Cecil Bailey captures Smith as he heads for another win at the 1960 Hants Grand National meeting.

the deciding round in Switzerland. As Jeff recently told me, *David has one fault which always troubled me and made my racing life difficult, he never knew when he was beaten!* Bickers finished the season as Champion, with Smith runner-up ahead of Czech rider, Miroslav Soucek.

'Black Bess' - a fledgling world-beater

With the C15 250 going so well in 1960, Brian Martin, with the full backing of Smith, embarked on the development of a unit construction 350 BSA, which with time would evolve into the championship winning 420s and 440s and would eventually become a full-blown 500. *Brian Martin and I became good friends as BSA teammates and when he became Competition Manager we really began to make headway, culminating in two World Championships. He looked after the technical side and although I helped out with that side, my main contribution was in the riding and analysis.*

The objective for Martin and Smith was simple; to build a powerful yet lightweight machine that would allow the rider to race more efficiently and their philosophy was neatly summed up in an article Smith wrote in the *MCN* of 18th August 1965: *' ... it is an accepted fact that the winner's machine is not always the fastest, but the lightest.'*

Smith began the 1961 season in great form with a hat-trick of wins at Hawkstone Park in March. Racing on a revised circuit didn't affect Smith's success as, using the C15 and his trusty Gold Star, he took the 250, 500 and Hawkstone Championship races. His form continued at the Hants GN in April, where he ran out the winner in the two-leg 500 event. But in August at Shrubland Park, he raced the experimental 350 to victory in the GN race, the little BSA immediately being dubbed 'Black Bess', by one of the journalists of the day, on account of its all-black motor.

Come September, the ACU Star contest was heading for an exciting climax at Thirsk, as Bicester's Dave Curtis appeared to be holding a slender lead over his arch rival. Curtis won the GN event and after finishing 2nd to Smith in the Star race he was declared the winner of the 1961 ACU Drivers' Star with an advantage of six points. However, controversy shrouded the Hawkstone meeting and which race, the Hawkstone Championship

1961

Smith, on the Gold Star BSA, takes the main event at the Hants Grand National meeting on Good Friday 1961. (CB)

At Shrubland Park on August Bank Holiday Monday, 1961, Smith riding 'Black Bess' slips up the inside of teammate John Burton on his trusty Gold Star to take the Grand National event. (MR)

or the 500, had counted towards the Star. In all the confusion Smith was eventually declared the winner, adding a fourth Star to his swelling trophy cabinet.

A gruelling season in Europe

Smith's pursuit of the 250 European Championship began badly, when he picked up an injury to his hand following a heavy fall in race one of the Belgian GP in April. But then he put together a very consistent run of results, including back-to-back GP wins in round three in Holland, where he was untouchable in the sand, and in Czechoslovakia, where he raced to a second leg victory in front of a crowd in excess of 100,000. At that stage Smith held a slender lead over Bickers, but the two riders swapped the lead several times, before a run of bad luck for Bickers saw him drop to third in the table; going into the British GP in July, it was Smith and teammate Lampkin who had the impetus in the title race.

However, the little BSA cried enough at Shrubland Park, as Smith made a vain attempt to stay with Bickers who was doubly determined to take his 'home' GP that year. Smith feels that the Greeves was the more reliable of the two British bikes at that time. *By the time Dave Bickers was winning the European Championship, the Greeves had been upgraded to a contender by Brian Stonebridge and was a sound reliable machine. The BSAs, on the other hand, were not. The engines were a particular source of problems, from the plain metal bearings, to piston seizure and the inevitable ignition troubles. Arthur and I became adept at changing C15 engines in 10 minutes, as this often had to be done in-between races! However, when the engines worked the two machines were competitive racers.*

As a result of his retirement in the home GP, Smith ceded the lead to his travelling companion Lampkin, who had finished second to Bickers. He then finished as runner-up to his teammate in the Swiss round, as Bickers drew another blank, but faded away in the last two GPs to finish the campaign in 3rd place overall behind his compatriots.

Even the snowy winter of 1963 could not stop the televised racing. Here, Smith holds a slim lead over Jerry Scott at the Winchester TV meeting in January. (CB)

1962

Top man

In the early '60s, Smith was such a dominant force in British motocross, especially as there were still 350 races being run in most of the big national events of the day. If Smith turned up at a meeting with his C15 GP bike and a brace of 350 and 500 Gold Stars, there were very few riders who would get a look in and the 1962 season was no exception.

- Smith takes a win in the 'TV Star' race at the two-day meeting at Long Plain Farm, Hambleton near Thirsk, in January, seeing off Lampkin and Vic Eastwood on his factory Matchless
- In March he wins the opening round of the 500 ACU Star at Hawkstone Park, ahead of Lampkin, Burton and Harris all on BSA!
- In mid-April, he takes the 500 Star race at the Wessex Scramble at Glastonbury, leading home Triss Sharp and Lampkin
- Wins his third consecutive Hants GN victory at Matcham's Park two weeks later
- Claims the Beenham 'Jackpot' in May, winning both legs to take overall honours ahead of BSA teammate John Burton and Derek Rickman
- Has a field day at Rollswood Farm in mid-July, winning the 250 GN, the Experts GN and, most importantly, the 500 Star race from Burton and Andy Lee
- At Shrubland Park in August, he shows his versatility, winning the 250 Star race from Bickers and Lampkin and adding the GN and Junior races for good measure
- Enjoys a clean sweep at Hawkstone Park in September, beating Alan Clough and Pat Lamper in the Brian Stonebridge Memorial in addition to wins in the 350, 500 and unlimited events
- As autumn sets in he records three wins at the ABC TV meeting at Clifton
- Finishes the year off in style by winning three finals at the December Scramble at Nantwich

World Champion or bust

Lest we forget, Smith was also busy travelling to and fro across Europe on a regular basis, in his attempt to capture the inaugural 250 World Championship.

He finished 3rd in the season-opening Spanish GP in February, winning race two ahead of teammate Lampkin, who took the GP victory. But he struck back by winning the Swiss GP at Lausanne on aggregate time after he and Lampkin finished with a win and a 2nd apiece. Incidentally, 4th on the day was a certain 18 year-old Belgian by the name of Joel Robert. At the end of May, Smith finished 2nd in the Czech GP, behind local hero Vlastimil Valek, and again finished 2nd in Russia in June, to Sweden's Torsten Hallman, who was beginning to hit form, though Smith still led the championship at this point.

The young Swede, who had finished 4th the previous season and would go on to become a four-time 250 World Champion was full of respect for Smith's professionalism as he told the *Motor Cycle* in January 1972. *'When one race was over, he'd always be working on his bike or dashing back to the factory to get things right for the next big meeting.'*

Smith could do little to halt the Swede's run of form, as he won consecutive GPs in Luxembourg, Finland and West Germany. However, Jeff, who had finished 2nd to Hallman in each of these GPs, must have hoped he could stop the rot in his home GP at Glastonbury in July, but ironically, this is where he lost his lead to Hallman. In race one he could manage no better than 8th place, though he improved to 3rd in the second, to score a single point and keep his championship hopes alive. But Hallman, racing in his home GP in the next round, sealed Smith's fate with victory over the BSA man with two rounds in hand.

After the disappointment of coming so close to a 250 title for a third year, BSA made the decision to change their focus, sending Jeff and Arthur Lampkin out on the road in an attempt to capture the 1963 500 World Championship.

Enter the 420

In early April, Smith took six wins at the two-day meeting at Hawkstone Park, five of them coming on the 350, but two weeks later he took the new 420 to a winning debut at the Hants GN, which counted towards the ACU Star, ahead of Derek and Don Rickman and it was the new 420 that BSA's 'likely lads' would be armed with for their new campaign.

And it didn't take them long to get to grips with the new bike. Having missed the first round in Belgium, Smith finished 3rd overall at the 500 Swiss GP, behind Sten Lundin and Bill Nilsson, but declared himself very happy with the new 420 BSA, telling *MCN*, *'It's now every bit as fast as Lundin's Lito.'* At the next round in Denmark he emerged victorious, winning both races from Husqvarna's Rolf Tibblin and Lundin, ably supported by Lampkin who finished 4th overall.

That season Jeff went up against two of the very best riders in the world in Tibblin and Lundin. The Swedes always had a very professional approach to racing, not unlike Smith's, with good levels of fitness and meticulous machine preparation. Lundin had been Champion in 1959 and '61, whilst Tibblin was the reigning Champion.

In the face of such opposition on an unproven machine, Smith had a very solid campaign in 1963, which paved the way for his success the following year. He finished 2nd overall in Holland and France, but failed to score in Italy, where Tibblin, who won both legs, stretched ahead in the championship. He then lost further ground on Tibblin and Lundin in the Czech and Russian rounds and although he won his home GP at Hawkstone Park and the final round in East Germany, he couldn't catch Tibblin and Lundin and finished the season 3rd overall.

National title number six *in absentia*

In addition to travelling all over Europe in search of the World Championship, Smith also completed a full domestic programme, including contesting the ACU Star contest. In July, Smith headed north for the Cleveland GN at Carlton Bank, Yorkshire, hoping to clinch his sixth title, but he could only finish 2nd to his main challenger Vic Eastwood on the factory Matchless. Then things were made a little more interesting, for everyone bar Smith, when he was selected for the Trophée des Nations team, as incredibly the 250 team meeting in Belgium clashed with the final round of the ACU Star series. As it turned out Jeff and the British Team were relegated to 2nd place by the Swedes though he still managed to hang on to his British title. Jeff takes up the story. *I had an eight point lead and Vic Eastwood would draw level with me if he won and I was not there. The ACU were not willing to change the date of the event or agree to put one more event in the schedule, nor would they allow me to withdraw from the British team. So I let it be known that I would pay £25 to anyone who beat Vic in that round. Andy Lee won and Eastwood was second making me the Champion and I happily paid Andy the £25.*

At Hadleigh, Essex in June 1963, local man Jim Aim pulled off a surprise when he beat the might of the factory BSA team of Smith, Arthur Lampkin and John Burton racing his 500 Triumph-powered Orcadian special. Here Smith on his Gold Star leads Lampkin on a 420 with Aim in close attendance. (MR)

Out front! At the Mortimer Club's Bargepole Scramble at Padworth in October 1963, Smith takes the 500 Star race on his lightweight 420 BSA. (CB)

Smith is pictured here racing in typical TV scramble conditions. (CB)

Unexpected bonus

In November 1963 Smith recorded a win that brought him immense pleasure, when he took the British Experts trial at Knighton on the Welsh border. Jeff takes up the story. *Having long since given up serious trials riding, I managed to beat Sammy Miller into second place. Clerk of the Course was Olga Kevelos who I phoned for confirmation after hearing I had won on the BBC. She told me I had tied with Sammy Miller and beaten him on the special test. She said she had heard he was going to protest the result, which he did, but I was confirmed as the winner. I was just thrilled to have won over Sam who was at the peak of his trials career at that time.*

The Entertainer

The onset of winter in 1963 brought Jeff an opportunity to add another trophy to his rapidly expanding collection, with the advent of the BBC Grandstand Trophy series. Chris Carter reporting in the MCN in October, told readers, '*Saturday saw the start of a new BBC television series starring those two well known entertainers Dave Bickers, the Coddenham "conjurer" and Jeff Smith, the Streetley "stuntman", who shone out like stars among a strong supporting cast, at a sundrenched Hawkstone Park.*' If you forget the 'sundrenched' part, that pretty much sums up the Grandstand series for the next four or five years. Smith, whose record was second only to Bickers in the BBC events, won two races at Hawkstone Park, the 500 race and the 500 Trophy race and by the time the series wound up at Cuerden Park, Lancashire in March 1964, he had won nine of the 11 remaining 500 rounds, to finish 37 points clear of his nearest challenger, BSA teammate Lampkin.

Despite the potential the 420 had shown over the 1963 season, Brian Martin let Smith know that there was a danger that the competition shop might be closed down in 1964. *He (Martin) gave me permission to make any arrangements I could, short of accepting an offer from another manufacturer. Late in 1963 I made arrangements to buy a Métisse kit from the Rickmans and obtained a Matchless engine and a Gold Star gearbox. For the 250 Class Husqvarna sold me a bike and also offered me the importership of Huskies into the UK. Fortunately for me a decision was made before Christmas 1963 that BSA would support only one rider in the New Year and I was chosen and, as they say, the 'rest is history'.*

A long time coming

1963 had been a good season for Smith and BSA, but 1964, even by their high standards, was exceptional. With the BBC Trophy series done and dusted, Smith could turn his attentions on the ACU Star and above all else, the World Championship.

On the domestic front, Jeff was in majestic form, dominating the opening rounds of the ACU Star at Hawkstone Park, the Hants GN and the Cheshire Motocross at Nantwich to put himself in a virtually unassailable lead in early April, after just three rounds.

Smith won two of the three races at the early season St. Anthonis Classic in Holland, but was edged out of victory by World Champion Tibblin, who had switched to a very powerful Hedlund. He then turned his attention to the World Championship, BSA having built him a new, lighter, 420cc for the championship, with a frame built in Reynolds' famed 531 tubing that carried the oil in the top tube, the GP bike weighing in at less than 250lbs.

Showing superb control of the factory 420, Smith is pictured at Hawkstone Park in March 1964. (MC)

At the first round in Switzerland in late April, Smith was level with Tibblin after the two 45 minute races, but Tibblin's aggregate time was six seconds faster, so he was awarded the GP. The second round in Austria went to Tibblin over Smith, as did round three in Denmark, though once again Smith lost out on aggregate time, and they finished in the same order when Tibblin convincingly won his home GP in Sweden, by taking both legs.

At this stage of the season Smith was riding consistently well and the BSA hadn't missed a beat. Unfortunately, for Jeff, Tibblin was simply outperforming him. Smith never lost faith, however, and the breakthrough came in the deep sand of the fifth round at Norg, Holland in mid-May, where he won both legs, though Tibblin followed him home with a solid 2nd overall. Smith slipped to 3rd overall in France, his lowest position all season, but bounced back immediately with victory in Italy.

Showdown in East Germany

At the half-way point of the season Tibblin had a comfortable lead over Smith, but from there on in, the man from Streetly turned on the pressure, with wins in Russia, Belgium and Luxembourg preceding, what for Smith was the decisive round at Schwerin in East Germany. *Tibblin was first and I was second in the first race, but closing fast. At the finish I was about 40 yards adrift. The second race was a ding-dong affair, Rolf led on two occasions and I on three. We lapped the field during our battle and I led Rolf over the line by about 40 yards. Fortunately the Germans were using electronic timing and were able to determine that on total time I had won by a fifth of a second! This was the moment of truth, as for the first time in a long season I had the advantage.*

With just one round to go, at San Sebastian in Spain in September, Tibblin had to win to have any chance of retaining his title. Ironically, poor preparation let Tibblin down, as the pressure seemed to get to him. After the East German round Smith and his loyal helper, John Harris, drove on to Spain, arriving on the Wednesday and giving themselves plenty of time to acclimatise for the GP on the Sunday. In contrast, Tibblin drove back to Sweden before setting out on the long drive to Spain on Thursday morning, arriving in San Sebastian late on Friday evening.

Tibblin's preparation was further hindered, when he decided that he wasn't happy with the Spanish petrol. Smith and Harris had run a test and had decided it was fine for the BSA. Tibblin, however, sent a mechanic off to France on the morning of the GP armed with his petrol tank, the poor man only returning a matter of minutes before the first race was due to start.

However, when the first race got underway it seemed to be a case of business as usual, with Smith deposing early leaders Lundin, and Jerry Scott on his Cheney, and Tibblin storming through to 2nd after a poor start. But then fate intervened, as the Swede's front wheel began to collapse and with just three laps gone Tibblin was out and Jeff Smith was the Champion. Smith also ran out the winner of the GP to register a perfect score in the championship which was decided on a rider's best seven results; in Smith's case his seven GP victories!

A true sportsman

Despite the intensity of their struggles on the track, Smith and Tibblin were good friends with tremendous respect for each other's talent and Rolf was soon out trackside, waving the new Champion on to victory. He was also the first person to shake Jeff's hand, telling reporter Chris Carter "I'm disappointed of course, but it's only a game and the best man has won!"

For Smith, at 30 years of age, the dream had finally come true and he had reached all the goals he had set himself 11 years earlier as the new boy at BSA. He had become British Trials Champion, British Scrambles Champion and now, after a gruelling 14 round series that spanned six months, he was the World Motocross Champion.

Incidentally, if you're wondering what happened to the home round in 1964, there wasn't one, as Britain hosted the MDN at Hawkstone Park in late August, where Smith showed his pedigree, winning both races and leading Britain to victory over Belgium, ably supported by Don and Derek Rickman, Vic Eastwood and Arthur Lampkin.

Fitter and faster

1965 was another exceptional season for Smith. He was in fine form in the BBC Grandstand races, though after missing the opening two rounds, the second as he was collecting his World Champion's gold medal at the FIM Congress in Prague, he couldn't catch Chris Horsfield, the Matchless man being in fine form that winter.

As World Champion, Smith had great confidence in himself and his bike for the coming GP season as

1965

he explained. *Retaining the title in 1965 was not difficult because my machine was stone reliable and at the time the best there was. Two graph lines crossed during those two years, the experience and fitness lines. I had about as much experience as I could have absorbed and with Maurice Herriot's help I was fitter than I had ever been.*

Herriot, a fellow employee at BSA, was a world ranked athlete who had won a silver medal in the Steeplechase event at the Tokyo Olympics in 1964 and he helped Smith with his fitness regime, getting him into peak shape over the winter of 1964/65.

Star quality

With a new level of fitness that set him apart from most of his competitors, Smith took his eighth ACU Star that year, but Dave Bickers, who rode a 360 CZ in three of the five rounds, and new teammate Vic Eastwood made sure he had to fight tooth and nail to win it. Having won the final round of the 500 Grandstand Trophy series at Cross-in-Hand, Sussex, on the last Saturday of March, he headed up to Hawkstone Park for the following day's opening round of the ACU Star.

However, unlike the TV race which Smith had led from start to finish, he had to work really hard for this win in Shropshire. In the 12-lap Star race, Smith fell mid-race whilst lying second and had to fight back to get on terms with Horsfield, Eastwood and Arthur Lampkin. As the race entered the final lap, Smith drew alongside Horsfield as they stormed the famous Hawkstone 'mountain' and Horsfield, in his haste, missed a gear and crashed into the fencing, leaving Smith to ride in unchallenged to the flag.

Smith pushing on at the 1965 Hants Grand National on the 440 BSA, where he took the Victor to victory in the second leg after being eliminated from the first with clutch-slip. (CB)

In the groove! Smith on his way to his fifth British 500 GP win at Hawkstone Park in July 1965. (MC)

Though he only raced in four of the five Star races that season, with three wins and a 2nd place to Eastwood at Hadleigh, Essex in June, he was too strong for his challengers. However, things might have been different had Bickers been able to ride at Hawkstone Park (it clashed with the 250 GP in Spain) and had Eastwood's gearbox not seized up at the Cumberland GN in April.

Smith went to the opening round of the World Championship in Austria as leader of the Star competition and as such was brimming with confidence. However, things didn't go to plan, as his BSA suffered a rare mechanical failure when the clutch burnt out in the first race. But a week later he took the first of six GP wins he would register over the course of the season, at Wohlen in Switzerland, winning the first race and finishing just two seconds adrift of championship leader, Sten Lundin, in race two to guarantee top spot.

Master tactician

Smith, who was renowned for his calculated approach to racing, rarely seemed to do more than was necessary to win a race. *I was extremely focused on winning and being in the right place at the right time was my focus. Early in my motocross career I realized that there was only one moment when it was important to be in the lead and that lead could be as little as half a wheel. Often the easiest way to win was to follow the man who was destined to finish second until the last lap, pass him at one of the predetermined spots and jump immediately onto his line, thus giving him no time to adjust and counterattack.*

Smith was the undisputed master of this strategy, carefully biding his time before striking to win yet another race. However, what was so often overlooked by the uninitiated was the work that had gone into winning the race before a single wheel had turned. *Such a strategy required an excellent knowledge of the course, gained by pre-walking and close study during practice, good racing experience and an ability to be strong at the end of the race combined with a trustworthy and reliable machine.* Smith also gained a reputation for being rather aloof and unfriendly, but as he explains it had more to do with his focus than anything else. *Gaining and applying these requirements took application and concentration. Thus I had little time for social intercourse and I was single minded and to some extent unapproachable.*

Winning spell

The win in Switzerland marked the beginning of a run that provided Smith with the platform for his second World Championship, as it was followed by victories in France, Sweden and Finland. The French GP at Tarare, was a huge success for the British contingent, with Smith leading home Jerry Scott, Lampkin and Eastwood in race one and winning the second. Scott finished in a career best second overall, though Swede Per-Olaf Persson spoilt the party by taking 2nd in race two to edge out Lampkin for the third step on the podium.

But the win in Finland in early May was marked by the presence of a new, almost sinister, rival to Smith. Indeed the *MCN* headline of the day, choosing not to commemorate Smith's win, simply stating: *EAST GERMAN SHADOWS JEFF SMITH.*

The East German in question was Paul Friedrichs, who within a few short years would become a triple-World Champion. As the reporter went on to observe, '*It was a game of cat and mouse with Smith the mouse! He didn't like it. … Even when Smith deliberately slowed down Friedrichs just stayed behind, disconcertingly confident.*' Smith won both legs from his 'shadow', but he clearly wasn't happy.

Whilst seemingly winning at his will on the GP circuit, Smith faced a stern challenge in the fourth round of the ACU Star at the Cotswold Scramble at Nympsfield in June. 250 GP runner Bickers, who had been given dispensation by Greeves to race a 360 CZ, rode a brilliant race, charging through the field to snatch the lead from Smith on the eighth lap of the 10-lap race. But then, in a moment of high drama, Bickers and CZ cartwheeled down the track with less than a lap of the race remaining. Smith and Eastwood gratefully slipped past before Bickers could remount and Smith scored his second win of the series to take a slim lead over Eastwood and Bickers to the final round at Padworth Park, Reading, in October.

Smith smokes the world's best for N°6

At the beginning of July, Smith went to Hawkstone Park, for what would turn out to be his last home GP win. He rode a typically cagey first race, moving steadily through the field from ninth on the first lap to second behind Eastwood, where he patiently sat, until with less than two laps to go he swept past his tiring teammate for the win. In the second leg, he trailed

Malcolm Carling spotted Smith catching up with the news in the paddock.

CZ man Tibblin, knowing that second would be good enough to win him the GP, though he had to fend off a spirited attack from Eastwood in the closing laps. As Smith mounted the podium, the 32,000 spectators hailed their Champion, as he took another giant step towards retaining the championship.

Smith often came under criticism from the motorcycle journalists of the day for tactics such as these. *Mainly the press did not understand my methods and would mistake a win where I carefully calculated what was required, as being 'lucky'. In the second race of a GP for instance, provided you had a good first race it was unnecessary to win the second race as long as you had good signals and placed yourself in the right position. Such an approach cut down significantly on race risk and ensured more comfortable success.*

Mission Impossible

After winning his sixth British GP, Smith had virtually guaranteed himself his second world title and at this stage the BSA management interjected with a plan to bring the BSA 'Victor' further publicity. *Mr. Sturgeon, managing director of BSA asked me to try and win one of the remaining rounds on a production Victor. The machine was similar to the 420/441 I had used during 1964, but had heavier wheels and some other compromises necessary for production in quantity. Although I rode the machine in several GPs the best I could do was a 6th place, which was worth one point in the World Championship!*

Smith soon reverted to his GP bike and eventually secured his second world title with victory in the deep sand of Berharen, Holland in late July, with a win and a 3rd place in the two legs. He dominated the first and despite a tumble at one-third race distance he recovered to finish comfortably ahead of the CZ pair, Friedrichs and Tibblin, the Swede having won the previous GPs in Italy and West Germany. The second leg saw another calculated ride from Jeff, who was content to trail young Dutchman, Jef Teuwissen and Tibblin, safe in the knowledge that third place would win him the GP and with it the World Championship.

Good things come to those ...

The World Championship may have been decided in his favour, but Smith would have to wait another 10 weeks before the outcome of the ACU Star would be known. In the meantime he put on a world class show of riding at the Thirsk International at Boltby in September, winning two of the three legs for a clear overall victory ahead of Jerry Scott and the consistent Brian Nadin.

Then after the long wait, at the Mortimer Club's meeting in the second week of October, Smith added his sixth straight 500 ACU Star, winning the aptly named 'Jackpot' Scramble, which counted towards the Star. In an exciting race which saw Jerry Scott lead for three-quarters of the race before his rear suspension gave up, Smith came through closely followed by Bickers, now riding the new pre-production 360 Greeves. Bickers challenged strongly and actually took the lead for a few fleeting seconds, but Smith eased ahead and held on for a narrow win, with Eastwood and Scott also in close attendance.

A turbulent season

After the highs of the previous two seasons, 1966 would be a trying time for Smith. It all started brightly enough though, with Smith, who had gone into the New Year with a perfect three races three wins ratio in the Grandstand

1966

Smith gives the new 'Titan' a good workout on its debut at the 1966 Hants Grand National. (CB)

Trophy, making it four out of four at the opening round of the year held at Caerleon in truly atrocious conditions. He would go on to add wins at Jewels Hill, Kent and Brill in Buckinghamshire, to regain the title he had lost to Chris Horsfield the previous winter.

BSA had also been working very hard over the winter to produce a bike they hoped would land them, and Smith, a hat-trick of World Championships and the new bike would soon be ready for its racing debut in the British Championship. *For 1966 BSA decided to make an extremely light machine with a full 500cc engine. The main direction was to make use of exotic lightweight materials such as titanium, magnesium and aluminium alloys combined with advanced designs and practices. This necessarily took most of the work, except for the actual building of the machine, out of the hands of the Competition Department. We had built two very successful machines, but now we were to enter a new world with many untried designs and ideas. This machine was made in five months beginning with preparatory designs in September/October of 1965.*

When the British Championship got underway at Hawkstone Park at the end of March, Smith took to the line on his trusty 440, but he was blown away by Bickers, who had signed to CZ and would be one of Jeff's rivals in the World Championship. Indeed for a short spell at Hawkstone, Smith was relegated to 3rd by Horsfield on another CZ, before recovering to finish 2nd, unaccustomed as he was to doing this, on the tough, demanding, Shropshire circuit.

The Titan enters the arena

Then at the Hants GN in early April, Smith debuted the titanium-framed, full 500cc Victor. However, Smith and the 'Titan' were completely upstaged by a supreme display of riding skill from Bickers (see p31) Smith relentlessly reeled him in during the first leg but Bickers had things under control maintaining a slim

At the 1966 500 British GP at Farleigh Castle, Smith launches the BSA uphill. (MC)

lead to the flag. In the second leg Bickers went straight to the front chased by Smith. The two superstars of British motocross then simply left the others trailing behind, but Bickers steadily extended his lead and had 11 seconds to spare over Smith at the flag. *With the first GP only a week away, we began to realise that this very advanced machine would need a long period of race testing before all the bugs would be worked out. The year turned out to be a frustrating mix of success and failure. The machine was troublesome from the start but showed great potential.*

Smith certainly had a frustrating time in the opening rounds of the World Championship. In the season-opener at Payerne, Switzerland, a loose float chamber on the carburettor and a broken chain eliminated him from each leg whilst well placed. A week later and the venue was Sittendorf, Austria, where unfortunately for Smith his luck had not changed. Whilst running 4th in the first leg the rear suspension started to play up and he had to settle for 5th. In the second race he was still in the paddock when the officials let the field go. 50 seconds later he powered over the line in hot pursuit of the rest of the field, but he could only claw his way back to 7th. However, it was worth the effort, as his fighting display was rewarded with 5th overall and his first championship points.

An upturn in form

Things greatly improved in Italy, where he finished 2nd overall behind Friedrichs and although he went out of the first race in Denmark he thrilled the crowds in race two, passing Tibblin, young Belgian Sylvain Geboers and Friedrichs for an emphatic and very popular win. He finished 6th in Sweden the following week, but

Smith pressing on at Farleigh Castle as he tries, in vain, to outdistance Don Rickman, who had won the first leg and was the eventual GP winner. (MC)

roared back to victory in the sixth round of the series at Tikkurila, Finland. On a dry, dusty track, Smith finished a close 2nd to Swede Gunnar Johansson in the first leg, before taking control of the second and beating the same rider by a comfortable margin of 30 seconds.

Things were looking up for Smith and he finished 2nd in the next round in East Germany. However, the man who won there, Paul Friedrichs, registered his fifth win of the series and was in peak form adding wins in Czechoslovakia and Russia to virtually guarantee him the championship.

A spanner in the works

When the GP circus headed to Farleigh Castle, Wiltshire in early June , Smith was lying 3rd in the championship one point adrift of Tibblin, but 27 points behind the runaway series leader Friedrichs. When the East German opted not to race at the British GP, a small window of opportunity opened for Smith. His task was now to win the British GP, held at the Wiltshire circuit for the first time, and the four remaining rounds! This was a tall order but Smith was never one to shy away from a challenge.

On a day that was dominated by home riders, Smith was upstaged by Don Rickman on his Triumph Métisse in the first race, the younger of the two brothers from New Milton, Hampshire, enjoying one of the most inspired day's racing of his career. Rickman beat Smith by 16.8 seconds with the Czech, Vlastimil Valek, filling 3rd spot. However, many of the 24,000 spectators in the crowd knew that the GP was not over yet and fully expected Smith to take the challenge to Rickman which is exactly what happened.

Smith's BSA teammate Jerry Scott led from the start, but couldn't hold off Rickman, who was really flying again. This time, however, Smith latched on to his rival, as the two of them pulled clear of the field. What followed was a titanic struggle, with Jeff trying to shrug off the man who threatened to end his dream of a hat trick of World Championships. After passing Rickman mid-race, Smith put the hammer down and began to stretch away from his adversary, but in Smith-like fashion, Rickman managed to stay close enough to the leader and when the racing was over and the race times added up, he was declared the GP winner by just 1.8 seconds.

Beautifully poised, Smith racing in the BBC Grandstand meeting at Naish Hill in February 1967. (RD)

Jeff Smith

After the disappointment of the home GP, Smith went to Holland three weeks later to try and salvage 2nd place in the championship. However, things went badly in the first race which was won by Tibblin with Smith languishing back in 5th place after an altercation with a tree. Things got worse in the second leg though, when the motor blew as he was contesting the lead with Tibblin and Bickers. As a result, Tibblin appropriated 2nd place from Smith and the top three positions were settled for the season.

Tragedy at Boltby

Smith was having a difficult time of things, but worse was to come. On 31st July 1966, Boltby, on the North Yorkshire moors, was the venue for the 21st North v South team challenge and the cream of British motocross assembled there in readiness for a classic encounter. However, as the first leg entered the fifth lap Jerry Scott from Poole in Dorset, fell and Smith and Dave Nicoll, who were in close attendance, had no chance to avoid hitting the prone rider. Tragically, 27 year-old Scott, who had been signed up by BSA that year and was seen as a potential World Champion himself, died in the accident. Smith was naturally shaken and it was the psychological rather than physical damage that affected him most. *Jerry was killed and I suffered a broken wrist and collarbone. Up to that time I had not broken any bones, so this was something of a shock and with the trauma of it being a fatal accident I feel I really lost something that day. I have always thought that since that accident I have never ridden with the same freedom and determination as formerly.*

Double break

Smith, who was the model professional, took time out to recover and managed to get himself into some sort of shape for the final round of the British Championship at Cadwell Park in October. But disaster struck again, when, just 150 yards from the start line, he clashed with Chris Horsfield who was having his first ride on the 360 Greeves. *He (Horsfield) made a mistake with either the gear change or brake lever immediately after the start as we were going up a rutted ramp which led to a jump over the road race circuit.* In the melée several riders fell including Jeff, who had no chance to avoid the back wheel of the momentarily stationary Greeves. Smith fell heavily making contact with the tarmac and breaking his other collarbone.

This injury effectively brought to an end the most disappointing season in Smith's long and highly successful career, with Bickers becoming the first rider to win the 500 Championship on a foreign machine and the first to win it on a two-stroke. Essentially, this marked the beginning of the end for both Smith and BSA competing at the highest level.

Smith still managed to make his second comeback before the season's close, racing at the second round of the Grandstand Trophy at Dodington Park in November, where he recorded a steady 5th place before adding points at the fourth round at Tweseldown on Christmas Eve, when he finished 4th, as Dave Bickers, who was running away with both series, raced to another stunning double victory.

Write him off at your peril!

As 1967 dawned, there was little Smith, or anybody else for that matter, could do about checking Bickers in

1967

Smith attempts to close down Dave Bickers (out of shot) at the BBC scramble at Hankom Bottom in March 1967. (BH)

At the 500 GP at Farleigh Castle in July 1967, Smith holds a slim lead over his friend and rival, Dave Bickers. (BH)

the Grandstand Trophy, as he rode on to become the first rider to win both the 250 and 750 Categories in the same series, Smith eventually finishing 8th overall in the 750 Class.

Jeff was getting back to his best though and at the early season international meeting at Lummen, Belgium, in February, he sent out a clear warning to his World Championship rivals; I'm back and I want my title back too! In race one, he had a great battle with Joel Robert, outsmarting the Belgian to win by 18 seconds, whilst in the second leg, the master tactician followed home Belgians Roger DeCoster and Jef Teuwissen for overall victory.

Luck deserts Smith

When the championships proper got underway Smith had his fair share of bad luck. At the opening round of the 500 British Championship at Hawkstone Park, he was eliminated when he picked up a rear tyre puncture, though he was back in the points two weeks later on a very muddy Nantwich track, where he took a hard earned 2nd place behind man of the meeting, Chris Horsfield.

In the World Championship there was a similar pattern, as he finished out of the points in Austria, when the chain broke in the second leg after a solid 3rd place in race one. But he took 3rd overall in the Swiss GP, won by Bickers, taking the second leg when his compatriot waved him through knowing that he had the GP wrapped up. It was a case of *déjà vu* for Smith, as three weeks earlier he had also finished 3rd to Bickers, at the third round of the home championship at Dodington Park, where teammate Eastwood split the long term rivals.

Better luck, but no catching Friedrichs

Following a disappointing East German GP, where he failed to add points, Smith bounced back in the best possible fashion, winning the Russian GP with a great second race win over home rider, and winner of the first race, Vladimir Pogrenyak, to re-ignite his title challenge. Also of note here, was Keith Hickman's gutsy ride on the Cheney BSA which earned him 6th overall, whilst Smith's win lifted him to joint 2nd with Bickers in the overall classification. In the following rounds Smith added points in France and West Germany where he finished 4th and 2nd respectively to consolidate 2nd place in the championship, though Friedrichs began a run of four straight wins in France that would see him retain his world title.

At the end of July, Farleigh Castle hosted the ninth round of the series, where Smith hoped to check his East German rival's progress. However, it was Friedrichs who treated British motocross fans to a masterclass, as he completely dominated the racing, winning the first leg from Eastwood and Don Rickman, now on a BSA Victor Métisse, as Smith could do no better than fourth. Then in the second leg, when Rickman retired mid-race with gearbox problems, Friedrichs pulled over to allow his friend and teammate, Bickers, to take the win and complete a CZ one-two on the podium. Smith, who lost out on second overall to his countryman, was far from pleased though, as he effectively lost the title at Farleigh Castle for the second consecutive year.

Friedrichs clinched his second World Championship at the next round in Belgium, where Smith had to give second best to the CZs, Friedrichs winning and Bickers taking the second step on the podium ahead of Smith. Although CZ dominated the second half of the season, with Bickers winning his second GP of the season in Luxembourg and Friedrichs taking his eighth win in the final round in Switzerland, Smith did manage to stave off his long term rival, Bickers, to hold on to 2nd place in the championship.

Refocussing attentions

The World Championship may have been lost, but the British Championship was still up for grabs, with Smith holding a slim four point advantage over Bickers and Eastwood, whilst Horsfield and Clough were still in with a shout a further two points adrift. So, on the day after his 33rd birthday, Smith headed off to the final round at the Kidston Scramble at Builth Wells, where he enjoyed a grandstand view as all the drama unfolded.

As young Welshman Andy Roberton on his CZ shot into a surprise lead, Horsfield was the first to crack, crashing as he attempted to pass an unphased Smith. Eastwood and Clough passed Roberton on the fourth lap, whilst Greeves' youngster, Bryan Wade, crashed out on one of the downhill stretches. As the race reached the half-way point, Eastwood led Clough and another surprise package, Terry Challinor on his 360 Sprite, with Smith back in 7th following Arthur Browning and teammates Banks and Arthur Lampkin.

Then Clough slipped past Eastwood and Challinor crashed out, to ease Smith's plight. The BSA man still needed to make up another position though and after getting past a tiring Banks he received a pit signal telling him he would be Champion if everybody held their places. With loyal lieutenant Lampkin chaperoning him to the line, Smith beat Clough and Eastwood by two points and was British Champion for a ninth time.

Smith was crowned British Champion for a final time and although he raced on until he emigrated to Canada in 1971, and had some great moments along the way, he was no longer the dominant force he had been.

Top Cat amongst the pigeons

However, he wasn't quite done with winning championships in Britain, as he pulled off a major surprise over the winter of 1967/68 when he dominated the 250 Grandstand Trophy, winning three of the five races and twice finishing 2nd in the others. Smith was riding so well that he finished 16 points clear of AJS' Malcolm Davis, who had to fight Freddie Mayes and Arthur Browning to see who would finish 2nd. *The 250 I used in 1967/68 was a marvellous device we made up in one of the remaining titanium frames. The engine was making 21 or 22 hp but had a beautiful torque curve which made it easy to ride. The whole machine, ready to race, weighed 199lbs. so it was really great fun. It was exciting seeing how well we could do chasing the youngsters and their 2-strokes.*

A new order

In 1968 Jeff was coming under increasing pressure from younger riders, not least of all on the BSA team. Eastwood was still looking to win his first major title and Banks, who had edged out Eastwood to take the 750 Grandstand Trophy, was beginning to show more self-belief. BSA had also recruited Cambridgeshire runner Dave Nicoll, who had been plying his trade in France for several seasons, and Oxfordshire man Keith

1968/9

Brian Holder catches Smith racing in the 500 British Championship at Wakes Colne in June 1968.

Hickman, who had demonstrated his potential the previous season when he achieved some outstanding performances in the 500 GPs racing Eric Cheney's 440 BSA.

Smith found it difficult to defend his British title, only registering his first points at the third round at Farleigh Castle, where he would post his best result of the series, finishing 2nd to championship leader Banks in the second race. However, he also added points in each of the four remaining races, to finish the season in 5th place, as Banks captured the first of his four British titles .

The '68 season also marked Jeff's final GP campaign when he accompanied Banks in his first full season of 500 GPs. Smith would finish on the podium on three occasions, in Sweden, Holland and Switzerland, bringing to a close a truly wonderful era.

The following season, 1969, was a very quiet one for Jeff, limited mainly to the televised races where he rounded off the 750 Grandstand Trophy with a fine 2nd place to fellow Birmingham man, Arthur Browning, to leap-frog up the table to 4th in the final standings.

One high point that season was his selection for the MDN team one last time and at Farleigh Castle in September, he turned in a solid performance to finish in 7th position in both races, therefore justifying his selection. Unfortunately, the British team could only finish 3rd, thus incurring their first home loss in the competition, though Banks, who suffered an electrical failure in race one, thrilled the crowd as he won the second race, beating the new World Champion, Bengt Aberg, in the process.

Motocross ma'am

Whilst competing in a motocross series in New Zealand in the winter of 1969/70 with Dave Bickers, Jeff received word that he was to be awarded an MBE as announced in the New Year's Honours list. *I had been aware that I might be included in the list, because Harold Wilson (Prime Minister) had written to ask me if the Queen was gracious enough to offer would I accept. Naturally I had written "Yes" even though I was no lover of Mr. Wilson's politics!*

1970/1

So, in March 1970 a very proud, Jeffrey Vincent Smith, took his family along to Buckingham Palace, where his many years spent representing his nation and promoting BSA were officially recognised when he received an MBE for 'services to motorcycling'. It was presented to him at Buckingham Palace by the Queen Mother who in her own inimitable style engaged Jeff in some friendly banter. *The Queen Mother said "Motocross?" and I said "Yes, ma'am", which was the form of address we were told to use. Then she said "We sometimes watch it on television". But maybe the most fun was when I told the taxi driver in the morning "Buckingham Palace - inside the gates."!*

Fun and games on an exotic lightweight or a calculated campaign?

As he entered the third decade of his career in 1970 Smith stunned the country's leading 250 exponents, when he campaigned another lightweight BSA in the British Championship. In the first big race of the year, the BBC Grandstand meeting at Hadleigh, Essex, John Banks, who hadn't raced a 250 in earnest since his days with Dot six years previously, shocked TV viewers as he borrowed Smith's bike to beat all the two-stroke aces. And when the British Championship got underway at a very muddy Hatherton Hall, Nantwich in April, Smith handed out a lesson to the youngsters, as he buzzed the little Beezer to third in the first race, after being left on the line, and surprised everybody with a win in race two.

Round two was at Tilton in June, where Smith continued to impress with 3rd and 4th place finishes in the two races, though AJS star Malcolm Davis seized control of the series with a double win. Davis was in a class of his own that year, but Smith and the little BSA finished every race they competed in with another excellent performance coming in Smith's native Lancashire, at Cureden Park in late July, where he twice finished runner-up to Davis. Unfortunately, he missed the final round at Beenham Park in October, as he was

It's the 1969 Motocross des Nations at Farleigh Castle and elder statesmen Smith and Bickers appear to be taking time out to discuss tactics. (BH)

away racing in the USA, allowing AJS' Andy Roberton to overhaul him for the runner-up spot.

Smith recently told me that he always meticulously planned out his racing year. *Once I had the list of important events, all other events were treated as testing or practice events. This meant that I knew exactly when I wanted to be very fit and my machines must be in perfect order. It allowed me to bring tremendous focus to events which were important and not be too concerned about others. Some years I rode in more than 60 events, so it made sense that maximum effort be required and expected at only a few. Obviously the series where I looked for success were the Star or British Championships, the BBC Grandstand events and World Championships.* It would seem from his success in 1970 that even in the twilight of his career he adhered to this disciplined approach to his racing.

The New World beckons

In 1972, Jeff upped sticks, much as his father had done 36 years earlier, and moved his family to Canada, having been head hunted for a job working for the Bombardier company to help develop the Can-Am motorcycle, as Jeff recalls. *By 1972 it seemed that motorcycling in the U.K. was destined for the scrap heap of history. I was offered a 3-year contract to help Bombardier build motorcycles from a clean sheet of paper and be well paid for doing it. In the end I had 17 rewarding years working for Bombardier. I never thought at that time that I would still be on this side of the Atlantic 38 years later but here we are and very happy about it.*

22 years ago Jeff and family settled in Wisconsin, where he lives to this day. *Irene and I have been happily married for 53 years, we have two children who between them have produced 3 grandchildren. We live close enough to see each other often and also meet at vintage events where our boy, James, also races a BSA. I ride in about 12 off-road events a year and from time to time I am invited to events for ancient warriors in other parts of the world. As long as they send me an air ticket I usually go! I am still involved with AHRMA (the American Historic Racing Motorcycle Association) and enjoy the events and the fellowship.*

Happy landings

Smith is clearly very content with his life in America and has no regrets about making the move. Indeed, he revealed a philosophical side to his character when he shared the following episode with me. *One winter night years ago, I was walking Rufus, a magnificent hound whose golden retriever mother had been courted by a wolf. There was a full moon, not a cloud in the sky, it was 25 degrees below zero fahrenheit and the snow squeaked as we walked. I thought "How did it all come down to this?" The only answer is that when we set out there's no way to know where we will wash up. Mostly we can't chart our lives and know the end, all we can do is look back down the years and know it was good.*

Jeff seems to have 'washed up' in a place that makes him very happy. How strange though, that his life's journey has taken him from Walsall, West Midlands, to Wausau, Wisconsin.

The years were certainly good to Jeff Smith, BSA and all of those who followed his career with interest. But lest any of you think the 'ancient warrior' has turned his back on everything that once mattered to him, let me put you at ease. Alan Clough, who was privileged enough to be in Smith's close circle of friends, once told me that Jeff stood for the three Bs - Britain, BSA and Birmingham. *Cloughy was right in many ways, I stood for all of those things and I still do. How could it be otherwise, considering that everything I am has origins in these entities? We, as a family, have not changed our nationality and retain our British passports, and I proudly call us English!*

Arthur Lampkin

Yorkshire's Finest

Photo CB

There wasn't much that Arthur Lampkin didn't win in the world of trials and motocross. He was a 250 and 500 GP winner, a stalwart member of the British teams in the Motocross des Nations and the Trophée des Nations and represented the nation in the International Six Day Trial in Garmisch-Partenkirchen in 1958 and 1962 winning Gold Medals on both occasions. He also captured both the ACU 250 and 500cc Drivers' Stars (British Championships) and was runner-up in the 1961 250cc European Motocross Championship. He was a prolific winner of trials events, with victories in the Scottish Six Day Trial, the Scott Trial in his native Yorkshire on three occasions, and the British Experts Trial. But, despite all of this he is probably best remembered as 'Mr. Television', a title he earned from his sterling efforts in the televised winter race meetings of the 1960s. As the old adage goes, 'When the going gets tough, the tough get going' and this was certainly true in Lampkin's case, though he didn't just go, he usually disappeared clean out of sight.

Arthur John Lampkin was the eldest of three sons born to Arthur Snr and his wife, Violet in May 1938. Though seen by many as being 'Yorkshire through and through', Arthur was actually born in Shooters Hill near Woolwich, where his father worked as a turner at the Woolwich Arsenal until the outbreak of the Second World War. At that juncture they decamped to the West Yorkshire village of Silsden, on the edge of Ilkley Moor, where his father established a precision engineering company.

First trial

Arthur's first contact with motorcycles came when he was given a 1937 side-valve BSA at the tender age of 12. It was the beginning of a life-long affection for motorcycles, but it wasn't all roses for the young Yorkshireman. When still only 15 years old he had a brush with the law; he was caught riding the BSA on the public highway! He was summoned to appear in court in nearby Skipton, where his father told the magistrate, "He was born on wheels and wants to be a trials rider."

A Triumph Tiger 80 followed the BSA and this in turn was followed by a 197cc James that Arthur started riding in trials once he turned 16. In his first season he rode it in the toughest one day trial of them all, the Scott, complete with L-plates and following a good ride in the Alan Jeffries trial he graduated to the expert ranks after just five trials.

1955

Aiming high

After several successful outings on the James he graduated to a 350 Royal Enfield Bullet, which was converted from a roadster. On the Bullet, Lampkin took part in his first Scottish Six Day Trial in May 1955, taking a Special First Class award at the end of a gruelling week. The winner of the trial was none other than Jeff Smith, who would soon become Lampkin's teammate and close friend.

1956

BSA support

In his early years, Lampkin was also befriended by one of Yorkshire's trials riding greats, Tom Ellis. Ellis, a BSA factory rider of some standing, used his influence to persuade the company to give Lampkin the use of a bike. So it was that whilst still only 17 years old, Lampkin was entrusted with a 500 Gold Star trials bike. He returned to Scotland in May 1956 and after day one he was one of four riders tied for the lead on a clean sheet. He had an outstanding week eventually finishing 5th overall and taking the over 350 Class in just his second Scottish. Lampkin loved the whole experience, telling Peter Howdle of MCN, 'It felt wonderful to ride a works bike'.

With his trials riding career going from strength to strength, Lampkin decided to try his hand at scrambling. His first event was at Post Hill near Leeds, though it was no fairy tale debut for Arthur. Riding a 350 Gold Star, he took an excursion into the bushes whilst trying to keep up with another Yorkshire great, Frank Bentham. However, he rapidly learnt the art of off-road racing and soon found himself on the BSA factory team as their youngest ever rider, following the departures of Brian Stonebridge, to Greeves, and John Avery who had stepped down to devote more time to his motorcycle business.

1957

As a fledgling BSA rider he was on a steep learning curve. By Easter 1957 he already had the measure of local ace Bentham, beating him on the moors at Boltby and going on to win both the Junior and Senior races at that year's Cumberland Grand National riding the 350 Goldie. Then in May he switched back to his trials bike for the Scottish, improving to 3rd overall, behind winner Johnny Brittain and his BSA teammate John Draper, who beat him on the special test.

Not surprisingly, the same year he captured the hugely prestigious Pinhard Prize (awarded to the best performance by an under 21 year-old in all areas of competition motorcycling), whilst still only 18 years old.

1958/59

1958 found Britain's most talented young motorcyclist on national service in the army, where he soon became Lance Corporal Lampkin, motorcycle riding instructor. As such, he managed to stay fairly active as a trials rider at least, winning the army championship and taking in his first trip abroad to Germany for the ISDT at Garmisch-Partenkirchen, where he rode a 350cc Gold Star to a Gold Medal. Then following his demobbing, in January 1959, his motorcycling career really started to take off.

That year he was in inspired form on the 500cc Gold Star scrambler, taking the coveted ACU Scrambles Drivers' Star by a comfortable margin of seven points from Derek Rickman and teammate John Draper, who tied on points with Rickman the younger (Don). The same season, he won the Cumberland GN again, and the Lancashire GN, and all this before he had reached the age of 20!

1960

Europe beckons

Given his predilection for the 500 Gold Star, he might well have welcomed a crack at the 500 World Championship, but for 1960 BSA turned their attention to the quarter-litre Coupe d'Europe (European Championship). The previous year Lampkin had ridden an experimental 250 to victory in the 250 race at the prestigious Experts GN meeting at Rollswood Farm near Redditch. This had obviously made an impression on BSA's Competition Manager, Brian Martin, who asked Arthur, in company with Jeff Smith, to spearhead their effort riding the C15.

Despite a very impressive start to the campaign, which saw him score podium finishes in the first and second rounds, it would not be until the eighth round in Finland that Arthur took his maiden GP victory. However, when his time came, he did it in style by winning both races. From there, he went on to finish a hotly disputed season in 5th overall, behind Bickers, Smith, Miroslav Soucek (Eso) and Stig Rickardsson (Husqvarna).

Although he retained the Cumberland GN trophy, Lampkin was no match for teammate Smith in the season long 500 ACU Star contest, where his good friend and rival dominated proceedings, amassing 28 points from a possible 32, to claim his third national title.

It was a similar story in the inaugural 250 ACU Scrambles Drivers' Star, where despite winning at the Lancashire GN at Cuerden Park near Preston, in August, he couldn't mount a sustained challenge to Dave Bickers, who took the title at the season's end with a 20 point advantage over Dot's rising star, Alan Clough.

However, in November he achieved one of his major sporting goals, when he won the Scott Trial in his native Yorkshire, a success he would go on to repeat the following year and again in 1965.

1961

Consistency is the key

In 1961 his main objective was to wrest the 250 European Championship from the hands of Dave Bickers and Greeves and after a steady start to the campaign, whilst Bickers blazed the trail, he emerged as a real title contender thanks to a run of consistent results. Blighted by bad luck in the opening rounds in France and Belgium, he bounced back to finish 2nd in Holland, 2nd in Czechoslovakia, 2nd in Poland, 4th in

Lampkin dives into the 'bombhole' at Shrubland Park in front of a packed gallery at the 1961 250 British GP where he finished second overall. (MR)

Luxembourg and 3rd in Finland. Back-to-back victories in Italy and West Germany upped the ante for the championship, and despite finishing 2nd to Bickers in the British round at Shrubland Park (see p19) another win in Switzerland, where he beat Smith into 2nd kept his championship hopes alive.

Looking at Lampkin's string of results in the championship, with hindsight one can only sympathise with the Yorkshireman. Such a run would ordinarily have won many a World Championship, but unfortunately for him, he came up against Dave Bickers riding at the very top of his form. By the time they set off for the twelfth round in Sweden, the Coddenham man had won five of the rounds. However, he had also retired from four GPs and if he failed to finish at Vannas, Lampkin could, conceivably, outpoint his compatriot. Unfortunately, for Arthur, Bickers was in imperious form for the Swedish round taking the GP by storm and consigning Lampkin to runner-up.

One for the scrapbook! The camera of Maurice Rowe captures Lampkin leading a very young looking Joel Robert, in the 250 GP at Shrubland Park.

Another Star

Lampkin may have lost out to Bickers in the European Championship, but he took the 250 ACU Star from his great rival and once again consistency was the cornerstone to his success. Over the five rounds, he never finished outside of the top three, finishing 2nd on two occasions and winning two of the rounds.

However, at Hatherton Hall, Cheshire, for the opening round, try as he might, Lampkin had to play second fiddle to Bickers, who was in tantalising form. In the Star race, Bickers took off like a scolded cat whilst Lampkin found himself trailing Roy Peplow on a very quick Triumph Tiger Cub. Surprisingly, Lampkin could do nothing about catching Peplow and Bickers pulled away lap by lap to record a winning margin of 400 yards. Then Lampkin rolled out his trusty 500 Gold Star for the Cheshire Motocross and a great battle ensued. Bickers set the early pace, but Lampkin forced past on the fifth lap with Peplow also getting in on the act. Lampkin and Bickers then eased away from Peplow and swapped places for several laps until Lampkin tired and settled for 2nd place.

But in late July Lampkin, in Bickers' absence, completely dominated the day's racing at Belmont near Durham, winning six races from six starts. The only riders to challenge his supremacy were the young Vic Eastwood, all the way up from Kent and racing a 250 AJS, factory Dot runner Pat Lamper and Andy Lee with his 500cc Fenman special. Arthur easily took the 250 Star race ahead of Lamper and Eastwood, leading from start to finish and establishing himself as the clear leader in the championship.

However, at Shrubland Park a fortnight later, Lampkin had no answer for Bickers who, racing on his local track, won the lightweight race for the fourth year in succession and closed to within two points of the Yorkshireman in the general classification.

Lampkin gets a break

But the East Anglian's luck ran out at the Gloucestershire GN at Tirley in mid-August. On this occasion the Star was a two-leg motocross style event and Bickers quickly got down to business as he headed the field in race one. But he was soon out of the race and loading up his bike for the long drive back to Suffolk, after the Greeves' engine had seized up just five laps into the race. With Bickers out, Lampkin turned on the style passing Greeves runners Joe Johnson and Freddie Mayes, as he sped on to victory. In the second race, young Bryan Goss gave the locals something to cheer about, when he raced to his, and Cotton's, first ACU Star race win in front of Lampkin, Mayes and Clough. However, Lampkin was the overall winner ahead of Mayes and Goss, the win guaranteeing him the ACU Star as he extended his lead over the hapless Bickers. It also brought him his second ACU Star in three seasons, as he became the first rider to win Stars in both the 250 and 500 Classes.

The final round of the championship was played out on the magnificent Glastonbury Tor circuit in September. Although Lampkin and Bickers had nothing to play for it didn't stop them putting on a fantastic show for the crowds who came to watch them. Lampkin got the drop on his rival from the start, but within half a lap Bickers had forged ahead. An enthralling tussle followed, as Europe's top two 250 riders slugged it out for the opening five laps until Lampkin uncharacteristically slid off. This gave Bickers plenty of breathing space, though fellow Greeves riders Joe Johnson and the Sharp brothers, Triss and Bryan, failed to capitalise on Arthur's lapse of concentration and he rode in to 2nd at the flag, but Champion in the Star contest eight points clear of Bickers.

With the Star race done and dusted, Lampkin won the Wessex Junior Scramble, but again had to give second best to a rampant Bickers in the Lightweight Scratch race.

World title tilt

In 1962 BSA gave Arthur a shot at his first World Championship when the 250 Class was upgraded and with Bickers missing, Lampkin might well have entertained thoughts of being Champion. Things started very brightly with a win in the season-opener in Spain, which he backed up with another victory in round three in Belgium. But as Jeff Smith began to take control, Lampkin started to fade, eventually slipping back to finish 3rd in the championship, as the super-talented Swedish ace, Torsten Hallman, stormed back to snatch victory from Smith.

In April, the BSA factory star came south to race at the Wessex Scramble at Glastonbury. Fellow British Champion, Bryan Goss, vividly remembers it for his encounter with Lampkin. "He was a brilliant rider. He'd won just about everything in the ITV meetings and I'd just gone on to Greeves. I remember beating him in the 250 and 350 races and Cobby (Derry Preston Cobb) was loving it. Then in the second 250 race with everyone waving me on I got to the top of the hill just in front, but he passed me as he jumped down the other side! He didn't like it when I beat him, but he was on my stomping ground and I gave him some stick! But I learnt a lot from Arthur."

Back in Europe for the Motocross des Nations (MDN) at Wohlen, Switzerland, in late August, Arthur suffered more disappointment, when after being selected to represent his country he had a day to forget. It started brightly enough, as the BSA man rode to a comfortable fourth place in his heat, but in the final he crashed on the first lap and lost a lot of time as he attempted to restart the BSA. In a one-sided contest, the Swedish team dominated the final, all five riders crossing the line abreast, ahead of Derek Rickman and Jeff Smith.

However, Lampkin, and the British team, took some consolation when they won the Trophée des Nations event at Shrubland Park a month later. Arthur played his part in the British team's victory recovering brilliantly from thirteenth, after stalling the little BSA half way round the opening lap, to finish 5th in race one, as teammates Bickers and Smith finished 1st and 2nd to set the team up for a win. In the second leg Lampkin was credited with a third place finish, though, as documented elsewhere, the British team crossed the line abreast for a famous victory taking the first five places.

1963

Contesting the 'blue riband' series

In 1963, his loyalty to BSA was rewarded with a crack at the 500 World Championship. Armed with one of the new 420 machines that BSA had developed from the C15 250, and in company with Jeff Smith, Lampkin set out on a gruelling campaign that saw Britain's likely lads travel to 13 different countries and cover more than 30,000 miles in a long and arduous season.

Incredibly, despite such a hectic schedule, Arthur managed to take time out for a week's 'holiday' in the Scottish Highlands, where he won the Scottish Six Day Trial riding a C15T! Having won the Scottish on Saturday, Lampkin boarded a plane bound for Denmark, to compete in the Danish round of the championship the following day, where he was in inspired form and finished 4th overall to register his first championship points.

Boosted by his recent upturn in form, he improved to take his first podium place in the 500 Class in Italy, with 3rd overall after finishing third in race two. The circus then moved into the Eastern European leg of the championship and the Czech GP, where a spirited ride in the second leg, when he briefly led the very rapid 263cc CZs of the home riders, Valek and Pilar, saw him finish 6th overall. He improved to 4th in Russia in late May, after finishing 4th and 5th in the two races.

Home GP podium and TV success

Back on home soil for the British GP at Hawkstone Park in July, the ninth of 12 rounds, Lampkin finished as runner-up to Smith, his best result of the season, with a brace of 3rd place finishes. It was a real treat for the 40,000 plus spectators who turned up, as they witnessed a great day's sport and had plenty to cheer about, as Derek Rickman filled the last step on the podium for a British 1-2-3. Lampkin's result moved him up to fifth place in the title race a position he would hold till the end of the championship.

Not surprisingly after so much gruelling travel, Lampkin had a quiet season on the home front, though as the year drew to a close he still found time to perform heroically in front of the TV cameras despite the adverse conditions. In the fifth round of the inaugural Grandstand Trophy series at Newport in December, he took a welcome win ahead of the Matchless of risng star Dave Nicoll moving him up to 2nd overall, behind Jeff Smith. He consolidated this position a fortnight later at Naish Hill, Wiltshire, with second place to Smith in the 500 race, following a memorable win in the 250 series where he inflicted the first defeat on the seemingly invincible Bickers-Husqvarna combination.

In an 'action packed' race Lampkin took the start closely followed by the Greeves of Bryan Goss and Alan Clough with Bickers harrying all three until he fell on lap four. At the same point Lampkin managed to shrug off the tenacious Goss, who then had to defend his position from the attacks of teammate Clough. Bickers fought back to briefly challenge the Greeves pair before committing another mistake and having to settle for 4th. Lampkin also clashed with Bickers and Eastwood, on his 500 Matchless, in the Unlimited Invitation race. Lampkin had the horsepower advantage with his 420 BSA, whilst Bickers had a considerable weight advantage with the svelte Husky and the diminutive Eastwood simply performed heroics with the AMC dinosaur. It was battles like this that typified the Grandstand series and captivated the viewers, making household names

Arthur Lampkin made his name riding Gold Star BSAs in trials and scrambles. Here he is locked in combat with Bicester's Dave Curtis on the factory Matchless at the Hants Grand National in April 1961. Curtis faired the better of the two, finishing level on points with Jeff Smith, though the BSA man had a faster aggregate time, whilst Lampkin finished fourth overall behind Don Rickman on his Triumph Métisse. (CB)

of their star performers. On this occasion, try as he might, and he tried mighty hard, Bickers couldn't match the speed of the factory BSA and Lampkin notched his second win of the day.

1964 Intermission

As the 1964 season dawned Lampkin dropped a bombshell, by announcing that he would be switching from BSA to ride the Villiers Starmaker-engined Cotton in company with his younger brother Alan, aka 'Sid'. However, although the news broke in early February, it would be a month before Arthur took his first win on the Cotton, at Colne, Lancashire (curiously the birthplace of Jeff Smith and Vic Eastwood). This followed a promising 3rd place in front of the BBC Grandstand cameras at Cuerden Park the previous day, where Arthur turned in a spirited performance and briefly held second place to Bickers in the 250 race, before Alan Clough passed him, the Greeves duo riding the much vaunted, all-new, Challengers.

Although he was racing the Villiers-powered 250 and competing in trials on a 250 Cotton, initially Lampkin continued to race a privately owned 420 BSA in the 500 races. However, as the season wore on there were rumours that Lampkin was to ride a 500 Cotton using a unit-construction Triumph engine in a Cotton rolling chassis, maybe inspired by the special that Clacton-on-Sea market gardener Norman Messenger had been campaigning since March. Wherever the inspiration came from the rumours bore fruit, when a Malcolm Carling photo of Arthur, on the Aly Cliffe owned Triumph-Cotton, graced the cover of the October 14th issue of the MCN. Inside Peter Howdle reported, 'ARTHUR LAMPKIN IS BACK!' The headline referred to Lampkin's win in the 500 Grandstand Trophy race at Clifton, Derbyshire, from John Burton and Chris Horsfield.

1965

Normal service is resumed

However, by Lampkin's standards the '64 season had not been as successful as he would have liked and for 1965 he returned to the fold at BSA, who in his absence had signed the younger, up and coming riders, John Banks and Vic Eastwood. However, the prodigal son soon returned to his winning ways, as he made history by becoming the first rider to win 250 and 500 Grandstand Trophy races on the same day.

This occurred at Yeovil in January, but although he won the 500 race at a canter, some 35 seconds clear of runner-up Derek Rickman, the 250 race was gifted him after leader Alan Clough's Greeves expired with a seized gearbox just 150 yards from the finish. With all the drama being transmitted to the homes of millions via a live TV feed, Clough bravely began to push the stricken bike for the line.

Clough, who was challenging Dave Bickers for the title that winter, remembers the occasion well. "I was leading the 250 race until the gearbox seized up in sight of the line. This was one of the first Challengers with the Albion gearbox and one minute you had six speeds, the next two, and this was a four-speed box! I had to push through something that resembled a swamp, and Arthur Lampkin pipped me right on the line, to win the race."

Confusion reigns in a 250 race at the TV meeting at Leighton in November 1964, but Lampkin on the Starmaker-engined Cotton (left) stays on track. (CB)

Arthur Lampkin

The two northern stars enjoyed a healthy relationship, however, and Clough had a lot of respect and admiration for Lampkin. "He was good at everything, Arthur, not brilliant, but he was damn good at everything. I got on well with him, he was a super guy".

Back on form

Lampkin was clearly happy to be back with the Small Heath outfit and was enjoying his racing again. A month later he was prominent in the International meeting at Brands Hatch, where he rode his 420 to 2nd behind Belgian 250 World Champion Joel Robert, on his flying 360 CZ in the up to 1,000 cc race and ran out winner of the Invitation event from Chris Horsfield (Matchless) and Bryan Goss (Husqvarna).

Other highlights that season included victories in the Hants GN in April and the Brain Stonebridge Memorial at Hawkstone Park in June, 4th overall in the British GP, also at Hawkstone Park, in July and victory in the Staffs GN in September. The Hants GN win was of great significance as it brought to an end Jeff Smith's five-year domination of the event. Smith was forced to retire from the first leg with clutch trouble paving the way for Arthur, who took the overall result from an inspired Jim Aim on his Kirby Métisse, with Jerry Scott in 3rd overall.

New blood at BSA

As good as Lampkin's results were in 1965, they couldn't match the glory of what was, arguably, the biggest win of his scrambling career which came in the

Lampkin making history at the BBC meeting at Yeovil in January 1965, when he became the first rider to win both the 250 and 500 Grandstand Trophy races on the same day. (CB)

Out front! In winning the 1965 Hants Grand National, Lampkin ended Jeff Smith's five-year winning streak. Here he is pictured leading the eventual runner-up, Jim Aim, on his Kirby Métisse. (CB)

1966

summer of 1966, in what was, by his standards, a quiet year. Following the recruitment of Banks in 1964 and Eastwood in 1965, Jerry Scott from Poole in Dorset, who had performed so brilliantly on Eric Cheney's Gold Star BSA the previous season, was the next young rider to join the BSA factory team. With a bigger team of riders, there was no longer a place for Lampkin on the GP team, with double-Champion Jeff Smith and Vic Eastwood getting the GP bikes.

That wasn't the only change. By the time the circus arrived at the Citadel circuit at Namur, Belgium, in August, Smith had ceded his crown to the young East German, Friedrichs and was nursing a broken wrist and collarbone following the tragic accident at Boltby that claimed the life of Jerry Scott. BSA asked Lampkin to substitute for his long-time friend and he did so with great aplomb.

Just reward

When racing got underway Britain, and BSA, had plenty to cheer about as Vic Eastwood stormed into the lead, pursued by Lampkin and Czech CZ runner, Zedenek Polanka. At the front, Eastwood began to stretch away from Lampkin until his engine cut out deep in the woods. Lampkin shot past, but Eastwood, aided by the fanatical Belgian fans, realised that it was just the plug lead that had come adrift and was soon back in the running. In a great show of determination Eastwood caught and re-passed his teammate to win an exciting first race.

In the second, home favourite Roger DeCoster was first to disappear into the woods, but Eastwood was once again the man on the move. From sixth on the first lap he took the lead from the Belgian on lap four and seemed to be cruising to his maiden GP win. But with the clock ticking down and just three laps

Any time, any place, any where. Arthur Lampkin, the Martini man! Here Ray Daniel catches Arthur on his way to victory in the 500 Belgian GP at Namur, in August 1966.

remaining he fell, allowing DeCoster to ride past into the lead, seemingly on his way to a home GP win, much to the delight of the partisan crowd. But Lampkin had other ideas. Having ridden past the stricken Eastwood into third place behind the new World Champion, Paul Freidrichs, Lampkin saw his window of opportunity and pressed on to pass the East German on the final lap. De Coster took the second leg, but Lampkin, by finishing 2nd, guaranteed his first 500 motocross grand prix win.

Whilst the hapless Eastwood could only reflect on what might have been and DeCoster rued a poor start in the first race, Arthur celebrated one of the greatest and most unexpected successes of his career. What made it even sweeter for BSA was that he'd done it on what Gavin Trippe, writing in the *MCN* described as a 'near standard production bike.'

When I was researching a magazine article on TV scrambles a few years back, Arthur told me: *I rode for BSA and I rode where they told me to ride. They wanted me winning TV races because it sold bikes.* Well I doubt that the GP was televised, certainly not back in the UK, but once again Arthur proved to be a true ambassador for BSA winning them a GP and plenty of publicity into the bargain.

Changing times

The mid-60s was a time of great turmoil for many in the motocross world. Following the introduction of the very potent 360cc two-stroke CZ in 1965, when Rolf Tibblin and rising star Paul Friedrichs had ridden them to GP success and Dave Bickers had demonstrated the potential the big two-stroke had to British fans, in 1966 Jeff Smith and BSA had relinquished their 500 World Championship title to Friedrichs on the 360 CZ.

Fearing an influx of big-bore two-strokes, the FIM had sanctioned a new racing category for 1966; the 750 Coupe d'Europe competition that was restricted to four-strokes only. Keen to keep abreast of developments in the racing scene, the BBC also decided to increase the bigger capacity in their Grandstand Trophy series from 500 to 750cc, though in this case the bigger two-strokes were also permitted.

Lampkin achieves the impossible

When the series got underway it was Bickers, who by that time had made the permanent switch from Greeves to CZ, that dominated the racing. But Lampkin, who had been conspicuous by his absence in the opening rounds, finished the year in style, winning the 750 Grandstand Trophy race at East Meon, Hampshire, on New Year's Eve. In doing so, he became the first rider to beat Bickers in any BBC race of the 1966/67 campaign. Although not one of his best races ever, Arthur kept out of trouble by following BSA new boy, Dave Nicoll, until the younger man slid off. But once in front he used all his guile and experience to protect his lead from the advances of Bickers, who had passed Chris Horsfield on the 360 Greeves, whilst Nicoll remounted to finish ahead of young Greeves factory rider, Bryan Wade, on another 360.

Though the year ended on a high for Arthur, brother Alan's finished on a low. Involved in a first lap *melée* with Arthur Browning and Vic Eastwood, he careered of the track and into a barbed wire fence after being struck by a wayward bike. 'Sid' was taken off to the nearest hospital suffering from concussion and was kept in overnight, thereby missing out on the seasonal festivities.

Less prominent

Though it may be nothing more than a coincidence, Arthur's time as a top runner on the domestic scene seemed to go into a downward spiral as the 'big' two-strokes came to prominence. Lampkin had ridden a James lightweight early in his trials career, had flirted with the Cotton in scrambles and would go on to ride Greeves, Bultaco and Ossa in trials, but he never really looked at home on a two-stroke.

When interviewed by Peter Howdle in the *MCN* in November 1961, Lampkin told the journalist his secret to success was riding every weekend. This is something he confirmed for me. *I rode in both trials and scrambles because they had seasons.* At that time a lot of off-road enthusiasts did likewise, but few competed as regularly and even fewer as successfully as Lampkin. But come the mid-60s he was riding far less frequently and although he still achieved some notable successes they were fewer and further between.

The 1967 season serves as a good illustration of this. When it kicked-off live on the TV screens, it was another Arthur, Browning, and his Greeves who were making the headlines. The young Birmingham rider caused a sensation as he took Cuerden Park, Lancashire, by storm, inflicting the second straight defeat on reigning Champions Dave Bickers and the big CZ. He would soon be referred to in the press of the day as 'King Arthur' a title he earned on merit, as

Lampkin pressing on in determined fashion at the BBC Grandstand meeting at Hankom Bottom, March 1967, where his best finish was third in the 'Handicap' behind the all conquering Dave Bickers and Alan Clough. (BH)

he provided the stiffest opposition to Bickers in both categories, though I'm sure Mr. Lampkin was none too pleased about it.

Though some way from his best form, Lampkin turned in a good performance in the televised meeting at Hankom Bottom, Hampshire in early March. He finished 6th in the 750 race won by Bickers, from Goss, Smith, Browning and Clough, but improved to a 3rd place finish in the televised Handicap race, behind Bickers and Clough.

The following month, he showed well at the National Wessex Scramble at Dodington Park, which hosted a round of the 500 British Championship. However, despite being handily placed in fourth position on the opening lap of the championship race, he struggled to get on the pace, fading to 7th at the flag one place ahead of brother Alan. But things went better in the first Invitation race where he finished 5th and he managed 2nd place to Bickers in the Wessex Senior. Then to finish off the day's racing, he took another 2nd place finish, this time to Don Rickman in the second Invitation.

A shift in the status quo

At the 500 British GP at Farleigh Castle, Wiltshire in July he was returning to his best, but was still some way short of the kind of form he had shown just 11 months earlier in Namur. The East German, Paul Friedrichs, treated the English public to a masterclass in motocross as he swept all before him on his way to his second world title. Lampkin, who finished 6th overall, couldn't compete with Bickers, Smith or teammate Eastwood, who took 2nd in the first race but had to retire in the second when he lost his rear brake pedal.

A further sign of how things were changing on the domestic scene came at the North v South team contest at Boltby near Thirsk in August. Racing on his

Above, the Two Arthurs! In April 1967, Lampkin leads Greeves' bright young prospect, Browning, as Jeff Smith concentrates on closing them both down. The event was the Wessex Scramble, held that year at Dodington Park. (RD)

Below, at the 1967 500 British GP at Farleigh Castle, Lampkin has teammate Vic Eastwood for company. Eastwood failed to finish, but Lampkin managed sixth overall. (BH)

Great action in this photograph from the camera of Brian Holder. Lampkin slides up the inside of Dick Clayton at the Wakes Colne International meeting, in September 1967.

native Yorkshire soil, Lampkin was still good enough to finish as the top scorer for the vanquished Northern team, but tellingly he was out pointed by Bryan Goss, two years his junior, Malcolm Davis and emerging star Andy Roberton, who guided the Southern team to victory.

In September he represented Britain in the MDN once more, at Markelo, Holland, where Britain won the event for the fifteenth time and notched up five consecutive victories. In this team competition where every place gained could prove vital, Lampkin played his part, finishing eighteenth first time out but improving to tenth in second leg. Fellow BSA man Eastwood was the sensation of the meeting, finishing as the individual top scorer, following his win in the second leg.

As the 1967 season came to a close, Lampkin was on hand at Builth Wells in October, to witness his long-term teammate, companion, friend and rival, Jeff Smith, win the last of his nine British Championship titles. In a typically calculated performance, Smith finished 4th, shepherded in by Lampkin, to win the championship by a single point from Alan Clough and Vic Eastwood. Looking back on this event, it effectively marked the end of a great era for both of them.

In his twelfth season of racing in 1968, some of the spark seemed to have gone out of his riding and his appearances in British Championship rounds, Grandstand Trophy events and even National meetings became increasingly rare.

However, having scored 3 points in the opening round of the 750 Grandstand Trophy at Canada Heights the previous November, he ventured south to Bury St. Edmunds in late January for round two, though he was out of luck on the day, with just 6th place in the Invitation race to show for his long trip. He faired even worse at Naish Hill, Wiltshire, the following month where he fell and failed to make the points for the second round on the bounce, if you'll excuse the pun.

Lifelong friends, Lampkin and Jeff Smith caught in action at the Lincolnshire Grand National at Cadwell Park in October 1967. (RD)

Contrasting fortunes

It's quite interesting to compare the form of Lampkin and Smith at this juncture in their careers. Whilst Lampkin was struggling in the 750 series, Smith, the elder of the two by some four years, was truly inspired, racing the titanium framed BSA with great gusto and was joint leader of the 250 series as the circus headed north to Kirkcaldy in Scotland in early March, for what was to be an eventful meeting.

However, it was quite like old times at Kirkcaldy, where in treacherous conditions Lampkin and Smith ran out the winners in front of the TV cameras. In the 750 race, Lampkin was trailing Eastwood on the first lap when the man from Kent presented him with a gift as he slipped off. Lampkin seized the opportunity with both hands, quickly putting distance between himself and local hero Jimmy Aird in the ensuing *melée* to take a comfortable win at the flag.

At the final round in Caerleon in mid-March, he could finish no higher than 5th, though he hung on to 4th overall in the 750 series behind teammates Banks, Eastwood and Hickman, whilst Smith, who had performed brilliantly throughout the winter on the lightweight BSA, wrapped up the 250 series with a win and a 2nd place at the same meeting.

The following weekend, he turned up at Chard, Somerset, for the opening round of the 500 British Championship and got amongst the points in the heavy going, taking 4th place behind teammates Eastwood and Nicoll and AJS' Malcolm Davis in race one. Sadly, he failed to add to those points over the championship, though things might have been different had the BSA's gearbox not seized up and thrown him off as he was leading Dave Nicoll on the sixth lap of the first race in round two at Elsworth, in April.

In search of new motivation

Incidents such as these and also witnessing Vic Eastwood's heavy fall at Hawkstone Park, in December of that year could have done little to inspire Lampkin,

Giving the factory BSA a good work out at the Haywood Scramble at Builth Wells in 1968. (RD)

Lampkin showed some good form at the 1968 Cambridge Grand National at Elsworth. Here he leads race one ahead of BSA teammate Dave Nicoll. Younger readers may be familiar with Nicoll, as he can still be seen on TV, supervising the starts of all the MX GP races today. (RD)

1969

who already felt that he was getting too old to remain competitive, and by 1969 he had pretty much rung down the curtain on his motocross career.

Though Arthur himself can't remember quite when he hung up his motocross boots, he did continue in the trials arena for many years eventually turning his attention to sidecar trials where he would also excel, winning the British Experts trial and finishing 2nd in the British Championship.

The Lampkin legend

Arthur Lampkin was quite simply one of the best British off-road riders ever, who served as an inspiration to a whole generation of young off-road motorcyclists including his brothers. Alan ('Sid') was a very good motocrosser who also excelled as a trials rider, matching Arthur with wins in the Scottish Six Day Trial and the Scott, which he achieved in the same year, 1966. His youngest brother, Martin, after briefly flirting with motocross and speedway, fully committed to the feet up brigade, going on to become the first World Trials Champion in 1975.

This was just the beginning of the Lampkin family's involvement in off-road motorcycling with further generations picking up the baton where the three brothers left off. Arthur's eldest son John became a top trials rider, whilst his brothers David and Stephen both had fun riding in trials. Martin's eldest son Dougie,

Taking care of business. 'Mr. Television' motors on at the BBC Grandstand meeting at Clifton in December 1968. (BH)

needs no introduction as a 12-time World Trials Champion (seven outdoor and five indoor) whilst his younger brother, Harry, has dabbled in motocross and enduro with some success and now a third generation of Lampkins from Silsden are beginning to have fun riding their trials bikes out on the moors.

However, it all started with Arthur John Lampkin and had it not been for the presence of a certain Lancashire-born teammate, he might well have been a multiple British Champion, maybe even a World Champion. Known for his dour Yorkshire demeanour, when said Lancashire-born teammate announced his imminent departure for Canada in 1972, Lampkin told *The Motor Cycle; I wish he'd emigrated 17 years ago when I first came across him, I'd have won a lot more trophies!*

It only seems fair that to follow that, I leave the last word on Arthur to his old friend and rival Jeff Smith. "Arthur's not really a Yorkshireman, as he was born within the sound of Bow Bells, which makes him a cockney! But he's the best Yorkshireman I know!"

Fred Mayes

Steady Freddie

Photo CB

Freddie Mayes emerged from a group of very talented young riders who sprang onto the scrambling scene in the Eastern Centre in the early '60s and included the likes of Dave Nicoll, John Banks, John Pease, John Louis and Norman Messenger. In a riding career that spanned 20 years, there were many successes; highlights included his selection to ride for Britain in the 1966 Trophée des Nations at Brands Hatch, competing on the GP circus for three years, winning Inter-Centre team events, with not just one but two centres, and winning multiple Centre Championships. But unquestionably, the pinnacle of his success was being crowned 250cc British Champion in 1966.

Fred was born in Haverhill, Suffolk in May 1943 and started racing at the tender age of 14, on a 197cc James, which his father, a keen motorcycling enthusiast bought for him. But had he not been so successful scrambling he may well have been lost to the road racing fraternity. *My first love was road racing. I had a friend called Ray Butler, who used to race, and I followed him around everywhere. But at that time you had to be 17 to go road racing, so I tried scrambling, thinking that I would switch to road racing after a year. But I got quite good at scrambling so I stuck to it.*

1960

Factory support

Like so many of his generation, Fred cut his teeth on a succession of 'lightweight' British two-strokes. Some promising results on the James, led to some help from Dot in 1960, in the shape of another 197 and Fred's name started to appear in the results. In June, he took 6th place in the up to 200cc race, won by Johnny Giles on a Tiger Cub, at the Cotswold Scramble and closer to home, he finished 3rd in the 250 race at the Cambridge GN in September.

Then in 1961 Fred replaced the Dot with a brand new MDS Greeves and he also got to ride his first 'big-un', a 500 Gold Star BSA, supplied by Cambridge dealer Claude Scott. Getting support like this at such an early stage of his career is something Fred remains proud of to this day. *I got the bike and all my spares for half price, and that was the last time I had to pay for a bike!* With some quality machinery at his disposal, Freddie's results steadily improved during the '61 season, peaking over the summer months.

1961/2

Centre excellence

At Wakes Colne in July, he became the Eastern Centre 200, 250 and 500 Champion, all in one afternoon. Not a bad day's work! And August proved a good month for young Fred, with some excellent results in the best company. At Shrubland Park he took

Despite his slight build, Mayes could handle a big bike as he demonstrates here, racing a Gold Star BSA in the 1962 Maybug Scramble at Farleigh Castle. (CB)

Fred Mayes

Racing a 250 Cotton, Freddie Mayes was a race winner in the BBC's 'Four-corners' team event at Tye Farm, Sudbury in November 1962. (MR)

Looking so stylish, Cecil Bailey captures Mayes racing a Matchless at the 1963 Minety Vale Scramble.

5th place in the 250 race, behind winner Dave Bickers, Arthur Lampkin, and the factory Dots of Pat Lamper and Alan Clough. He also rode the Gold Star to 6th place in the prestigious Shrubland GN event. Then three weeks later, at the Gloucestershire GN, he came an excellent 3rd overall in the two-leg motocross style 250 ACU star race on the Greeves and raced the Goldie to 3rd in the 500 race behind Lampkin and Smith. However, his season ended prematurely at an Open to Centre meeting in Gloucestershire a few weeks later, when he broke a leg.

Factory rides

But this decidedly grey cloud most certainly had the proverbial silver lining. Whilst still laid up in bed, he was approached by BSA Competitions chief, Brian Martin, who offered him a trials bike for the winter. The offer extended to a season scrambling a 250 C15 and a 500 Gold Star. Fred enjoyed some success on the Gold Star, notably at the Wessex Scramble at Glastonbury in April, where he took an excellent 4th place in the 500 ACU Star race behind Smith, Triss Sharp and Lampkin. Then the following month he made the short trip to Tye Farm, Great Cornard, for the Suffolk Grand National, where he got the better of Dot factory riders John Griffiths and Alan Clough in the main event.

But he was soon tempted away to Cotton, with the promise of a 250 trials bike for the winter in addition to a 250 scrambler. His first ride on the Cotton proved to be a winning one; racing close to home at Littleport, Cambridgeshire in October, he rode John Draper's 250 to victory. A month later he managed to win a race, which was televised on the BBC's Grandstand programme, again at Tye Farm. The meeting preceded the Grandstand Trophy Series and was a 'four-corners' match race, with Fred representing the winning Eastern team.

However, it wasn't the most successful venture and with hindsight he wishes he'd waited for a new offer

Fred Mayes

from BSA. *The 420 that was being developed would have suited me, being so much more compact than the Gold Star.* (Fred stands just 5' 6" in his race boots).

After a relatively quiet 1963 on the Cotton, he signed to James in 1964 to race the Villiers Starmaker-engined 250. But on his first outing on the bike he crashed heavily whilst racing in treacherous conditions at the Wakefield Grandstand Trophy meeting and had to be hospitalised. The James experience was not one of Fred's best, but there were some positives, such as 5th place in the 250 ACU Star race at the Cotswold Scramble in June. In addition to the little James, Mayes was also riding a TriBSA at this stage of his career hitting form at Brill in July when he shared the winning with Brian Curtis. But by mid-August he had left James and was campaigning a new Greeves Challenger, once again courtesy of Claud Scott, and was beginning to find some good form again.

Privateer Mayes in good form

In the Eastern Centre Championships at Woodham Ferrers, Essex in August, he won the 250 Class ahead of Pete Smith and John Pease, added the 400-650 Class on the TRiBSA, from Jim Aim and Dave Clark, and then gave the Challenger another run out in the supporting Senior race, where he fought off a determined challenge from Norman Messenger on his 500cc Triumph-engined Cotton. At the end of the race he was full of enthusiasm for his new Greeves, telling reporter Claude Jolly, *It goes like a bomb.*

That same year, he took the Lightweight (up to 250) race at the Cambridge Grand National from John Louis (Greeves) and John Banks (BSA) and the Junior 201 – 350 race from Banks and Louis. He was also starting to make his mark in the 250 ACU Star competition and in spite of only scoring points in two of the rounds, he finished the contest in 7th overall.

Fred was always a very consistent performer, a quality that would stand him in good stead in his championship winning year, and he hit a good run of form in the 250 Grandstand Trophy series on the Challenger with a string of 4th place finishes, often chasing home a trio of works Greeves riders and going on to eventually finish 6th in the series, as the best privateer.

Greeves call-up

Form like this didn't escape the attention of Greeves' talent spotter extraordinaire, Derry Preston Cobb, and for 1965 Mayes was invited to join the Thundersley team. It was a dream come true for Fred, as he would team up with one of his idols, the former European Champion, Dave Bickers. It was an association, which played a big part in Fred's career. *David and I became close friends when I was at Greeves. Being fairly local, Greeves would often invite me along to do testing at Wakes Colne and riding with David like that was a great help to me.*

It must be remembered that at this time, in addition to Bickers, Greeves already had riders such as Alan Clough, Bryan Goss, Malcolm Davis and local lad John Pease on their books. So it was testament to Fred's continued progress that the Essex factory signed him up to ride for them.

Mayes didn't disappoint his new employers, getting in the points in the ACU Star races in April, at the Hants Grand National, where he finished 3rd, and the Cambridge Grand National where he took 4th place. He also had a fine win in one of the invitation races at Elsworth, keeping his Greeves ahead of John Giles' Triumph and teammate and Grand National winner, Alan Clough.

Freddie was also in good form in the 250 Motocross event at Hadleigh, Essex, on Bank Holiday Monday, where after finishing level on points with Bickers, he took 2nd place in a unique, two-man, two-lap race-off to decide the result! Back in the ACU Star he took a fine 3rd place in round three at the Cotswold Scramble at Nympsfield, in mid-June, behind teammates Bickers and Goss, the result moving him to third in the points standing.

Grand Prix debut for a rising star

Then in July he rode his first Grand Prix, the 250 event at Glastonbury, where two steady rides saw him finish 9th and 11th, for a solid 7th overall – just outside the points. Then in the ACU Star race at the Lancashire Grand National at Cuerden Park the following month, he finished an excellent 3rd, behind teammates Bickers, to whom he'd loaned his second bike, and Clough.

Over the season Mayes had made considerable progress on the factory Greeves, maturing into an accomplished rider and in the final reckoning for the ACU Star, he finished joint third, with Clough, behind winner Bickers and Bryan Goss to complete Greeves' domination of the series.

A fine study of Mayes, racing in the BBC Grandstand meeting at Leighton, in March 1966. (CB)

1966

Friendly counsel

After a promising first season on the Thundersley machines, Fred started the 1966 season in a good frame of mind, his confidence boosted by some advice from his former mentor at Greeves, Bickers, who by then had moved on to CZ.

David told me that he was only going to ride three of the 250 Championship rounds that year, as CZ wanted him to concentrate on riding the 500s in the GPs, and the British Championship. He told me, "You could win this boy, if you can just be consistent." But I think that he really believed he could take it himself with three wins.

The season started quite well for Mayes, with a brace of 2nd place finishes in the 250 BBC Grandstand Trophy races at Leighton near Frome and Crowborough in Sussex, which saw him finish 6th overall in the series.

A trip to Spain in March, for the 250 Grand Prix in Barcelona, with Bryan Wade, who had stepped in for the injured Bryan Goss, Malcolm Davis and Don Rickman, was no doubt a good experience, but it could have done little to boost his confidence as he struggled to find form at this level and there were few signs to suggest that this would be a special season for Fred.

Fortunately, however, one of Mayes' best attributes as a rider was always his consistency and his rides during the 1966 250 British Championship season proved to be no exception. He finished 3rd in the opening round at Nantwich, improved to 2nd at both the Hants GN meeting at Ringwood in April and the third round at the Stroud Valley club's Cotswold Scramble, and then posted 4th at Wakes Colne in July, where Bickers and Goss ran amok.

In the season that he became 250 British Champion, Mayes duels with Norman Messenger in the opening round of the championship at the Hants Grand National in April 1966. (CB)

Another showdown with Bickers

So, thanks to a string of steady results, he went to the final round of the 250 Championship at Builth Wells, knowing that the only rider who could beat him was his old sparring partner, Bickers. On a clearly superior machine, Bickers had won at Ringwood and Wakes Colne and knew that a win in the final round would clinch yet another quarter-litre title for his trophy cabinet.

Badger Goss, a close friend and travelling companion of Mayes, was to have a big say in where the title wound up that year and had this to say of Mayes. "Fred was one of the smoothest riders ever. He stood up everywhere, and was so neat and tidy. He was also a good friend and I was so pleased that he got to win the championship."

That year Dave Bickers was bidding to become the first rider ever to win both 250 and 500 Championships in the same season and having clinched the 500s at Cadwell Park, the previous weekend he was in confident mood before the deciding race at the Kidston Scramble. And in typically determined style, it was Bickers, needing to win to make history, who shot into an early lead in stark contrast to Mayes who was left floundering. *I got a terrible start. But in that first lap, I probably rode the fastest I ever rode in my life and I'd got through to second by the end of the lap.* Fred then came under pressure from teammate Arthur Browning and they were riding so hard that they had soon reeled in Bickers. *When we caught David he tried to slow things up, to throw us out of our stride.* But Bickers lost valuable time and unbeknown to him, Goss was on a very determined charge through the field.

At two-thirds race distance, Goss swept past the leading trio and once in front, was never headed. Bickers tried in vain to catch Goss, but Mayes was oblivious to

At the Stafford Grand National in August, Mayes demonstrates his smooth, unflustered riding style. (RD)

Mayes (right) and his good friend Bryan Goss are in good spirits in the paddock of the 250 Swiss GP at Payerne in April 1967. (BH)

the drama unfolding ahead of him. *After Badger came flying past me, I stalled the engine on a drop and Arthur passed me again. Then I got a bit despondent as I wasn't aware that Badger had also passed David and I thought I'd blown it.* At the chequered flag, Goss was a comfortable winner ahead of Bickers and although Mayes could only manage 4th that was good enough and the championship was his by a single point. Bickers' predictions were right on the money; Fred's consistency won him his crown, but had Bickers won at Builth Wells, the three wins would have been enough!

Development role

As British Champion, Mayes was in demand and found himself being head-hunted by Norton-Villiers at the end of the '66 season. They wanted a top rider to help develop their prototype Starmaker-engined motocrosser, which was to be the forerunner of the AJS Stormer. It was hard for him to leave Greeves, but the offer proved too good to refuse. *They made me a fantastic offer. The retainer wasn't brilliant, but they were very generous with my expenses. I remember going out to the Eastern Block countries to do the GPs, and receiving £1500 when I got back. That was a lot of money!*

The relationship started quite promisingly, with Mayes racing what had officially become a Villiers Métisse to victory at the end of February 1967 in a 'Somerset mud-bath' at Steart Hill Farm, Sparkford. Local man Bryan Goss was the star of the meeting, but Fred was the one making news as he came home 1st in the Experts only race ahead of new teammate Andy Roberton and Malcolm Davis (Greeves). Then in the 250 British Championship round at the Cotswold Scramble he gave the Cotton-framed 'Norton-Villiers' (see p220) its first major win in the second 250 race, where he beat Arthur Browning and ex-teammate Alan

Mayes is pictured racing the Métisse-framed Norton-Villiers at the 250 British GP at Wakes Colne in July 1967. (BH)

Clough, who was now racing a private Husqvarna. In the next round at the Cleveland Grand National in July, he turned in another solid performance taking 3rd behind the Huskies of Goss and Clough, who extended his lead over Mayes to eight points.

Mayes rode well in the GPs in 1967, gaining valuable experience, though he was plagued by mechanical problems all season. Typical of this was his bad luck at Wakes Colne in July, when an oiled plug eliminated him in the first race and he was also forced to pull out of the second race mid-way through whilst well placed.

Midland Champion

By September, the project was labelled an 'AJS' and at Hawkstone Park, Mayes took the Midland Championship to give it a winning debut. He also led the Brian Stonebridge Memorial race in the same meeting, until a stray rock hit the timing cover causing the AJS to splutter to a stop. As it was an on-going project, Mayes had to contend with frequent changes being made to the bike, which did little to help him in his struggle to retain his British title, but had Lady Luck smiled more kindly upon him, Fred believes he might well done just that.

I had some really good results on the Norton-Villiers, but in a couple of the races (including the penultimate round at Hintlesham) the engine cut-out momentarily and I lost a couple of places in each race. In the final race of the 250 British Championship at Cadwell Park in October, he finished 5th and was edged out of runner-up spot in the championship by Bickers, who took the tie-break with Mayes by virtue of winning the previous round at Hintlesham Park.

More reliability needed

Although he had managed to get some impressive results on the Norton-Villiers, by the end of the season, Freddie was looking for a more competitive machine

Photographer Brian Holder was on hand to catch Mayes making his CZ debut at West Stow Heath in October 1967.

and found it in a twin-port CZ that Dave Bickers put at his disposal. It proved to be a good combination, as he followed his new sponsor home in the 250 race at the Player's Winternational Meeting at West Stow Heath just a few days after collecting the bike and two weeks later he rode the 250 to victory in front of the BBC cameras at Canada Heights in both the Grandstand Trophy race and the support race.

Although Fred raced so many machines over the years, it came as no surprise when he singled out the CZ as his favourite all-time bike. *I would pick out the twin-port CZ David lent me in the winter of 1967/68 as the best. I won the opening TV scramble on it and although I only raced it a few times it made a great impression on me. It was a great bike and it handled so well.*

Fast Montesa

Despite such a promising start on the CZs, an offer from the Spanish Montesa concern for the 1968 season was too good to refuse and he made his debut in front of the BBC TV cameras at Naish Hill in February and although he couldn't repeat his winning form from Canada Heights, he finished in a creditable 4th place in the 250 race. This was followed by another 4th place in the next round at Kirkcaldy, Scotland, behind a resurgent Jeff Smith, local man Jimmy Aird, and Malcolm Davis. However, despite lying 2nd as the TV circus moved on to the double-header final round at Caerleon in March and having a chance of toppling Smith, Mayes could only add two points from the two races with 6th place in race two, though he did hang on to claim 3rd overall in the series.

Out front! On his 250 Montesa, Freddie (25) hits the front at the 1968 Hants Grand International, followed by no less than eight fellow British Champions. Smith (8), Bickers (14), Davis (18) with Banks on his shoulder, Lampkin (9), Clough (21), Roberton (22) and Allan (16). Also visible are the Swedes, Arne Kring (34) and Hakan Andersson (35), Keith Hickman (11) and Joel Robert (3), far right following in Bickers tyre tracks, whilst overall winner Sylvain Geboers can be seen over Smith's left shoulder.(RD)

In the 250 British Championship he was his usual consistent self, scoring points in every round. On the factory Montesa he scored a couple of 4th places in round two at the Wessex Scramble at Glastonbury in April, and had his best ride in round three at Carlton Bank, Yorkshire in July, where he added to his points tally with a fine 3rd place in race one behind winner Chris Horsfield and Vic Allan. After switching back to a CZ again for the final round at Nantwich he finished 5th in the series just a point adrift of Greeves' Arthur Browning.

In the company of his old friend Dave Bickers, Freddie travelled out to the GPs for a third consecutive season, though tellingly he was also on his third bike in as many seasons. He was in sparkling form on the Montesa in front of the home fans in Barcelona, at the season-opening Spanish GP, where he was the sensation of race one. Mayes tailed GP regular Marcel Wiertz on a Bultaco for eight laps until the Montesa gassed up, allowing Torsten Hallman, Don Rickman, Sylvain Geboers and Joel Robert all to slip past. He held on to eighth place until just 200 yards from the finishing line when he struck a straw bale, locking the back brake on and dropping him to 12th place at the chequered flag. In race two he faired worse, crashing out in a first corner incident with Wiertz.

The bad luck continued for Freddie in Belgium, as he was caught up in another first corner melee when Belgian sand ace Jef Teuwissen crashed heavily. Mayes' Montesa was damaged in the resulting chaos and he was forced to retire after battling away for six laps. This was fairly typical of his season in Europe and despite contesting most of the rounds over the '68 season, he again failed to make his mark at this level.

Mayes, on the factory Montesa, heads Champion to be, John Banks, on the works 500 BSA at the 1968 Battle of Newbury meeting. (RD)

So fast it flew!

Though the racing proved hard and not very rewarding for Mayes, there were plenty of interesting moments on the road and the following dramatic incident from their travels sprung to mind for travelling companion Bickers. "We were getting on pretty well until we got to Yugoslavia. My mechanic was driving and he took a corner a bit too quick and the trailer stepped out and hit a lamp post. My CZ was OK, but Freddie's Montesa flew out and went bouncing down the road. We can laugh about it now, but I'm not so sure he saw the funny side of it back then!"

There might even have been a suggestion of foul play, as Fred, tongue in cheek, explained. *The 250 was a great bike, there was nothing quicker in the GPs. David's mechanic used to get so rattled. He worked so hard on the single-port CZ, but wherever we went the Montesa would always beat it off the practice starts. When we went to the Czech round, he even wanted to take it to the factory to strip it down and discover why it was so quick!*

Success close to home on CZs

From 1969 until 1972 Fred rode CZs for Dave Bickers and the decision was made that Fred would concentrate on racing close to home, mainly competing in the Eastern and South Midland Centres, though he did take in the occasional British Championship round. Then from 1972 to 1977, which marked the end of his competitive career, he raced CZs for another close friend, Mick Berrill. In 1975 when the British Championship changed to a single class, Fred participated in the Support Championship and amassed

1969-72

enough points at the season's end to earn 'promotion' to the top flight. But he didn't take this up, as he felt he could earn more money from winning races in the Support series, which he thought was wrong. But despite the highs in his career he is probably best remembered, as a prolific race winner in the Eastern and South Midland Centres.

Today, at the age of 67, Fred, as his father before him, works in the building trade. He still competes in the occasional Pre-65 motocross and actively participates in trials, with a modern Montesa and a Greeves TFS that he has prepared for Pre-65 events. Also, when time permits, there's nothing he enjoys more than a round of golf in the company of his younger brother, and fellow British Motocross Champion, Geoff.

Right, stylish as ever, Mayes is back on a CZ at the BBC Grandstand meeting at Clifton in December 1968. (BH)

Below, Mayes racing at the 250 British Championship event at Tilton in March 1969. (RD)

In 1975 Mayes returned to the British Championships in the Support series. Here he is pictured racing the 400 CZ to victory in the first round at Matchams Park in March. (CB)

Alan Clough

Good Things Come To Those Who Wait

Photo BH

As a Dot rider competing in the support races at the British Grand Prix at Hawkstone Park in the early '60s, Alan Clough looked on in awe as his idols, Jeff Smith, Dave Curtis and the Rickman brothers did battle. A few years later he had become a force to be reckoned with, competing on the same stage as his erstwhile heroes, and for many was a model professional. Though a top contender for many seasons, especially in the 250 Class, Clough was only British Champion on one occasion, but no rider has ever been a more deserving Champion.

Clough races the works Dot to victory in Britain's oldest Scramble, the Southern Scott, at Tweseldown, in December 1961. (CB)

Alan Clough was born on New Year's Day, 1939 and was raised in Cheadle Hulme, in the suburbs of Manchester where he still resides to this day, living just a quarter of a mile from where he was born.

Alan's father and older brother both had motorcycles and his first bike was a Francis-Barnet, which he bought whilst working as an apprentice central heating engineer as a means of transport. Interest in scrambling had started before that however, when as a teenager he attended meetings run by the local Cheadle Hulme club at a course in a disused brickyard near his home. *I remember watching Johnny Cox, a local Manchester 17 Club rider, who had a Francis-Barnett with his own special cylinder head on it which went like the clappers.* He also remembers riding his bicycle there and then 'racing' it round the track at the close of the day's racing.

1957-60 Late starter, but quick learner

Inspired by what he had seen, he joined the Cheadle Hulme Club in 1957, bought himself a DMW and started racing at the comparatively late age of 18. He first competed at a Cheshire Centre meeting at Bowstone Gate Farm, near Stockport. *I was very wild and kept falling off. I was competing against a lot of big four-strokes on my little 197 DMW. It was fitted with Earles type forks and they kept bending every time I crashed!*

The early days were spent competing locally where he found plenty of inspiration. *Bill Barugh, the legendary Dot works rider, was very kind to me at the start of my career, then there was Roger Kyffin on the Triumph, Jack Matthews on his Gold Star, Derek Warburton on a converted 500 HT Ariel and the Bickertons, Dennis on a Gold Star and Stuart on a Dot, they were the guys to beat in the Cheshire Centre.*

Headline material

The young apprentice learnt quickly and after graduating to a 197 Dot he was soon winning races in his native Cheshire Centre. But it was in his second year on the Manchester-built bike that he really started to click, winning his first big event and hitting the headlines in April 1960. '*CLOUGH THE UNBEATABLE*' the *Motor Cycle News* declared, as he won the 250, 1000 and the Cheshire Motocross races at Oulton Park on Good Friday, beating established northern aces such as Terry Cheshire, Jack Matthews, John Griffiths and Norman Crooks.

Dot support for local rider

With his confidence boosted, Alan, under the guiding influence of Roger Kyffin (an experienced Cheshire Centre expert and prolific bike builder), headed off to his first trade-supported event, the Cotswolds Grand National, where he had an excellent day on the Dot finishing 5th in the 350 race and 3rd in the up to 200s. There was one spectator in the crowd who took particular interest in his performance that day, as Clough explained. *Burnard Scott Wade* (the owner of Dot Motorcycles) *was there and he offered me a 25% discount on my spares for 12 months, which was good, and after that they gave me a bike, which was even better. So I was off and running then.*

He certainly was, and in his first season on the factory supported bike he went from strength to strength, as he developed into a very fast rider with a lot of natural stamina. In September at Hawkstone Park, where he always performed exceptionally well, the reporter waxed lyrical on his showing. '*Outstanding is an understatement when used to describe Alan Clough's performances in the 350 and 500cc races*'. In the inaugural 250 British Championship that year, he also managed to keep Dave Bickers honest, finishing as runner-up to the new British and European Champion.

Temporary setback

However, his rise to the upper echelons of the British motocross scene took a severe setback before the season was up. A month after his headline-making performances at Hawkstone Park, he was lying in a

At Wakes Colne in June 1962, Clough, right, challenges the European Champion, Dave Bickers. (DK)

bed at the Derby Infirmary Hospital. A broken hip, incurred in a fall whilst racing at Clifton, Derbyshire in September had brought his season to a premature end: Clough was hospitalised for the next three months.

The accident at Clifton sidelined him for nine months, but incredibly he came back fitter and faster than before and was soon making the headlines in the MCN again. 'Alan Clough is Back! After 9 months absence from the scrambles game, the 250 Dot rider returned in fine form to Hawkstone Park on Sunday.' This was August 1961, when he finished 2nd to Joe Johnson in the 150-250 race, won the 150-350 race and pushed Dave Curtis, on his full-500 works Matchless, all the way in the 300-1000 race. Two months later at the Bredbury and Romiley MC meeting in October where Clough won the Lightweight and Top Twenty races, the headline in MCN ran: 'ALAN CLOUGH VS DAVE BICKERS: AND THE DOT COMES OUT ON TOP'.

To round off a meritorious season, Clough won the prestigious Southern Scott Scramble at Tweseldown in mid-December, where he got the better of established southern expert John Clayton on his 500 Gold Star.

He started the 1962 season as he'd finished off the previous one, winning. Now it was in the meetings broadcast by ABC Television that winter, where he won races at Mansfield, Bredbury and Clifton. The form continued into the spring, as at Hatherton Hall, Nantwich, another of his great hunting grounds, he was the man of the meeting. In very sticky conditions, he won the 1000 race and the Motocross, but tellingly lost out to Bickers in the 250 race, which counted towards the ACU Star, where he could only finish 6th after falling three times. However, he went on to finish 3rd in that season's 250 ACU Drivers' Star, behind Bickers and just one point adrift of fellow Dot works rider, John Griffiths.

Grand Prix debut
The same season he won the support races at the 500 British Grand Prix at Hawkstone Park and turned in a sterling performance in his first Grand Prix, the 250 event at Glastonbury, where he finished fifth in the first leg, improved to fourth in the second and took a highly respectable 4th overall. He was the second Brit home, after the victorious Bickers, and headed the likes of Don Rickman and Jeff Smith.

His ride in the GP must have impressed the selectors for the Trophée des Nations team, as he was duly chosen to represent his country for the first time, in the team event at Shrubland Park in late September. Clough played his part in Britain's historical win, when the host nation's full compliment of five riders, Jeff Smith, Dave Bickers, Arthur Lampkin, Don Rickman and Clough crossed the line abreast in the second leg for a sensational victory. *Yeah, getting selected was brilliant and it was great to win. I think crossing the line together was Smithy's doing, because the Swedes had done it to him the previous month in the Motocross des Nations. I did my bit and I wasn't last!*

Greeves steps in
Clough's form in those early years hadn't escaped the notice of the people at Greeves and as the season drew to a close, they stepped in with the offer of a contract for 1963. *Garth Wheldon, approached me to ask if I would like to race for Greeves, with a handsome signing-on fee being paid by Shell. So we went down to Southend and they promised me the chance to do the GPs as well. So I was signed to go out and ride all the rounds with Dave Bickers, which was exactly what I wanted to do.*

So began a long, and largely happy, association with the Essex company. Clough joined Greeves at a time when they were planning the transition to the new Villiers Starmaker-engined machine and there was much anticipation in the air with Bickers making his return to the GP stage. They were exciting times for Clough and he recalls those early days at Greeves and heading off to conquer Europe in the company of Bickers with great affection. *When I first went to Greeves from Dot, we teamed up to do the GPs. Dave was the first guy I went abroad with and he looked after me and showed me the ropes. We travelled together and it was kind of strange, as he was my hero and my companion at the same time.*

GP promise
Things started really well for the new partnership, with Bickers winning the opening GP in Spain, though Clough's maiden GP was marred by a mechanical failure when one of the aluminium cylinder head bolts stripped its thread. But at the Italian round at the end of March, Clough was outstanding, finding himself on the podium after twice finishing as runner-up to the great Torsten Hallman. Following some very exciting racing (Clough actually led Hallman for five laps in the first leg) the cool Swede proffered the young Englishman some advice, as Clough recalls. *I remember Hallman was leading and I was going too fast and I jumped right over him, and he didn't like*

that. He came over to me and said "There was no need for that you could have had us both off!" But after that we got on OK, especially when I was a Husky rider.

An excellent 3rd overall in France in round three suggested that Clough and Greeves could mount a serious challenge for the title. But sadly, despite such an encouraging start, the Greeves teamsters struggled for the rest of the season and Bickers was so dismayed with the Greeves that he bought his own private Husqvarna. *David did quite well (on the Greeves), but I wasn't quite good enough. The Husky and the CZ were the thing to have, and we were racing against Hallman, (Joel) Robert, (Vlastimil) Valek and (Victor) Arbekov and they were all really competitive. Although we did really well in England, we just didn't have the bikes for the GPs.*

Zut alors!

Clough's reading of going on the GP circus in search of titles mirrors that of many riders I have spoken to. *We went away and did our thing, but it was expensive and it was always nice to get home. We got start money, but it wasn't really a lot.* Being on the road in those early days could be difficult. *We tried to survive on trout and chips, but we couldn't always get it. In Belgium we often ate horse steaks, which you could have bounced off the floor! One of the first things you learnt in French, was 'Bien cuit. S' il vous plait' – 'Well done, please.' I couldn't stand garlic at that time, but it was difficult to find anything without it. Omelette and chips was our other favourite.*

Soon after joining Greeves, a fresh-faced Clough (standing, second from left) and Dave Bickers (seated on right) share a joke with Derry Preston Cobb (in the wheelchair), Bob Mills (left) and Competition Shop manager Bill Brooker (standing at the back), as they collect their GP bikes from the factory at Thundersley in 1963. (Photo supplied by Bill Brooker)

How did Malcolm Carling catch this shot? Clough hustles the 250 Challenger, with 'banana' forks, to victory in the 1965 Cambridge Grand National at Elsworth in April.

Like many before him, and a whole lot since, Clough found it difficult adapting to racing on the continent. *I seemed to ride better against the top British people than I did in the GPs for some reason. Perhaps I was a bit overawed. I didn't really spend enough time over there. The tracks tended to be dry and dusty compared with Britain, and the deep sand in Belgium and Holland was something we didn't get a lot of racing in England.*

Though Greeves came in for a lot of criticism for becoming complacent after the European Championship success and not developing the bikes, Derry Preston Cobb did a very good job of contracting the best young riders to put the East Anglian marque on the map nationwide and maintain sales of bikes, as Clough explained. *Mr Preston Cobb wanted a northern lad, because we were at different ends of the country and we only met up at the nationals and the British Championships at that time. So all around here I would be winning on Greeves, with Badger in the south and west, and David in East Anglia doing the same. So really he'd got the country covered.*

The Challenger is a contender

Once on the Challenger model, from 1964 onwards, the results improved, as did the moral in the Greeves camp. In the 250 British Championship Clough finished as runner-up to Bickers for a second time, the Suffolk man having been persuaded to return to the fold with the promise of a new improved machine.

Clough certainly took to the new model. Highlights from the season included Nantwich in April, where the headlines in the *MCN* read: 'ALAN CLOUGH BLOWS OFF JEFF SMITH'. The event was the Cheshire Motocross and he beat the works BSAs of Smith and Lampkin over

1964

Out front! Clough was on top form at Hawkstone Park in July 1964, winning all four of the day's major finals, including the Brian Stonebridge Memorial and the Midland Championship. (RD)

15 laps on his 250 Challenger. In June he was runner-up to Bickers in the 250 ACU Star race at the Cotswold Scramble, which consolidated his 2nd place in the title race, then at Hawkstone Park the following month, he had one of the best day's racing in his career. He won all four of his finals against top opposition, most pleasing of all being the Brian Stonebridge Memorial, which he won from Dutch Greeves' factory runner, Fritz Selling, and Dot rider Brian Hatton. He also won the Midland Championship in front of John Giles (Triumph) and Joe Johnson (Matchless Métisse), with his other wins coming in the 350 and 500 races.

The Challenger was good for me initially. It was lighter, had a different riding position, and it suited me, but Dave wasn't very keen on it so they altered it again, which didn't really work for me. Clough had a little chuckle as he picked out a photo of himself on a factory Greeves. *Just look at those handlebars! David altered them. How did I ever ride with them?* (The Greeves of that period had very high and very wide bars)

A further indication of just how good Clough was at this time can be taken from his performance in the Thirsk International at Boltby, in September 1964. After three gruelling races he and the new 250 World Champion, Joel Robert, had to be separated on time. Clough lost out to the Belgian wonder-boy by just five and a half seconds after tying on points.

Mixed fortunes

Clough mixed up his racing in 1965 his main aim being the ACU Star competition, though he also took in some selected GPs. These included a promising 3rd place in race one of the French round behind Robert and Russian, Victor Arbekov, who would go on to

1965

become World Champion that year. In Belgium he went one better, finishing 2nd in race one though he was mysteriously absent from the second. He had better luck on home soil though, winning the Cambridgeshire GN at Elsworth in April after chasing Bickers home in the 250 ACU Star race.

Then at the Luxembourg GP he crashed heavily and dislocated his shoulder. As a result he missed the third round of the 250 Star at the Cotswold Scramble and the penultimate round at the Experts GN at Larkstone in August, but was back to full fitness for the final round at the Lancashire GN later that month, where he had a great day's racing, taking the Star race ahead of his Greeves teammates, Bickers and Fred Mayes, and the GN race from the Lampkin brothers, Arthur and Alan.

He also made a promising debut on the new 360 Challenger that Greeves were developing in response to the 360s coming out of the CZ and Husqvarna factories, finishing 2nd to Goss in the first leg of the Staffordshire GN in September that year.

Kingpin at Greeves

As 1966 dawned, Clough emerged as the senior rider at Greeves, following Bickers' departure to CZ. As such, he found himself coming under increasing pressure from his younger teammates, Arthur Browning and Freddie Mayes, who had both joined Greeves the previous season, and another raw talent in the shape of Bryan Wade who would officially join Greeves mid-season.

1966

The third front fork in less than a year! Clough's Greeves now sports a Ceriani fork as he powers it through the Somerset mud at the BBC Grandstand meeting at Leighton in March 1966. Clough finished fourth in the 250 race, but raced the 360 model to runner-up to Jeff Smith in the 500 Trophy race. (CB)

Alan Clough

Wade remembers that although Clough was a big star, he always had time for him. "Alan Clough was on my list of targets when I started riding. He was a very likable character and I remember him and Jack Matthews were always having a good laugh together. The other thing that stands out in my mind was that when the race meeting had a hundred pound first prize for the last race of the day, more than likely he would win the race."

Wade's comment reminded me of a headline the MCN ran on Wednesday June 1st 1966; 'GREEVES GOLD DIGGERS AT BOLTBY'. The report went on to explain that the marauding Greeves teammates, Clough, Browning and Wade, had finished 1-2-3 in the main event of the day the £100 Northern Motocross. Reporter, Colin Hutchinson added '...with £100 pinned to the chequered flag for the first man home, Clough took less than 40 minutes to blaze his way to a cash century.' However, Browning pushed him hard initially, before coming under pressure himself from the teenaged Wade. But by that time Clough had been around for a while and he soaked up the pressure before easing away from the youngsters to win by 12 seconds. *Yes, the £100 races did seem to suit my mindset. I remember winning the £100 race at Builth Wells too. It's true I seemed to do very well in those!*

Opportunity knocks

With Bickers concentrating on winning CZ a 500 British Championship in 1966, a window of opportunity opened for Clough to grab some silverware, in the form of the 250 title, following several years of near misses. After showing good form in the BBC Grandstand Trophy series over the winter, the campaign started well, with second at the opening round at Nantwich in March, and a storming third in round two at Ringwood on Good Friday after being last away from the start. But at Stroud, Gloucestershire, mid-season, the heavens opened producing a quagmire of a track and although Clough led from the start, he dropped the Greeves whilst still on the first lap. Never one to quit, he fought back to finish the race but was out of the points and that left him struggling to catch series leader Mayes.

At that time, the championship still consisted of just five races of about 30 minutes duration each. Bickers then piled the pressure back on both of his ex-teammates, with a comfortable win in the fourth round at Halstead in July, whilst Clough's disappointing fourth

Ray Daniel was on hand to capture Clough's Husqvarna debut at the BBC meeting at Naish Hill in February 1967.

behind Mayes, virtually put paid to his chances. At the final round at Builth Wells (see pp95-96), Mayes did just enough to secure the title, with Clough finishing the season in 3rd behind Bickers on the CZ.

Despite a few flashes of brilliance, including wins in the Lancs GN on the 360 and the Brian Stonebridge Memorial at Hawkstone Park, his third victory in this event, ultimately it was a disappointing season for Clough. It's interesting to note that by the end of the season he was struggling to match his younger teammates, Browning, Wade and Mayes, especially in the televised meetings.

The Swedish connection

Clough needed some new impetus and he certainly found it with his switch to Husqvarna. *I left because the Greeves wasn't competitive anymore. We have a short life racing and if you want to earn a living you have to be winning. It was make or break time for me. I gave up a factory Greeves and spent a grand of my own money on two Huskies, but it was the best investment I ever made.*

In March 1967 Clough races the 360 Husqvarna to victory in the opening round of the 500 British Championship at Hawkstone Park. (RD)

You couldn't go wrong, they were light, fast, purpose-built and everything about the Husky was right.

Once on the Husky, everything clicked into place and he hit the form of his life. Concentrating on the home championships in the 1967 season, though he did venture abroad for a few GPs, it seemed at one stage as if Clough might achieve what Bickers had audaciously attempted the previous season and become the first rider to win both British Championships in the same season though he recently assured me that was never his goal for the season.

In the 250 Class, he soon 'set out his stall', with a race win in the opening round at Chard in March, where he was just too strong for long time rival Bickers. Two weeks later, he started his 500 campaign in the same vein, winning round one at his beloved Hawkstone Park. Having lost out to Bickers the previous day in the final round of the 250 Grandstand Trophy at Builth Wells, Clough got the better of the 'Coddenham Flyer' as he slipped past him at three-quarters distance and eased away to win comfortably at the flag. In his race report, a suitably impressed Gavin Tripp described it as, '*27 minutes of agony and 9 minutes of glory*'.

Praise from the highest quarter

At the time, Clough rated this as his best ever win and it really boosted his confidence for the rest of the season, as he explained. *If you could take Dave Bickers and Jeff Smith apart at a meeting then you felt you'd really done something. David was exceptional. He had the flair. He could just jump on any bike and win! Smithy was the most professional and so determined and they were the ones to beat. That day it was just so easy that I couldn't believe it. Smithy came over to me at the end and said, "There was*

On international duty at the 250 Swiss GP at Payerne in April 1967, Clough demonstrates his seemingly effortless style. (BH)

just no way, I could have lived with you round here today." That was really special to hear.

Round two of the 500s was at another of his favourite haunts, Hatherton Hall, Nantwich in April, but in atrociously muddy going, he could manage no better than 4th behind winner Chris Horsfield on the 360 Greeves, Jeff Smith and Vic Eastwood, though he maintained his lead in the championship ahead of Eastwood and Horsfield.

After a long spell with no overall results in GPs, Clough chanced his hand in the 250 GP at Payerne, Switzerland in April. The gamble paid off, with a fine 4th overall from sixth and third places in his first GP on the Husqvarna. Indeed, he was only kept off the podium by the interloping Paul Friedrichs, the 500 World Champion trying his hand in the 250 GPs for a change.

The Belgian jinx

No doubt encouraged by his fine showing in Switzerland, Clough opted to ride in the Belgian GP in April rather than contest the third round of the 500 British Championship at Dodington Park and it was a decision which arguably cost him the 250/500 double that year. When I questioned Clough on this he told me, *Yeah, it probably did, but I was on a contract with the factory and you had to do what they wanted you to do.* Sadly, he also suffered in the deep sand of Hechtal, falling twice in the first race and missing out on any points despite finishing seventh in the second leg.

Indeed Belgium seemed to be holding a hex over Clough at that time. A ride in an International event there in June resulted in a damaged knee, that threatened to end his season and which would have long lasting repercussions. At the end of the season,

Clough racing the Husqvarna in the 250 British GP at Wakes Colne in July 1967. (BH)

reflecting on his success, Clough told the *MCN*, 'The knee injury is the result of a 'long dab' in a Belgian event in June. I didn't fall off, but it hurt a lot then and it's hardly stopped hurting since'.

In search of the double

Back on home soil, his task eased as Bickers was away contesting the 500 Russian GP, Clough won round two of the 250 Championship at the Cotswold Scramble, but only after Norton-Villiers' teenage sensation Andy Roberton was denied when he lost his chain mid-race. Roberton's teammate, Fred Mayes, came through for 2nd with Arthur Browning taking 3rd on his Greeves. Clough, who was already nursing his injured right knee, now led the title chase from Mayes and Browning.

A week later he was back in the saddle adding another six points to his 250 Championship tally at the Cleveland GN, where he finished 2nd to Bryan Goss but ahead of Mayes, with the reigning Champion now emerging as his closest rival for the title.

The August Bank Holiday was a key weekend for Clough and his title aspirations as he travelled down from his home in Poynton to Tirley, Gloucestershire, for the penultimate round of the 500 British Championship on the Sunday, before heading east to Hintlesham, near Ipswich, for the 250 Championship round, which had reached the same stage. It's worth reflecting here, that Alan faced a round trip of nearly 600 miles to take in these two events.

By the end of the championship race at Tirley, Clough must have been rueing his decision to miss Dodington. However, nobody could fault his bravery and commitment, as despite still being troubled by his injured knee, he took the challenge to his rivals and shot to the front to lead the race for the first four laps. John Banks then got past him, and Vic Eastwood, in his haste to stay with Banks, tangled with Clough causing them both to fall. Meanwhile that wily old protagonist, Jeff Smith, was moving up the field and when Eastwood and Bickers both went missing within a lap, he was through to second. As Banks tired, Smith pounced for

At Hintlesham Park in August 1967, Clough finally realised his dream as he was crowned 250 British Champion. (BH)

the victory and seized the initiative in the title hunt, as rivals Eastwood and Bickers both failed to score and an exhausted Clough managed to add just one point to his tally.

Happy Monday

However, on the drive up to Suffolk for the August Bank Holiday Monday meeting, he must have had plenty of time to think out his strategy for the 250 Championship race and when he went to the line, he knew a good result would see him crowned Champion. A calculated ride by the Cheshireman, saw him finish third behind Bickers and Malcolm Davis (Bultaco) which was enough to net him the title with one round to spare. I count myself privileged to number amongst the crowd that day that saw him finally win the title he had been chasing for eight long years.

Clough, who had ridden consistently well all season, went to the final round of the 500 Championship at Builth Wells in October with an outside chance of making history by clinching the 250-500 double. Having secured the 250 title the pressure was lifted and he took the race victory, following a pulsating battle with Eastwood, but lost the championship to the race

In October Clough was vying for a unique 250-500 British Championship double and is clearly pushing on here. But despite victory in the final round at Builth Wells, he couldn't prevent Jeff Smith from winning his ninth national title. (RD)

In good company! Clough leads Jeff Smith and Malcolm Davis at the Hants Grand International in April 1968. (RD)

craftsmanship of Jeff Smith, who in finishing 4th did just enough to take the title, beating Clough and Eastwood by a single point. Reflecting on his season, Clough told MCN, 'Never before had I wanted to win as much as I did that race and I think that this determination must have shown in my riding. I was a bit disappointed, but Vic and I had a great race. It would have been really good to be double-Champion, but I'm nicely satisfied with one win.'

Clough across America

However, winning the 250 title had its perks. As reigning British Champion, Clough was invited to participate in the forerunner of the Trans-AMA series in the autumn. *The first time I went out there was with Hallman, Heikki Mikkola and Torlief Hansen and I went there as British Champion. The four of us rode Huskies and a San Diego dealer (Edison Dye) who was the importer for the States, put the series together. The first meeting was at Saddleback Park and I raced a used 250 Husky. Hallman was second and I was third. Then we moved on to San Francisco before hopping, skipping and jumping our way across the States for* about six weeks. I enjoyed it; it was a great experience and we were very well paid.

On his return to British soil, Clough had to address the problem of that nagging knee injury, which had failed to clear up. After careful consideration, he opted to take a break from racing, have an operation and convalesce over the winter. But when racing began again in earnest, he was fit and strong, having spent several months training with the local football team, Stockport County.

Full factory Husky?

If 1967 had been Clough's best season yet, 1968 promised to be even better. His success in the British Championship on the Husqvarna led the Swedish manufacturer to offer him full factory support with machines supplied through British importer, Brian Leask. Clough was on the ACU grading lists for both the 250 and 500 Classes in 1968 and with Leask's blessing he opted to contest the blue riband 500 category.

There were signs that Clough's recuperation from his operation would be successful with some fine results

Clough had an excellent day in front of the BBC Grandstand cameras at Clifton in December 1968, winning both the 250 and 750 Trophy races. (BH)

coming early season. These included a good showing at the opening 500 British Championship round at Chard in March, where he challenged for the lead in race one before taking a tumble, but then fought back to win the second race. Although he failed to score in round two at Elsworth, he was back in the points at the third round at Farleigh Castle, where he finished third in the second championship race.

Lack of parity leaves Clough frustrated

Things started well enough in the GPs too, with a third place in round two in Italy, behind the CZs of Roger De Coster and Petr Dobry. This augured well for the rest of the campaign, but sadly those would be the only points he earned all season. Clough found that whilst gaining the support of the Swedish manufacturer, their management clearly had a pecking order when it came to getting the best bikes. At this time Husqvarna were naturally pinning their hopes on home grown talent, such as Bengt Aberg, Ake Jonsson and Christer Hammergren and Clough found himself some way down the food chain. Speaking to *MCN* at the end of the season, the normally jovial Clough was clearly disgruntled with the situation. '*I had to ride a 360, while the other Husqvarna works men were given 400s and 420s. The season was disastrous. Now I'm not interested in chasing world titles unless a factory wants to sponsor me fully.*'

Clough shed some more light on the situation when I spoke to him in person. *My knee was never the same again after the operation in late '67. I couldn't put it down, I was always tweaking it and it was very painful. But the bike definitely wasn't as good as those the Swedish boys were riding. I remember I was over with Smithy at a French meeting and I was promised a 420. So I drove up from France, all the way to Sweden, and all they had for me was a bare engine, not even an exhaust or carburettor. It took me a while to get it sorted, but it was never right from the start. Vic (Eastwood) had a 420, but he spent more time out in Sweden, and he knew the Swedish lads better than I did, and they helped him out where they could.*

Upturn in form

Disappointing as the GP campaign had been, Clough showed glimpses of the previous season's form as he raced to victory in the Cotswold Scramble in late June ahead of the factory Greeves of Vic Allan and Arthur Browning. Later in the year he narrowly missed out on the Gloucestershire Grand National in September, when John Banks beat him to the line after the two riders came together a hundred yards from the flag, but he enjoyed a morale boosting double win at the final round of the 250 British Championship at Nantwich in October, although these were the only points he scored in the competition all season.

Winter wonderland

That win on one of his favourite hunting grounds seemed to serve as a catalyst to reignite the rest of his season, as he soon returned to his winning ways and that beaming smile returned to his face. He was in fine form for the third round of the Grandstand Trophy Series at Clifton in late December, winning three races, a double in the 250 and 750 Trophy races in addition to one of the invitation races. The highlight of the meeting was his duel with Malcolm Davis, a battle which would continue throughout the year for the 250 Trophy and would only be resolved at the final round at Kirkcaldy in March where 3rd place secured Clough his second major trophy in as many years. Though not as prestigious as the British Championship, Clough remains proud of his achievement over the winter of 1968/69. *Yeah I have a miniature silver camera to commemorate that, there weren't many of those about.*

With such good form from the winter, much was expected from Clough in the 1969 season, however, by his own admission he never fully recovered the form he had shown in the '67 season.

1969

Ton up in rural Cheshire

After missing round one of the 250 British Championship at Tilton in March, Alan had one of his vintage days at round two. Racing on a track that had been so good to him over the years, Clough devastated the field at Hatherton Hall, Nantwich, in late March, where only fellow veterans Jeff Smith on his lightweight 250 BSA and Dave Bickers could stay with him. Arthur Browning led the first race, but Clough and Smith both slipped through on the third lap and held close formation till the flag. In race two, Bickers and Vic Allan hit the front early on with Smith and Clough tagging along, but then Allan and Bickers slid off in turn, whilst Clough desperately tried to hold on to Smith's back wheel. His efforts weren't in vain as on the last lap after a coming together at the foot of the hill, Clough just managed to edge Smith out for his second win of the day. To cap things off, he outpaced Bickers and Greeves' rising star Malcolm Rathmell, to win the Cheshire Motocross and increase his winnings to a nice round £100.

In the next round of the championship at Hadleigh, Essex on the May Bank Holiday Monday, Clough and a young spectator had a narrow escape, when Alan lost control of his 250 whilst leading the first championship race. He got out of shape after catching a molehill and followed his cartwheeling Husky down the track, the bike tearing the trousers of the young boy who, not surprisingly, got the fright of his life! However, Clough remounted and fought back to finish 6th and salvage a single championship point. He put things right in race two though, where after leading a scrap with Goss and Bickers in the early laps he was passed for the lead by race one winner, Wade. However, Wade couldn't shake of his pursuers and Clough, Bickers and Allan all came through on the last lap. Clough's points haul moved him to the top of the championship standings ahead of Vic Allan, Malcolm Davis, who had a poor day, and Wade.

California trumps Gloucestershire

However, it was at this juncture that Clough was invited to race in the USA for a second time, and he didn't need much persuading to go! The Trans-AMA was too good an experience and too lucrative an opportunity to miss. Unfortunately, though, this meant that as the 250 Class hopefuls went to the line for round four of the championship at a very wet and muddy Cotswold Scramble at Nympsfield, Clough was enjoying breakfast in America, California to be more precise, where he scooped the 250 race in San Francisco.

Clough only missed one round of the British Championship, whilst plying his trade in the USA and was lying second just two points adrift of former Greeves teammate, Bryan Wade, when the series came to a thrilling climax at Tirley, at the end of August. However, sadly for Clough he didn't figure in the excitement (see pp179-180), as he was forced out of the first race with ignition failure. Bryan Goss sportingly loaned him his spare 250 Husqvarna for the second race, but Clough was clearly out of sorts with the bike and finished a lowly 10th in the race slipping back to 4th for the season.

Clough was selected to represent Britain in the 1969 Motocross des Nations, held on home soil at Farleigh Castle in September. Here he is pictured leading teammate Jeff Smith. (BH)

A change is as good as a rest

Then in the autumn of 1969, Clough surprised many motocross aficionados by linking up with his old friend and rival, Dave Bickers, to race CZ. *I was looking for a new challenge and Leasky was very understanding. Looking back I don't think the left-hand gear change did me any good and it just didn't suit me really. It was a bit of a camel to ride, although the engine was pretty good.*

His CZ debut came at the penultimate round of the 500 British Championship at Beenham Park in mid-October, where his best result was a 4th place in a 250 race. But the following week, he turned in a great performance on the Czech bikes at the final round at Builth Wells. He finished 5th in race one and improved to 3rd in the final race, behind winner Goss and fellow CZ convert, Malcolm Davis. He also finished a fine 3rd in the 250 race, chasing home British Champion, Wade, and Davis.

Easing back

Sadly the switch to CZ proved to be largely unsuccessful and after just six months he made a winning return to Husqvarna at Hawkstone Park in March 1970. But the successes were fewer and further between; runner-up to Bryan Goss at the Wessex Scramble in April, second to Goss again in race one of the 500 British Championship meeting at Wakes Colne, a win in the first leg of the Midland Championship at Hawkstone Park in September and another of those lucrative £100 race wins in the Kidstone GN in October.

By this time, Clough had been racing for 14 years and though many, such as the evergreen Vic Eastwood, raced far longer, Clough was feeling the effects and his enthusiasm was on the wane. *The travelling every weekend was getting me down. I was always doing 400-mile round trips and I just got tired of it. In the early days my*

Clough caught in forceful mood at Beenham Park in October 1969, during his brief spell racing CZs. (BH)

brother would occasionally go with me and share the driving and when I raced in Europe, Don Hitchcock sometimes accompanied me, but by the early '70s I was on my way out. It's no good half doing something, so I decided that that was going to be it.

It wasn't always a chore though, as he fondly remembers. *My favourite place to stay on my travels was the New Inn in Gloucester, and the Lampkins and Smithy used to stay there. It was a great place to eat, with T-bone steaks being the order of the day. If Smithy had won he would buy Gaelic coffees for everyone he liked and myself and my wife were privileged enough to be liked by Jeff. There weren't many,* he joked, *I think it was just the Lampkins and me!*

Business time

On retiring from the sport in the early '70s, Clough went into the world of business, initially importing Italian Cimatti lightweights. He then ran his own shop after buying out established local dealer Harry Cartwright of Stockport. Mr Cartwright, who had ridden for BSA in the Scottish Six Day Trial, had been a BSA and Triumph main dealer and became a Honda specialist when the little step-throughs took everything by storm. *We expanded a bit, getting BMW because no one else had them in the area, but in the end there was no money in it really and after 14 years, I sold up and took early retirement.*

Today Alan is a fit, trim septuagenarian, who keeps in shape by playing two 18-hole rounds of golf a week if time and his grandchildren allow! *I play off a handicap of 13, which is not bad for a 71 year-old. Being so competitive you can't just stop, you have got to do something. It might be fishing for some, but when I took over the business Mr Cartwright got me interested in playing golf. It's a competitive sport and I'm with a good set of lads again. It's great, and I can't think of anything else I'd rather do.*

Reflecting on his racing days Alan told me: *I think they were a super set of lads and the camaraderie was always there, even though the competition was fierce. I couldn't live with Badger on the fast grassy tracks of the south and south west, but then he couldn't handle the bumps and the sand of Hawkstone Park which I loved and at Shrubland Park, which was David's track, we both had to give second best. I only ever had two set-tos, one with Dick Clayton and the other with Arthur Browning. In both cases I had the lead and they tried to come bundling past. When I didn't move out of the way, there was contact and down they both went. Dick's never really forgiven me, but I spoke to Arthur and that was it, we've never had a cross word since.*

One thing is for certain. Alan Clough was one of the most popular riders of the period and that popularity extended from the spectators to his fellow riders. Had there been a 'Rider's Rider' award, I'm sure he would have won it many times over, as he is a true sportsman and a very worthy British Champion. As his former competition manager at Greeves, Bill Brooker, put it "He was an absolute gentleman."

John Banks

The Man Who Would Be King

Photo BH

Today John Banks is known to many in East Anglia for supplying their Honda, Mitsubishi and Suzuki cars. However, 40 years ago he was a household name throughout the country, performing heroically in front of audiences in their millions on Saturday afternoons in the televised winter motocross meetings where he was one of the most successful riders. You couldn't fail to notice Banks. He was a strapping six-footer, who weighed in at close to 15st, with a brash, intimidating riding style. It may not have been pretty, but it sure was effective and Banks was the 500cc British Champion on four occasions between 1968 and 1973 and was twice runner-up in the 500cc World Championship.

John Banks was born into a wealthy Bury St. Edmunds family in April 1944. His father, Fred, had his own building company, and would later serve as mayor of the town. Although there was no motorcycling history in the Banks family, there was a little 98cc Excelsior knocking around home, on which John roared around the garden until he rode it into the fish pond one day! However, although he didn't share his son's passion for motorcycles, Fred Banks could see that he was ready for something more suitable and agreed to buy him a Greeves Scottish trials bike from Dave Bickers. *Dad was never really that interested. He never came out to the races, but he always encouraged me, bought me whatever I needed and gave me time off work to go and race when I was working in the family building business as an apprentice plumber.*

Developing a taste for victory

Banks always had a reputation for being hard on bikes and within a few months he had, in his own words, "ridden the Greeves into the ground". A replacement was bought and on the new bike he took his first premier award in his third trial and it was clear that a new talent was rapidly emerging. *At that time I was riding against the likes of Doug* (Theobald, a life-long friend), *John Kendall, and John Pease, all top Eastern Centre trials riders and it sort of went to my head. After a couple of wins I expected to win every time I went out.* A few defeats dented his ego, but he had tasted victory, and he liked it.

Like so many youngsters at that time, John idolised Dave Bickers (six years his senior), the local boy who'd made good as European Motocross Champion. Bickers, on his Greeves, had fiercely contested the 250 European and British Championships of 1960 and '61 against the BSA C15s of Smith and Lampkin (who would later become Banks' teammates) and he had followed events with great interest. *Jeff rode every day, ate the right food and was very fit. Nobody had more commitment than him. He didn't have the raw talent that Dave and Arthur had, but he made himself a better rider. He was an inspiration to so many of us.*

Scrambling debut

So it was no surprise when he decided to try his hand at scrambling. *I worshipped Dave and I told my dad that I wanted to give scrambling a go, so he bought me a 250 Greeves.*

His first competitive outing came at Cockfield, near Bury St. Edmunds in May 1961, where he received his first lesson from a master. *Dave (Bickers) soon cut me down to size. But he took a liking to me and during my early years we travelled around together a fair bit.* Indeed, Bickers would continue to be a guiding light for John throughout his career.

Banks learnt quickly, competing against the likes of Dave Nicoll, Norman Messenger and John Pease in Eastern Centre Junior races. It was around this time that Theobald, by then a works trials rider for Dot, put in a word for his friend with the Dot management. *Doug took me up to the factory in Manchester and I was given a trials bike to use. But I was set on going scrambling and when Burnard Scott Wade got word of my results on the Greeves, he phoned up to offer me a bike.*

The Dot days

The works scrambler came in early 1962, when John was still only 17 years old. He produced some sparkling performances on the Manchester-built bike that season, especially at Shrubland Park, where in August he took 5th place in the 'Junior' (up to 250) race, won by Jeff Smith, and finished 3rd behind Chris Horsfield and Bill Gwynne in the up to 350 Support race at the Trophée des Nations meeting at the same venue in September.

The following season, 1963, Banks was thrown straight in at the deep end, as Dot sent him out to compete in the 250 World Championship. In the company of his illustrious neighbour, Bickers, he set off on the GP trail and just a few days after his 19th birthday he climbed onto his first podium, in Switzerland, finishing 3rd overall in just his fourth GP. Then at the Dutch round he briefly led the first race, but after twice coming together with Champion to be, Torsten Hallman, he crashed into a tree and had to retire injured. However, at Shrubland Park in June, he turned in another excellent performance in his first home GP, when he finished an excellent 3rd behind Hallman and Vlastimil Valek, giving the Suffolk crowd something to cheer about, after Bickers had been sidelined in race one. However, he had to retire from race two with a broken rear wheel when well-placed, ruling him out of an overall position and the accompanying points.

Following such early promise, he was acclaimed in the motorcycle press of the day as Britain's 'New Hope', being seen by many as a natural successor to his friend and mentor, Bickers. But if anything, Banks feels this early success worked against him. *I came up too quickly really, there was a lot of pressure on me and I*

A young John Banks seems to be making a good impression on the men in white coats! He is pictured racing the 250 Dot at the 1964 Hants Grand National at Matchams Park near Ringwood. (CB)

was expected to go right to the top. Interestingly, although he would soon win a factory ride with BSA it would be several years before he established himself as a genuine world title challenger.

When he first went to Dot he joined Alan Clough, John Griffiths and Pat Lamper. *I travelled out to some of the GPs with John Griffiths, who was a good rider, and though the bikes weren't going that well, I got some good results. But even at that time I was hard on the bikes.*

Dave Bickers remembers him as being nothing short of reckless in those early days. "We would go out to the GPs and he would never walk the track or ride himself in, he would just take his bike out on the track in practice and bulldoze his way round." It should be noted, however, that he was still only 18 at the time and clearly youthful exuberance got the better of common sense. Sadly, the Dot was no match for John's forceful riding style and far from being 'Devoid of trouble', it regularly broke down.

CZ try-out

Then in the winter of 1963 in company with Bickers he went out to the CZ factory to try a 250. *Dave was on good terms with the Czechs and we tried the CZs. Joel (Robert) was there trying them too. They offered me a ride but I turned it down. Joel accepted and the rest is history.* As Robert took the 250 to World Championship glory in 1964, Banks must have been kicking himself. *Yeah, maybe, but I was already hankering after a 500.*

Despite missing out on a CZ ride, 1964 began well for the young East Anglian, as he made the front page of the *MCN* on January 15th: 'BANKS JOINS THE TV STARS,' read the headline, accompanied by a photograph of him hustling Jeff Smith and Dave Bickers in the televised Invitation race at Clifton. Then at Westleton, in his native

Now on a factory BSA, Banks is pictured negotiating a tricky bank at the 1966 Inter-Centre Team Scramble at Hatherton Hall, Nantwich where he played his part in the Eastern Centre team's victory. (RD)

Suffolk in early March, he was the sensation of the 250 race. In front of the BBC cameras, he led Bickers, on the new Greeves Challenger for several laps, before getting out of shape on a downhill stretch and allowing the more experienced man through for the win.

Undeterred by the Czechoslovakian trip, Bickers tried to fix up his young friend again, this time closer to home though in South London. Bickers takes up the story. "John told me that he really wanted to ride a 500. So I took him down to Plumstead (the AMC factory) to meet Hugh Viney (the Competition Shop manager). I walked in and said. 'Hugh, this is John Banks, and he'd like to ride one of your 500s.' He looked at us and replied. 'That's good. He can go into any one of our showrooms and buy himself one.' And that was the end of the negotiation." It was a reaction that I'm sure Viney must have lived to regret as AMC's loss would become BSA's gain.

Factory BSA comes Banks' way

Banks' luck would soon change however, when BSA's Competition Manager, Brian Martin, invited him to try one of the developmental 420s. At that time the Small Heath factory was restructuring its team after losing the services of John Burton and the Lampkin brothers. Martin had been keeping tabs on Banks' progress and in one of his first meetings on the 420, he led two races at Hawkstone Park in July 1964, only missing out on a win in the Midland Championship when the plug insulator broke. Martin was suitably impressed however, and Banks was invited to join the team. Thus began a long and successful association with BSA.

Initially Banks rode in the shadow of his erstwhile heroes, Smith and Lampkin (who had returned to BSA after a largely unsuccessful year on the factory Cotton), but although Banks had tremendous respect for Smith as a rider, he is quick to admit that the two of them, who came from very different backgrounds, never really saw eye to eye.

Then in late 1964, Vic Eastwood, who had been a thorn in the side of Smith on his works Matchless, was signed to the Birmingham concern. But if Banks was bothered by the arrival of Eastwood at Armoury Road, he didn't show it. *For some reason or another, Vic didn't really bother me. Although he could go well sometimes, he wasn't really someone I feared racing against.*

Out on the track though, Banks was being outperformed by his new teammate from Kent, who was in sparkling form. In 1965 Eastwood finished runner-up to Smith in the ACU Drivers' Star and 4th in the World Championship, whilst in contrast, Banks was struggling to find any real consistency on the BSA. A measure of the difference between the two at the time can be taken from that year's 500 British GP at Hawkstone Park, where Eastwood finished 3rd overall, behind Smith and Rolf Tibblin, whilst Banks found himself racing in the 500 Support race, though he did emerge as the winner from Jim Aim and John Lewis.

1965/66

He found some form over the summer of 1966 though, winning the Experts GN at Hawkstone Park in June, ahead of teammate Lampkin and Brian Nadin, and the Midland Centre Championship at the same venue in September. An eventful race saw Banks locked in combat with Eastwood and Hawkstone supremo, Alan Clough, with all three riders sharing the lead in the race. Clough led in the early stages until he missed a gear at the top of the hill allowing Banks to slip through. Eastwood then passed Clough and swooped past Banks as they came down off the hill. But Banks bravely retook the lead and held it to the flag.

By 1967, both Eastwood (who had finished as runner-up to Smith in the British Championship on the last four occasions) and Banks were beginning to believe they could move up to the leader's role at BSA. By then Smith was 33 years old and there were signs that he was losing his competitive edge. Banks had also had his first taste of the 500 GPs, riding in selected events, where he gained a lot of experience and was showing a lot of potential as the campaign closed, taking a podium place at the Luxembourg GP behind Bickers and Christer Hammergren, and finishing 5th overall, and best Briton, in the final round in Switzerland. But events that took place over the winter of 1967/68 would send the young pretenders, Banks and Eastwood, on very different paths in the coming season.

1967

A new self-belief

Banks' first major title win came when he captured the BBC Grandstand Trophy from Eastwood, who had clawed his way back into contention after a disappointing start to the series. The BSA teammates arrived at the final round at Caerleon, South Wales, level on points, with the scene set for a thrilling finale. As it was, neither rider finished the race and the title went to Banks, courtesy of a superior win rate in the series. However the win bolstered Banks' confidence and

At Hintlesham Park in August 1967, local photographer Dave Kindred catches Banks leading fellow East Anglian Jim Aim, on his way to victory in the Hintlesham Grand National.

served as a springboard for the highly successful years that followed. On receiving the trophy, he informed the watching TV viewers, *I want to be World Champion.*

A matter of weeks after winning the title Banks found his growing status at BSA confirmed when Eastwood was sensationally sacked by the Small Heath concern. Increasingly frustrated by, as he saw it, playing a supporting role to Smith and having to scratch around the competition shop for spares, he spoke out to the BSA management, who decided to 'let him go'. Eastwood then signed to Husqvarna, through importer Brian Leask, whilst Banks and Smith readied themselves for the coming GP season.

1968

Banks makes his mark

The 1968 season was arguably Banks' best ever. At 24 years old, he retained the BBC Grandstand trophy, edging out Arthur Browning and Keith Hickman, added the ITV World of Sport Trophy, which he dominated, became 500 British Champion and only missed out on the World title by a solitary point to the East German Paul Friedrichs, who took his third consecutive title. It was a phenomenal effort, though some would argue that he tried to achieve too much.

In the British Championship Eastwood was his main rival, after the expected challenge from Smith had failed to materialise. Whilst still BSA mounted, Eastwood had notched a win and a second at the super muddy series opener at Chard, whilst Banks had failed to score. But after switching to Husqvarna, Eastwood took a while to acclimatise to the bike and by the time he had returned to his winning ways, Banks was in complete control. His best round of the season came at the Maybug meeting at Farleigh Castle, where he recorded an excellent double win. He took the first when he pipped teammate Keith Hickman and Eastwood in a close race and then in the second, he led the same riders until Hickman's rear wheel broke up and Eastwood's rear brake arm broke leaving Banks to cruise in to the finish ahead of Smith and Clough.

1968 saw John Banks come of age. Here he is pictured leading Belgian CZ ace, Sylvain Geboers, at the Hants Grand International. Geboers took the overall victory, whilst Banks finished fourth overall, though a year later he would stand atop the rostrum. (RD)

He also won races at Wakes Colne in June and the final meeting at Kidston in October and at the close of the series had won four of the ten races staged and finished runner-up on four occasions, leaving him 13 points clear of his closest rival, Eastwood. BSA riders dominated the series, with new recruits Nicoll and Hickman finishing 3rd and 4th respectively, whilst the veteran, Smith, rounded out the top five.

Grand Prix glory, world title heartbreak

There were few signs at the beginning of Banks' first full 500 World Championship campaign that he would be a real contender for the title. It took four GPs before he registered his first points (though this was also true of the reigning Champion, Friedrichs), opening his account with 4th place overall in Finland, where he took his first race win at this level in the second leg. He was 4th again in East Germany and then improved to runner-up at the Czech round. Then it was Eastwood's turn to shine, as he won the home GP at Farleigh Castle (he would also triumph in Luxembourg that year). Banks was bitterly disappointed not to add points in his home GP, especially in the absence of Friedrichs, and had to sit out the second race after injuring a foot.

If his form in the first half of the series had been disappointing, in the run in to the championship's end it was sensational. He scored points in each of the remaining rounds, winning the French and Dutch GPs and finishing runner-up in Belgium and Switzerland. As a result he grossed five points more than Friedrichs, but sadly, for Banks, the rulebook stated that the title would be decided on a rider's top seven results and Friedrichs' win in the Swiss round proved decisive, with the East German retaining the title by the narrowest of margins, a single point!

Naturally Banks was disappointed at losing the title in such a way, but looking back on it today, he has nothing but praise for his East German rival. *Paul was incredibly strong and so fit. He was the toughest competitor I ever raced against. He mastered the 400, which was a*

The 1968 500 British Champion is pictured racing in the fourth round at Wakes Colne in June 1968. A second place to Vic Eastwood and a win in race two saw him ease clear of his main title challenger, Eastwood. (BH)

real beast (44 bhp and 220 lb). *It was so fast. Joel* (Robert) *and Roger* (DeCoster) *simply couldn't handle them and they soon went back to the 360s.*

Banks hits top gear

1969 promised to be Banks' year. On the home front Eastwood, runner-up the previous year, would not figure in the British Championship following a bad fall at Hawkstone Park in December 1968, which left him with a broken right leg that would keep him out of action for almost two years. And in the World title hunt Friedrichs, who was turning 30, was giving five years away to his younger adversary and the CZ now appeared to be less reliable than it had previously been.

Banks went into both championships on the crest of a wave, having retained the BBC and ITV trophies over the winter of 1968/69. BSA had always sent strong teams to the televised meetings, as they saw winning in front of audiences in their thousands as the best possible publicity for their product, even though the toll of racing virtually all season long might prejudice their GP runners come the series' end. Jeff Smith was the only rider who managed to win the BBC Trophy, the British Championship and the World title in one season, and although Banks had great stamina and determination, he lacked the overall level of fitness that Smith and Friedrichs possessed at their best.

Invincible?

He was showing no signs of tiring in the British Championship though, where he was in scintillating form winning nine of the ten races held, and amassing 75 points, more than double that of runner-up Vic Allan (Greeves). However, it wasn't all plain sailing, as he had to come from behind in virtually all of the races drawing on his renowned stamina and growing experience to pull him through.

John Banks

After dominating the opening rounds at Brownrigg near Penrith, and Wakes Colne in April, he left it very late to catch race leader Arthur Browning in the second race at Cuerden Park, Lancashire at the end of August, only passing him in the run-in to the finish line. Then at Beenham Park for the Jackpot Scramble in mid-October, he found himself in a real dog fight in the first race, with Andy Roberton, on a surprisingly potent 370cc AJS. Roberton actually caught and passed the reigning Champion and, to the delight of the crowd, headed him for four pulsating laps. But Banks bided his time, before passing and pulling away from the gallant Welshman. Then in race two, Vic Allan took the battle to him, leading for 21 of the 24 laps, before Banks caught and passed him as he made the mistake of easing back prematurely.

Goss spoils the party

The only other rider to win a 500 British Championship race that season was Bryan Goss in the final round at Builth Wells in October. Goss, who led the first race until he was put out at mid-distance with a whiskered plug, made sure in the final race, passing Malcolm Davis after a couple of laps and running away with it, whilst Banks, who was handicapped by a poor start, battled back to finish 5th at the flag.

Banks had also posted a warning to his GP rivals as the World Championship season approached, winning the Hants Grand International (HGI) at Matchams Park on Good Friday. Having narrowly lost out to Sylvain Geboers the previous year, Banks had to fend off three more top Belgians, in the shape of Joel Robert, Roger

The Changing of the Guard! As a teenager Banks idolised local hero Dave Bickers, as a young man he travelled to GPs in his company, but by 1969 Banks had the upper hand on his good friend. Here he leads Bickers in the ITV meeting at Morestead Down, Hants in March. (RD)

To the winner the spoils! Banks is pictured with the Hants Grand International Trophy after racing his BSA to victory in April 1969 (RD)

DeCoster (4th overall) and Jef Teuwissen, who finished runner-up on the day.

Most GP observers were expecting Banks and Friedrichs to pick up their own personal battle where they had left off in Switzerland the previous season. But the challenge was to come from another quarter, as the Swedes, Bengt Aberg and Arne Kring, blitzed the opening rounds. Aberg won the first GP at Sittendorf, Austria in April, whilst Banks fought hard all day to gain the runner-up spot. He was out of luck in the next round in Sweden, but bounced back to take his first race win of the 1969 campaign on his way to 2nd overall at the Dutch GP, where Kring took his second consecutive GP win.

Banks breaks through the Soviet Block

At the Italian GP at the end of May, he was forced out of race one with water in the electrics. But in a heady two-week period in June he put together back-to-back winning rides behind the Iron Curtain, in Czechoslovakia and the USSR, to hit the front in the title chase as it reached the half way stage.

Despite a disappointing 'blip' at the West German GP, where the BSA again suffered a mysterious electrical problem eliminating him just two laps from the finish of race one, Banks seemed to have timed his challenge to perfection. He was hitting peak form just as the series wound up with an intense programme that took in five GPs in as many weeks over the summer. First up was the famous Citadel circuit at Namur, Belgium, where Banks had to give second best to rising Belgian star DeCoster, losing out on the GP victory by 3.4 seconds after they had both finished with a win and a 2nd place. But in spite of this, he strengthened his lead in the title by finishing 2nd overall.

Reliability issues

But then the reliability of the British four-stroke was found wanting, as a succession of electrical and tyre problems forced Banks out of four consecutive GPs allowing Aberg to stretch ahead in the series. The title was once again decided at the Swiss round and Banks' preparation took a severe setback when he clouted a post in Saturday's practice, though after receiving pain-killing injections overnight, he valiantly took to the line on Sunday. However, in the heat of racing it was the BSA and not Banks that broke down, suffering a rear wheel puncture in the first race and a gearbox failure in the second. Aberg was Champion and a dejected Banks finished the season as runner-up again.

The disappointment of not lifting the world crown weighed heavily on John Banks. With Bickers and Smith now retired from the GP scene, the hopes of a nation fell firmly on his broad shoulders. To this day he resolutely believes that he should have been World Champion in 1969, and while many cite his fitness level as the determining factor, he is adamant that it was the BSA's lack of reliability and some questionable 'politics' that really defeated him. *Aberg's Husky was very fast, but my BSA was a match for it. But the electrics really let me down in (West) Germany and I didn't finish a race. (He also suffered the same fate at the French round). The problem was that we never had enough parts. The parts at BSA were spread out over too many people and we were fighting over bits and pieces. Then there were the tyres. BSA were contracted to Dunlop, who helped finance the*

Motoring on in typically determined style, Banks sends up a dust cloud at the Motocross des Nations at Farleigh Castle, September 1969. (BH)

GP campaign. I wanted to use Trelleborgs, but I had to use Dunlops and I picked up so many punctures.

Had the bike been more trustworthy, he might well have clinched the title. But BSA were on a downward spiral and in the coming seasons the bikes would become less reliable and naturally, less competitive. With little or no money available to the Competition Shop for development, BSA's glory days in the GPs were numbered. Sadly, though he still managed to perform quite brilliantly on home-soil, Banks would never mount a serious world title challenge again.

Banks' erstwhile teammate at BSA, Jeff Smith had this to say of him. "John Banks was the best motocross rider who never won a European or World Championship. He certainly should have been, but when the opportunity presented itself luck was not with him and he lost the 500 World Championship by one point!"

Injuries curtail Banks' efforts

After the successes of the previous year, 1970 must have been a huge disappointment for Banks when he was sidelined for most of the season with a knee injury. The defence of his titles started badly, when he lost the BBC Trophy to fellow BSA rider Dave Nicoll, who was in inspired form during the winter months. Then at the opening round of the British Championship, the Cambridge GN at Elsworth, Banks picked up an innocent looking injury, which would prove to be very costly. After edging out local favourite Nicoll in the first race, he sprained a knee in the second forcing him to sit out the rest of the meeting. The following weekend saw Banks compete in the final round of the ITV series at Winchester, where he pipped Greeves' Vic Allan, who finished equal on points, for the title thanks to a higher win rate than the Scot.

1970

Banks may have won the battle, but he effectively lost the war. He tried to ride through the knee injury and gallantly took off on the GP trail for another season, but after clouting another post in the opening Swiss GP at Payerne in mid-April and then aggravating the knee again, he decide to cut his losses, having surgery on the knee that would keep him out of action until September. By that time he had surrendered his British title to Bryan Goss and had missed out on most of the World Championship rounds.

Banks returns and pushes himself to the limit

For Banks, the 1971 season was a time for him to reassert himself as the country's top motocross rider. It also saw the arrival at BSA of Vic Allan, who had finished as runner-up in the last two 500 British Championships, and the highly talented, 23 year-old, Andy Roberton. Thanks to his consistent riding in 1970 on the Greeves, Allan was on the ACU's grading list and BSA decided to send him along to the GPs with Banks.

Eager to stamp his authority on the British Championship, Banks showed his mettle at the opening round at Hawkstone Park in March. Riding his new GP bike he fought off Husqvarna's young-gun, Bryan Wade, to take the first race. Then in a dramatic second outing he was comfortably in control of the race leading teammates Roberton and Hickman, when the engine cut out on the last lap. *I'd lapped everyone down to third place and then the battery just died on me. I had to push through a huge hole and across the finishing line having just done a 30-minute race and I remember thinking, 'I can't push it any further.' But the crowd was urging me on and I got there in the end.*

Despite collapsing after crossing the finish line, the effort was worth it, as he was rewarded with 3rd place, and took the lead in the title hunt, gaining a psychological, as well as numerical, advantage over his rivals. That season he went on to win his third British Championship. How important had that push to the finish line been?

Banks was always hard on his bikes. Here he is pushing the works BSA to the limit during his championship winning campaign in 1971. (RD)

At the 1971 500 British GP at Farleigh Castle in July, Banks is chasing World Champion Bengt Aberg (Husqvarna) with intent. He led both races, though sadly he could manage no better than fifth overall. (RD)

Allan soon demonstrated that he had the speed to be a threat to Banks in the months ahead, winning the Battle of Newbury and the Cambridge GN events early in the year, but his season ended dramatically at the 500 Italian GP in April, when he crashed heavily on the bone dry circuit, breaking his leg.

Following a complicated day at Farleigh Castle in May where he salvaged 2nd place in race two, Banks returned to his winning ways in the first race at round three at Nympsfield. Meanwhile, Bryan Wade, who won the second race, was beginning to believe that he might just be able to write himself into the record books as the first double championship winner (250 and 500 in the same season).

In July, Banks and BSA headed back to Farleigh Castle, for what would prove to be BSA's final 500 British GP. In front of a patriotic 12,000-strong crowd, Banks got a great start and led the first race for eight glorious laps. Then fate struck when his rear brake cable broke and he lost a lap having a new one fitted before battling back to finish a creditable 9th. Another great start in the second race saw Banks move past World Champion Aberg on the second lap. Again Banks was looking really good, but coming under increasing pressure from Ake Johnsson (Maico) and Friedrichs (CZ), he fell on lap 10. He quickly remounted salvaging 3rd place though he was unable to close down the two leaders. It had been a magnificent effort, which was rewarded with 5th overall, though it had promised so much more.

Dear John!

Less than a month later Banks, along with his teammates, received news from BSA that they were pulling the plug on the Competition Shop and therefore would be recalling the factory bikes. After seven great years with the Small Heath concern, it was all over for Banks. *I wasn't really surprised; I knew it was coming, though we thought we'd go the whole season. The problem was that there wasn't anything special coming out of BSA; it was just the same old bikes.*

Help came from an unlikely quarter when in a truly sporting gesture, John's great rival, Bengt Aberg, stepped in and contacted Husqvarnas' competition manager, Bror Jauren. As a result Banks was offered the use of the injured Arne Kring's machine, which he rode for the first time at the West German GP.

After a below par performance in West Germany, *I was so used to pulling a four-stroke and the Husky was spinning all over the place.* Banks rapidly adjusted to his new mount and shrugging aside the disappointment of being made redundant by BSA he was soon back on the pace in the GPs, scoring good points at Namur, with an excellent 5th overall.

Back on home soil he made the trek up to Cuerden Park in August, where first and second places on the Swedish bike in the penultimate round of the British Championship meant that he couldn't be caught in the title race and for the third time in four seasons he was British Champion. His main challenger, Bryan Wade ran out of sparks whilst leading the first race, thereby ending his dream of doing the championship double.

Husqvarna's loss is CZ's gain

An excellent 3rd place finish in the second race of the Motocross des Nations at Vannes in northern France in September, seemed to have secured Banks' future with Husqvarna. But incredibly, at only 27 years old, he was told by Husqvarna that they considered him too old

When the BSA Competition Department closed down in 1971, Banks was lent Arne Kring's factory Husqvarna, on which he went on to secure his third 500 British Championship. Here, the newly crowned Champion is pictured racing the Swedish two-stroke at the final round at Tirley in August. (RD)

to take on. Banks didn't dwell on their decision though, and with the help of his valued friend, Dave Bickers, he made contact with the people at CZ, who were more than happy to sign him up. When he tried Bickers' CZ he found he was happier with it than he had been on the Husqvarna. *It was more like the BSA, with more power in the bottom and mid-range and I found it easier to slide around.*

In 1970, Banks had been part of a four-man squad that BSA sent to contest the Trans-AMA series in the USA, with Dave Nicoll just edging him out to take the series and when he signed to CZ, they immediately sent him out to the USA to compete in the 1971 series. Banks was impressed with things in the US, and feels that he was better known in the USA than he was at home. *In America you go there as a star and people want to take you places and show you things. We were taken to Hollywood and saw all these big houses and met the stars, a lot of whom would come to the races. You'd be there and you'd see people like Steve McQueen walking about.*

Banks stayed with CZ in 1972, but despite getting some good results and being a strong British

Banks is pictured on the factory CZ at a muddy 1972 Cotswold Scramble at Nympsfield. (RD)

Out front! Ray Daniel's magnificent photo catches Banks at his best, as he races the Cheney BSA to victory in the first round of the 1973 500 British Championship at Hawkstone Park.

Championship contender, he never looked truly at home on the Czech bike. He still had his moments in the British Championship though, like at Tilton for example, where he was his old dominant self, taking both championship races with ease. But after running second to Wade for most of the season, he slipped back to third at the championships' close, after a disappointing ride in the final round at Tirley.

1973

Back on a thumper

For the 1973 season, to the delight of many motocross fans, Banks placed his trust in a British four-stroke again, when he linked up with ace bike-builder, Eric Cheney. He had also been approached by Alan Clews, creator of the Clewstroka (later to be known as the CCM), but Banks plumped for Cheney, because he felt he was more experienced than Clews. The Cheney-Banks partnership was one that would bear fruit, but one that ultimately left both parties feeling frustrated.

On the Cheney BSA, Banks was soon himself again and demonstrated that on this bike, he could regain the 500 title. At the first round of the British Championship at Hawkstone Park in March, Banks finished 2nd to reigning Champion Wade in a thrilling first race, where the gallant Husqvarna ace battled a flat rear tyre (see p189 and 191), and then dominated the second, lapping everyone down to 4th placed Norman Barrow (CCM). At the day's close Banks led the championship and he was never headed all season.

A fall and no points for the Suffolk man in the first race at round two in Devon, must have lifted his rival's hopes, but then Banks moved up a gear winning the second race comfortably. Then in round three at Builth Wells in June, he scored another impressive double win. In the first race he did it the hard way after misjudging the start and coming round 15th at the end of the first lap. However, he decimated the field and after 15 minutes he deposed Jimmy Aird on his Maico to hit the front. In race two, he made no mistakes, taking the lead mid-way through the first half and motoring away from his pack of pursuers. Wade, who had finished 4th in race one came through to the runner-up spot to maintain his title challenge, whilst Aird followed his excellent 2nd in race one with 3rd place, to finish as the second highest points scorer on the day.

However, the most exciting contest of the day was the non-championship 500 race, which much to the delight of the crowd, saw the four-strokes of Banks and Lancastrian Bob Wright (CCM) go head to head. Wright led in the early stages, whilst Banks once again stormed back from a poor start. Once on level terms, Wright and Banks traded places until the final lap, when they came together and Wright bit the Welsh dust. Banks rode on to his third win of the day, whilst Wright remounted to finish a well deserved 2nd.

Title number four

Banks went to the Rob Walker Scramble at Frome in August, knowing he had a great opportunity to secure his fourth title. But Wade was in no mood to relinquish his crown and came out fighting. He led both races though he failed to finish either, a jamming throttle eliminating him from the first race, whilst a recurring knee injury forced him to abandon the second. With Wade out, there was no pressure on Banks, who rode on to record two more wins, and put the seal on his fourth British Championship.

Although the series finished on a low for Banks, following a disappointing day at the final round at Wakes Colne, his performance in the championship was his best since his almost faultless 1969 campaign, as he finished with more than twice the points tally of runner-up Wade, who edged out Wakes Colne double race winner, Eastwood.

Razzmatazz Banks style

There were some flashes of his former brilliance in the GPs too. Banks forced the Cheney to the front in both the Dutch and French GPs, though he failed to finish either, but at the very first US GP, at Carlsbad Raceway, California, 3rd and 4th place finishes saw him finish 2nd overall, his best GP result since Namur in 1969.

Once again, Banks was really impressed with the level of professionalism he encountered in the USA. *Alan Greenwood (the US representative for Cheney) was so organised and the publicity was amazing. The bike was excellent too; I never really liked the forks we had on the Cheneys, but that one handled really well.*

However, in spite of such success, following the Motocross des Nations at Wohlen, Switzerland, where he was once again best Briton with two superb rides finishing 4th and 3rd, Banks announced that unless he and Cheney could find a sponsor he would quit grand prix racing. Sadly, despite a fund set up by Vic Vaughan, a West Country scrambler and Cheney fan, to keep the all-British package on the GP circus, Banks and Cheney couldn't agree terms and the relationship was over, though John's GP career certainly wasn't.

An Ossa and a CCM - Strange bed fellows

After failing to sign Banks in 1973, Alan Clews thought he'd missed out again when Banks stunned the motocross world by signing to race for the Spanish manufacturer, Ossa, in January 1974. The deal, set up by Ossa's UK importer, Cliff Holden, was that he would debut the Ossa in the 250 GP season-opener in Spain, and then race and develop it in the 250 British Championship.

However, Clews was not to be denied again, especially when a week after Banks had signed to Ossa his top runner, Bob Wright, penned a deal to race for another Spanish manufacturer, Montesa. As Banks deal with Ossa was exclusively to ride the 250, Clews didn't hesitate, signing Banks to race in the British Championship and the GPs. At the time, he was still Britain's most consistent GP performer, and Clews felt his experience would be invaluable in helping CCM in their first GP campaign.

This was an exciting period in British motocross history, as the battles between the resurgent British-built four-strokes (Banks and his Cheney were frequently challenged in 1973 by Bob Wright, Norman Barrow and Jimmy Aird on their CCMs) and the increasingly larger capacity two-strokes, such as Wade's 460cc Husqvarna, provided great entertainment. As such, many motocross fans of the day weren't too disappointed to discover that Banks was switching his allegiance from Fleet, Hampshire, to Bolton, Lancashire; the important factor for them being that he would still be on a British-built four-stroke.

Banks, who rode for CCM for four seasons, suffered a disappointing start to his British Championship campaign, netting just nine points from the first five

Racing the CCM in 1974, Banks had an indifferent season by his standards, but finished on a high with a double victory in the final round of the 500cc British Championship at Tirley in August. (CB)

races, before coming into form in the second half of the series. He won the second race at Tilton in June, added points in both races at the Lancashire GN, despite suffering with an injured back, and won both races at the final round at Tirley in August.

However, it all came too late, as Vic Allan had sewn-up the championship at Cuerden Park, and long term adversary Eastwood, on his factory Maico, edged Banks out of 2nd place in the title following a tie on points. To add insult to injury, Eastwood took the tie-breaker on the strength of two runner-up spots behind Banks in the final round.

Upsetting the form books

That season, Banks suprised many with his form in the 250 British Championship on the Ossa and, arguably, his best performance came at Brownrigg Fell, Cumberland in April. Luck, however, was not on his side, when a stray rock wiped off a footrest whilst he was closing in on leader Vic Allan in race one.

With some help from Dave Bickers, a spare CZ peg was hastily fashioned to fit the Spanish bike between races and Banks took off like an angry hornet in race two. He shot into the lead and proceeded to carve out a commanding 25-second lead. Meanwhile, Allan had fought back from a poor start, passing Malcolm Davis and moving up to 2nd. Banks still remembers how the race played out. *I was leading Vic Allan on the Bultaco with one lap to go when the exhaust broke and I could only crawl up the hill and he passed me on the line!*

At the close of the day's racing six points were all Banks had to show for his efforts, but he had demonstrated what he and the Ossa were capable of. Not a bad showing for a man who hadn't regularly competed on a 250 since his days with the Dot factory, 10 years earlier. He went on to finish 6th in the title despite more mechanical failures and having to miss the final round, as he was jetting off to the USA to contest another Trans-AMA series, this time for CCM.

Post 1974

John Banks raced on until the late '70s, enjoying his fair share of success, especially on the CCM. In 1975, the first season of the new format British Championship, he showed flashes of his former brilliance such as another stunning double victory at Tirley in August. In a season marred by a mysterious illness that left him feeling dizzy and short of breath, he would eventually go on to finish in 5th place in the championship.

The following season Banks began to wind down his riding career as he began to devote more time to his business interests. With his building company flourishing, he had opened a new motorcycle shop in Bury St. Edmunds and was also running a motocross team, consisting of himself, Stuart Nunn and talented teenager Jonathan Wright. Obviously something had to suffer and although he still managed to finish 4th in the British Championship, his points total was less than half that of the new Champion Graham Noyce.

Déjà-vu

1977 found him in sparkling form and he was often the only rider to present a serious challenge to Noyce. In the opening round at Hatherton Hall, the scene of many of his best rides over the years, despite riding with a heavily strapped shoulder, he twice finished runner-up to the Champion, but it was to be a season

Spectacular action! Banks on international duty on the CCM. (RD)

Banks giving the CCM its head at Builth Wells, October 1977. (RD)

of mixed fortunes and great frustration for the former Champ. In an interview with *MCN's* Nick Harris in October he declared *"I can hardly believe I'm so low* (6th place in the British Championship). *I am riding better now than when I last won the championship riding the Cheney"*. However, once again, as at the height of his BSA days, he was plagued by a combination of bad luck and bike problems and failed to score in eight of the twelve races that counted towards the championship.

However, in the 500 GPs he would prove that he could still run with the best as he mounted his best campaign since 1971. He finished 5th overall in Italy and 6th in Canada, before taking 4th overall in front of a wildly enthusiastic crowd at Farleigh Castle in July, following a storming ride in the second leg which saw him finish 2nd to, World Champion to be, Heikki Mikkola on his factory Yamaha. Sadly, he would just miss out on a top 10 place for the season after adding just one point in the three remaining rounds.

'Wizard' new bike

In 1978 Banks took on a new challenge, when as a 5-star Honda dealer, he decided to promote the product he was selling. With some support from Honda UK, he launched the Merlyn Honda; a bored-out, breathed on, 360cc Honda XL trail bike engine housed in a frame of his own design. Banks gave the bike a sensational debut, riding it to victory in the Shellsport TV meeting from a frozen Hadleigh, Essex circuit in February. It was just like old times, as he and Vic Eastwood, also on a Japanese powered four-stroke hybrid, the Hagon Yamaha, disputed the lead, Eastwood actually passing Banks on the last lap only for Banks to edge him out at the flag.

Time to move on

But sadly, things did not continue in the same vein and what was essentially a good bike was marred by continuous gearbox problems and the venture was shelved. Banks returned to CCM, but only gained a few points in the British Championship, in what was to be his last competitive season. Banks' business interests were occupying more and more of his time and this also hastened his retirement from the sport after 16 years of competition.

Today, after establishing a successful network of car dealerships in East Anglia, John oversees the family-run business, leaving the day-to-day management to his daughter, Melanie and sons, Mark and Justin, who followed in their father's footsteps and were both top motocrossers in their own right.

I leave the last words on John to his closest rival over the years, Vic Eastwood, who once told me. "*I raced against many great riders, too many to list and John Banks was very good and was unlucky not to have been World Champion. He was bloody fast and he got results and that's what mattered. He was unlucky really, but there's only one person who gets to be World Champion and the rest of us simply make up the numbers.*"

It wasn't always about the cut and thrust of racing. Here Banks (left), Chris Horsfield (with one of his sons) and Dave Bickers (right), have some fun in the paddock at Hintlesham Park, August 1967. (DK)

Malcolm Davis

Cheltenham Gold

Photo BH

Malcolm Davis was a rider who just oozed class. A very talented trials rider in his youth, he enjoyed factory support from DMW and Dot at seventeen and, whilst still in his teens, was signed up to ride for Greeves. Spectacular in his early days, he matured into a fast, stylish, rider who, as many observed, never really seemed to be trying too hard. As an AJS development rider he took 250cc British Championship titles in 1968 and 1970 and added a third in 1973, giving Bultaco their first British motocross title in the process. He retired from motocross in the late '70s, but was tragically killed in a road accident whilst competing in the President's Trophy trial in Devon in 1980.

Bill Cole captured Davis racing his 250 Greeves at Tirley during his first season of scrambling in 1961. (Photo supplied by Bob Light)

Malcolm Davis was born in Cheltenham in March 1944, into a family with a keen interest in motorcycling. His father, Les, had taken to motorcycles on returning from the Second World War and played motorcycle football for Cheltenham Town, before going on to become a leading ACU official in the Western Centre.

But when Malcolm was growing up, his father and older brother, Tony, were more interested in equestrianism. The brothers Davis were pretty much inseparable in their youth, but whereas Tony was a gifted rider, good enough to represent his country, Malcolm, the younger by two years, shared none of his equine talents. As Tony told me, *He was like a sack of potatoes in the saddle! A horse once bolted with him in the saddle and Malcolm decided there and then that enough was enough.*

First awakenings

At that time, Les and Irene Davis were the publicans at the *Air Balloon*, on the Gloucester to Cirencester road, and it was on the land behind the pub that the boys got their first taste of motorcycling, as Tony recalls. *We had a field behind the pub and a big wood at the back and one day we tried a friend's bike around the field and that was it really, the bug bit. Malcolm got an old 98cc James and we used to rush around the fields on it. Then we got a second bike and we'd race around together, though I have to admit that even then Malcolm would beat me most of the time.*

Before the Davis boys were old enough to legally compete in trials an uncle on their father's side took them under his wing. *Uncle Reg used to follow Johnny Draper absolutely everywhere and we'd get to see John Avery too. 'Drapes' was local, he lived just across the hills from us, and we had some wonderful times at scrambles and trials in the Western Centre, which was probably the*

Malcolm Davis

most popular at the time as a lot of great riders came from Gloucestershire.

However, Malcolm was also a very talented cricketer, especially with the bat, and before too long he would have to choose between cricket whites or racing leathers. The choice was not a difficult one to make though, as by that time he had, quite literally, been 'schooled' in off-road riding.

Encouragement had come from an unexpected quarter. Jack Nelson, Malcolm's headmaster at the Grammar school at Upfield, near Stroud, was an off-road motorcycling enthusiast who laid on an interesting line in extra-curricular activities that included scrambling on a BSA Bantam! Indeed, it was Nelson who loaned his 197 Greeves for Malcolm's first competitive outing in a scramble at Prestbury near Cheltenham.

A talent in the making

But prior to that, as a 15 year-old Malcolm competed in a few local trials held on private land, though he was itching to go scrambling. However, Les Davis brought a firm hand to bear, as Tony recalls: *Father told him "In your first season you're going to concentrate on trials."* If you can ride trials you can cope with scrambling, so his first full-season was trials all through the winter and he did very well. He came everywhere with me and I'd just got my first factory ride with BSA, so I was doing the nationals and he rode one or two of those, which did him some good.

Malcolm was so smitten with motorcycles that he even set up business, Dave Bickers style, trading in premises behind the pub that had formerly served as stables! With his father overseeing the venture, it wasn't long before they moved things up to the Barton Street site in Gloucester, where Malcolm Davis Motorcycles would trade for many years.

With Tony's trials riding going from strength to strength, he headed off to Scotland in May 1961 for the Scottish Six Day Trial, though he went alone as Malcolm had other plans in mind. *He said "Davis", he always called me Davis, "you've got your Scottish to go and do, I've got my scrambles to do."* So he rode his first scramble while I was away in Scotland and I missed it. But he finished the three races he went in and Johnny Draper told me later, "He's more than natural, he'll take on from me."

Factory support

In his first season of scrambling, Malcolm did enough to impress the Dot management, the Manchester company stepping in with the loan of a trials bike and a scrambler for 1962. He won his first national trial on the Dot, taking the Beggar's Roost on Exmoor and beating James' factory runner Bob Cooper and Sammy Miller on his works Ariel. Davis also had a good day on the 250 scrambler at the Warwickshire GN in May, bagging a brace of 2nd places, to Richard Croft in the 250 race and Ken Sedgley, who would become a close friend, in the 350. He also ran out 3rd in the GN, behind winner Terry Sleeman and Ernie Greer and to top it all, got his photo in the *MCN* alongside the report on the meeting.

The talent was there for all to see and in recognition of his meteoric progress, that same season, aged just 18, he won the coveted Pinhard Prize awarded to the outstanding performance by an under 21 year-old in motorcycle sport.

Before the year was out, Greeves came along with an offer of support. *Malcolm took the offer and father bought him two Greeves of his own. Then Bill Brooker (Greeves' Competition manager), who had been keeping tabs on Malcolm, took his bikes in and went to town on them. I remember he had a good day next time out winning everything and Cobby* (Derry Preston Cobb) *said immediately "Give him some bikes!" and Malcolm had full factory support from then on.*

Greeves works ride

This came about in 1963, when the Essex factory contracted him to ride in both trials and scrambles. His first outing on a factory bike came in the St. David's trial in January and the same season he took the Beggar's Roost and Kickham nationals, before scooping the 250 Cup in the Scottish. He was equally at home on the scrambles bike though and was soon picking up points in the 250 ACU Star, the first coming at the Wessex Scramble in March, where he took an impressive 3rd behind teammate Bryan Goss and Chris Horsfield on the factory James.

That summer he really began to blossom as a rider, taking a big win in the 250 race at the Rob Walker Trophy Scramble at Frome, beating Ernie Greer and Joe Johnson, and a week later was on fine form at the prestigious Experts GN meeting which was being held for the first time at Larkstone, Warwickshire. In the 250 Experts, run over two legs, he finished 2nd overall behind Dave Bickers, who at the time was on the Husqvarna, but ahead of Pat Lamper (Dot), Fred Mayes (Cotton) and Greeves teammate Alan Clough.

Heading for an interesting landing, Davis is pictured racing the factory Greeves at the BBC Grandstand meeting at Beeston, Cheshire in November 1963. (MC)

At the end of August, Davis enjoyed a good day's racing just eight miles down the road at Tirley. Although he didn't feature amongst the winners, he got some good results in very good company, not least of all 2nd to Goss in the up to 250 race and 3rd behind works Matchless riders Vic Eastwood and Horsfield in the Tirley Championship. Malcolm was on his way!

1964 was an excellent season for the young Greeves rider, who was now armed with one of the factory Challengers and June was an exceptional month. At Longleat, Wiltshire, he took the 250 race ahead of Greer and Jerry Scott, though he had to give second best to Goss in the up to 1000 race. Two weeks later Malcolm made the trip to the Isle of Man, though not for the TT races! The GN Scramble was traditionally held during TT week and this one was laid out on a disused golf course at Douglas Head. Manxman Geoff Cannell, who reported on the meeting, noted that the Greeves teamsters '*completely monopolised the GN event*' with Malcolm finishing 2nd to his senior teammate in both the 250 and the GN events.

A star is born

For Greeves, the 250 ACU Star was always a target and Malcolm faired well in the season long series. He opened his account with a fine 3rd at the Cotswold Scramble, later that same month, behind teammates Bickers and Clough, though the best was still to come. At the end of June the 250 British GP was held at a new venue, Cadwell Park in Lincolnshire. Malcolm went there with his confidence buoyed by recent results, knowing that he could run with the best 250 riders in the country. In the event, he turned in a sensational performance, chasing two-time World Champion Torsten Hallman through the field in the first race and almost catching Goss for 4th place. In the second race, he kept his head and split teammates Clough and Goss, a second 5th place finish gaining him a podium place in his first GP in the illustrious company of winner Joel Robert and Bickers. Malcolm had arrived!

Good run continues

Davis held his form and in August finished 3rd to Bickers and Clough in the Lightweight race at Shrubland Park which counted towards the ACU Star. A week later he had a field day on home soil at the Gloucester GN at Tirley, taking the four major finals and becoming the first rider ever to do so. In the main event, the Tirley Championship, he used his 252cc Greeves to inflict defeat on Mike Peach, on his 500 Cito, the Sussex man being unfortunate enough to pick up a puncture whilst leading.

Despite such good form, Malcolm was the surprise selection for the Trophée des Nations team, though he was a little out of his depth in the treacherous sand of Markelo, Holland. However, in the true spirit of the event, he gamely battled on to finish both races in 15th and 21st to help secure Britain third place behind Sweden and Czechoslovakia.

In the final round of the ACU Star contest at Farleigh Castle in October, Malcolm finished a brilliant 2nd to Bickers though he was shaded for 3rd place in the final standings by Ernie Greer who, by finishing 4th in the race, beat him by a single point.

On the limit! Davis is pictured 'challenging' the Greeves at the Wilts Border Scramble in 1964. (CB)

In glorious weather, Davis is the star of the Longleat Motocross in June 1965. (CB)

I always remembered Malcolm as a silky smooth rider, who at his best appeared to float across the track. But looking back at photos of him racing in his youth (see photos on previous pages) he appeared to be quite wild. Tony confirmed this. *Yes he was*, before quickly adding, *but not as wild as Wadie (Bryan Wade)! Malcolm had a style all of his own. Today I can't tell one rider from another, but in those days you could tell them apart by their style. Bickers, the Rickmans they all had a style of their own.*

1965 Trial period

After such a successful year scrambling, Malcolm had a different focus for 1965. That year he devoted more time to trials riding, as he took a serious crack at the ACU Trials Star, eventually ending the season as runner-up to the great Sammy Miller. On the motocross front, he raced in most of the winter TV scrambles and also took in several meetings racing on the continent, often in the company of his good friend Ken Sedgley, a fellow trials and scrambles rider.

The year started brightly with a double victory in the 250 and Invitation races at the Southern TV meeting at Hankom Bottom in February. Then in March he switched channels to entertain BBC viewers at the final round of the Grandstand Trophy series at Cross-in-Hand, Sussex. Davis was in sparkling form as *MCN*'s Chris Carter noted. '*With Dave Bickers and John Griffiths in Spain, the baby of the Greeves team, Malcolm Davis, made sure that the Greeves gaffers knew that there was a capable understudy at hand with a well-taken 'Spring Double''.* Carter was referring to Davis' wins in the invitation races, over Roger Snoad, on another Greeves, and Dave Nicoll (Matchless) in the first and Horsfield (Matchless) and Johnny Giles (Triumph) in the second. However, in the earlier 250 race he surprised many of the armchair viewers with his speed, as he caught and

Davis was in great form at the 1966 Hants Grand National, where he is pictured leaping the 250 Bultaco Métisse. (CB)

passed none other than World Champion, Jeff Smith, in a last lap dash for the line.

Keeping your employer happy

The 'Gaffers' certainly did take note of his performance, as in recognition of Malcolm's sterling efforts Derry Preston Cobb sent him a letter dated 5th April 1965, in which he wrote: *I've been meaning to write you for the past few days to say how very pleased I am that you are again at the top of your form, as you certainly slayed the opposition at last week's TV scramble.*

In May, he was dicing with ex-teammate Goss, now on a Husqvarna, and the Rickmans at Farleigh Castle in the Maybug Scramble, though his best result was only 3rd in the 250 race won by Goss from Don Rickman on the Bultaco Métisse. However, a month later he was the star of the Frome club's Longleat Motocross, winning the two leg 250 event, beating Fred Mayes (Greeves) and Arthur Browning (Bultaco Métisse) and adding 3rd, behind Don Rickman (Métisse) and Brian Curtis (Matchless Métisse), in the Experts Unlimited race.

As the year wound down, Malcolm, along with most of his contemporaries, was back on TV, taking a couple of 5th place finishes in the BBC scrambles at Builth Wells and Lyng, Norfolk, as another Grandstand Trophy series got underway.

Getting the thumbs up from Bultaco

1966

When the 1966 season dawned, Malcolm had made the switch to a Bultaco Métisse, having had the opportunity to get a good look at the bike at close quarter whilst dicing with Don Rickman all across the south and west of England in 1965.

He was soon picking up points in the 250 Grandstand Trophy races at Nantwich and Leighton, having briefly led the round in Somerset. He was out of luck at the opening 250 ACU Star race at the Hants GN in April, when having led for four laps the Bultaco whiskered

During his brief return to Greeves, Davis is pictured landing the Challenger at the top of the big hill at Hankom Bottom, during the BBC Grandstand meeting in March 1967. (BH)

a plug allowing CZ's Bickers through for the win. Incidentally, Bickers' form was so good at Ringwood that Malcolm was the only rider to head him all day.

At the Maybug Scramble at Farleigh Castle, Davis again took the challenge to the seemingly invincible Bickers-CZ combination. In the 250 Invitation he got the Bultaco out front, but within half a lap Bickers had powered through on an uphill stretch and Davis, who lost top gear on the four-speed gearbox, had to settle for 2nd. Then in a captivating 250 Maybug race, Davis took the lead again, this time holding it until three-quarters distance when Bickers demoted him and went on to win by a machine's length. Though having to settle for second best, running the twice European Champion so close must have done wonders for Davis' self-esteem.

A very eventful third round of the ACU Star took place at the Cotswold Scramble at Nympsfield, held in atrocious conditions following a deluge the previous day. Davis soon demoted early leaders Clough and Goss, but with the rain teeming down it was Malcolm's turn to come to grief on the tricky water splash, losing places to Goss, Mayes and Browning, before the latter was obstructed by a back marker on the last lap allowing Davis to 'slip' by for 3rd place at the flag.

On form, home and away

That season Malcolm took in a few 250 GPs and following a disappointing trip to the Belgian round, where he got the Bultaco out front in both legs but failed to finish either, he travelled to Luxembourg in June and this time the trip reaped rewards. With Torsten Hallman a non-starter and Robert and World Champion Victor Arbekov non-finishers, the lesser lights of the 250 GP circus had a chance to shine. Davis scored 6th overall and a single championship point, his first for two years, from 9th and 4th place finishes.

A nice shot for Bultaco lovers, Davis is pictured racing the 250 in the British GP at Wakes Colne in July 1967. (BH)

Back on home soil, he also found form, registering his best result in the ACU Star in the fourth round at Wakes Colne in July. From the start it looked like there would be a three-way tussle for the race, as Malcolm latched on to pacesetters Bickers and Goss, but after five laps he had dropped back. But two laps later Goss went out with a broken rear shock and Malcolm rode home to 2nd and six points towards the championship, where he would eventually finish 5th after missing the final round at Builth Wells in October.

Malcolm had the ability of being able to raise his game when he came up against the world's best, as he proved again at the Thirsk International at Boltby in September. Though a bit thin on overseas riders, the organisers had managed to attract the reigning 250 World Champion, Torsten Hallman, who clearly started the event as the favourite. However, the first 250 race turned into a domestic affair, as Davis built a strong lead before Bickers started to reel him in. Lap after lap Bickers reduced the deficit, finally usurping the Bultaco man on the final corner to win by less than a second, with Hallman finishing strongly to take 3rd. Next time out Bickers was away at the front shadowed by Hallman, whilst Malcolm had to fight off a Greeves posse of Browning, Clough and Mayes, to bag the runner-up spot and finish ahead of the World Champion.

Back to Greeves ...

In 1967 Malcolm returned to the fold at Greeves and continued to mix scrambling and trials riding, naturally excelling in both domains. At the Grandstand Trophy event at Cuerden Park in January, he slugged it out with Clough, for 2nd place in the 250 race behind Bickers, the situation only being resolved in Clough's favour in the last few yards. Then the following day, he was out on the trials bike, taking a narrow victory over brother Tony, on a factory Cotton, in the Len Drake Trophy trail in Worcestershire.

When the 250 ACU Star got underway at Chard in early March, Davis got a poor start and was then eliminated when his chain broke. Later that month at Hawkstone Park, he took 4th place in the 250 race behind Clough, now on a Husqvarna, and teammates Wade and Browning. This was then followed up with 2nd to fellow Greeves man, Horsfield, in a very muddy 250 race in the Cheshire Motocross at Nantwich. However, within a few days Malcolm and Greeves had parted company.

At the end of April, without a factory bike to ride, Malcolm took a 250 Cotton straight off his showroom floor onto the track at Dodington Park, where he finished 2nd to Roger Snoad on his factory Montesa in the 250 Wessex Lightweight Race, but ahead of ex-teammate Allan on his Greeves.

... and then Bultaco

However, it wasn't long before Malcolm was back on a Bultaco and this time it was a full-factory bike. However he made a rather ignominious debut on the Spanish bike in the British Championship at Nympsfield in June, where after taking the start, he fell heavily on the second lap, which ensured he would play no further part in the meeting. But at Tirley in late August, he won the 250 race before adding a 6th place finish, in good company, in the Tirley Championship. Eastwood, on his factory BSA took the win from Bickers, the BSAs of John Banks and Smith, with Davis on the 250 chasing Keith Hickman on his Cheney Victor all the way to the flag.

The following day Malcolm travelled east for the fourth round of the 250 British Championship at Hintlesham Park near Ipswich, on August Bank Holiday Monday. After a barren spell in the 250 Championship, he was on top form in Suffolk and, with the Bultaco really flying, he took a comfortable 2nd to Bickers in the championship race before inflicting a rare home defeat on Bickers in the Lightweight race.

Brimming with confidence, he raced to another 2nd, this time to Goss, in the final race of the championship at Cadwell Park in October. Once again he got the better of Bickers, though it was suspected that somebody had tampered with his CZ the previous night, the East Anglian's bike apparently being down on power in the race.

Later that month at the magnificently titled Kaj Bornebusch Trophy Scramble on the Oxenbourne circuit on the South Downs, Malcolm wheeled out a 360 Bultaco for the first time, racing it to victory in the 500 race leading home Vic Allan on his 360 Greeves and Dennis Smith on a 360 Husqvarna.

The AJS years: Part 1

With his form improving on the 250 and a big bike added to his stable, Malcolm surprised a lot of people in the sport when he signed to AJS for the 1968 season. The Villiers-engined AJS had evolved from the Norton-Villiers project (see pp96-97 & 220-221) though it still remained largely unproven. In search of a leading rider, AJS had approached Bryan Goss in October, with the Dorset man taking the 250 to a winning debut at Horton Common mid-month. However, things didn't work out for Goss and within a few weeks he was back on his trusty Husqvarna. Davis was signed in his place and the rest, as they say, is history.

TV debut

1968

Malcolm's first ride on an AJS came in the opening round of the 1967/68 Grandstand Trophy series at Canada Heights, Kent in November, where he scored 6th place in the 250 race, the winner being former AJS man Mayes, who was now racing CZs. In the non-televised 250 race, he was actually closing down leader Mayes when the plug lead came off.

The BBC series were run over just five rounds that season and after being left on the line with an oiled plug at the second round at Naish Hill, Wiltshire in February 1968, Davis was struggling to make up ground. Round three was at Kirkcaldy, where in treacherous conditions seasoned campaigner Jeff Smith stayed on board, whilst others fell all around, to win from Scotsman Jimmy Aird with Davis coming through for 3rd place. Malcolm also had two very good outings on the 360 in the Unlimited races, splitting the factory BSAs of Eastwood and Smith in the first and beating Arthur Lampkin and fellow AJS man, Dick Clayton to take the second.

Following the cancellation of the 250 race at Bury St. Edmunds, the final round at Caerleon featured a double-bill of 250 races. Freddie Mayes led the first race from Davis in the opening laps. But then Malcolm slipped through into the lead and Smith started to close down Mayes and Roberton, now racing a Husqvarna. Mayes succumbed to the pressure and slid off and Smith got the better of the Welshman to guarantee his third BBC Grandstand Trophy, whilst Davis took the

A determined Malcolm Davis flies the 250 Bultaco at Hintlesham Park, Suffolk in August 1967, where he won the Lightweight race. (DK)

Out front! On the AJS at the Cambridge Grand National at Elsworth in April 1968 where he won both 250 races. (RD)

Davis won his first 250 British Championship in 1968. Here he is pictured battling with Don Rickman on the factory Bultaco in round two at Glastonbury in April. (RD)

AJS to its first televised victory. With the trophy won, Smith blitzed the last race leading from start to finish and leaving the young guns to fight for the minor places. Greeves' Arthur Browning toppled Roberton, whilst Davis finished 4th and was pipped by the hapless Mayes, for runner-up spot.

Mixed fortunes

AJS had ambitious plans for their riders, sending Malcolm out to contest not only the 250 British Championship, but also the 250 GPs. On the home front, he made a winning start in round one at the Cumberland GN in April, easily beating fellow AJS man Clayton and Roberton. *MCN* reporter Gavin Trippe was clearly impressed: *The only conclusive ride of the day came from Malcolm Davis on the AJS. With a surprising hard core of spectators and sheep watching in spring-like weather, the invader from way down south belted his AJS home in front of the rest in the first race, even having time off for a laugh and a joke with friends on the way round.*

Tony Davis remembers Malcolm soon being at home on the AJS. *He just took to it, though it was certainly not the best bike of the day. He just knew how to ride it, though it did let him down now and then.* Indeed it did, as for example in the second race at the Cumberland GN. Davis and Clayton soon established themselves as the leaders and looked to be heading for an AJS one-two, when after 20 minutes first Malcolm's bike stopped with an electrical failure and then Clayton's AJS seized up.

Round two came closer to home, at Glastonbury later that month, but Davis was forced out of the first race with mechanical problems and had to fight hard to take 2nd place in race two behind man of the meeting, Don Rickman, who won both races and now led the title chase.

Davis was the sensation of the 250 British GP at Dodington Park in August 1968, though sadly the same could not be said of the AJS! (RD)

Ups and downs in the GPs

A week later Malcolm set off for his second GP of the season in Belgium, having finished both races in the opener in Spain, but failing to score any points. He had an inspired day in Belgium, racing to 5th and 7th place finishes, to take 4th overall in the GP, won by Sweden's Olle Petterson, and his first points since Luxembourg in 1966.

It was 'crazy season' in the 250 GPs back in May 1968, as three GPs in France, West Germany and Luxembourg were run off within a week! There was no luck for Malcolm in France and things got worse on the hazardous West German circuit, where he crashed heavily and was rendered unconscious. But he recovered in time for the Luxembourg round and clearly had his wits about him, as he once again finished 4th overall, behind the big three, Hallman, Robert and Bickers.

The 250 British Championship reconvened at Carlton Bank, Yorkshire, in July, where Malcolm toiled for his points in the absence of Rickman, taking 4th place in the first race, after the engine had lost power mid-race, though he improved to 3rd place in the second and some invaluable points, despite an altercation with a tree!

In his time as a top trials and motocross rider Malcolm had many famous victories, but ironically the event he is probably best remembered for was one where he failed to finish a race, the 1968 250 British GP. But let's regress a little. In the first week of August Malcolm made the long trip north for the Swedish GP. In the deep sand of Hedemora, Davis and Wade put on a fantastic show in the first leg gating well and chasing Joel Robert in the opening laps. Robert was in a class of his own, but the young Brits stuck to their guns and there was nothing the great Torsten Hallman could do to close the gap on them. Then, between races, the organisers decided to water the track, much to the detriment of Davis and Wade, who both fell on the greasy surface denying them a potential GP victory, as Robert had exited early in race two with an engine blow-up.

Over the winter of 1968/69 Davis battled Alan Clough for the 250 BBC Grandstand Trophy. Here they dispute air space over Clifton, Derbyshire in December 1968. (BH)

So close and yet ...

A week later, his confidence boosted by running with Robert and Hallman, Malcolm set off for his favourite circuit, Dodington Park, Old Sodbury, for the 250 GP. Racing in his native Gloucestershire, on a British-built bike, he thrilled the crowd and showed the world's elite riders what he was really capable of on his day. The circuit, set in the rolling countryside of South Gloucestershire, provided the perfect setting for Malcolm to showcase his spectacular riding skills.

In race one, he swooped past both Hallman and Robert on the technical downhill sections of the course to take the lead, only to go out three laps later when the plug cap disintegrated. Race two brought further disappointment for the home fans, when after getting himself into another race winning position and building an eight second cushion over Robert, the local man experienced more electrical gremlins and the AJS coasted to a halt mid-race. As Tony Davis told me, *They could hear the groans back in Gloucester!*

A change of fortune

Huge disappointment that the GP had been, Davis was back on his bike a week later, racing to a resounding double victory at Cureden Park near Preston, in the penultimate round of the 250 British Championship. With a new exhaust system fitted to the AJS there was no holding Davis in the first race, as he lapped everybody down to 5th man Allan. In the second race Browning led for two laps before Malcolm raced past on a tricky downhill section to take control. The double win moved Davis into the championship lead for the first time, with one round to go.

The final round was at Hatherton Hall, Nantwich, in October where Malcolm rode intelligently to outpoint his main rivals Don Rickman and Andy Roberton. On the day, the reigning Champion, Clough, also did him a favour by winning both races, as although Rickman and Roberton both got a 2nd place apiece, Davis' 3rd place in race one was good enough to make him British Champion and to bring

AJS their first national title since Geoff Ward had taken his third 500 ACU Star in 1954.

1969

TV star

The season ended brightly for Davis and AJS, as Malcolm rode to a fine win in the opening round of the 250 Grandstand Trophy at Dodington ahead of a very rapid Fred Mayes–CZ combination and Eastwood on the Husky. Eastwood top scored in the second round at Lyng, where Davis finished 3rd behind a second Husky ridden by Clough. However, Eastwood's challenge ended prematurely when he broke his leg in a fall at Hawkstone Park in December. Things looked more promising for Davis though and as the 1969 season dawned, he bounced back in the penultimate round at Caerleon in late February, winning the 250 race to set up a winner takes all scenario with Clough, as they went to the final round in Scotland level on points.

But before that, Malcolm had to turn his attention to the defence of his 250 crown, as the British Championship kicked off at Tilton in March. This he did in style, passing early leaders Aird and Goss, to race to victory in race one from the Greeves of Browning, Allan and Wade. In the second race he took a tumble soon after the start, but showing great character, he battled back from 20th to eventually finish 3rd behind race winner Goss, and Allan.

Star quality lacking in Scotland!

The following week saw the final round of the Grandstand Trophy at Kirkcaldy, but it proved to be a long drive in vain for Davis, as he lasted just three laps before the AJS seized up allowing championship rival Clough to race on to finish 3rd and claim his first TV trophy. Curiously, teammate Roberton's progress was also checked; the AJS pulling up with the same problem, the official verdict being that the bikes had been run on 2-star rather than 4-star petrol! However, later that month Malcolm suffered the same fate in both legs of the second British Championship round at Nantwich. Now, what was it Tony Davis was saying about the reliability of the AJS?

Trouble brewing

That season Malcolm went through a particularly torrid time in the GPs. At the Spanish GP in April, he led both legs until water penetrated the engine of his AJS causing it to splutter to a stop on two occasions and in Switzerland, a broken spark plug in race one and a broken chain in race two meant he had failed to finish a single GP race all month. A frustrated Davis reacted angrily, telling reporters: *I've had plugs break on the bikes about four times and when it's happened once, it shouldn't happen again. The whole thing is really annoying as the bikes are fast enough and handle beautifully.*

In early May AJS announced that they had sacked Davis for 'not trying hard enough', though this was clearly not the case. Given the reliability of the AJS, this would seem to be a very harsh, not to mention rash, decision, as at the time of his dismissal he was well placed in the 250 British Championship, lying 3rd with three rounds still to come.

The dismissal from AJS arguably marked the low point in a very successful career. But within days things were looking up again, as Malcolm signed to race CZs in a deal brokered by Dave Bickers. He was out on the Czech bikes at the Maybug Scramble at Farleigh Castle and had victory in sight in the 250 Maybug, when he was baulked by a back marker allowing his new 'boss' to slip through for the win. However, he gained his first win on the CZ in the second 250 race, when he beat Browning and Bickers.

After an exciting, but ultimately frustrating time at the Dutch GP in June, when his throttle cable broke whilst he was disputing the lead with Robert and Petterson, he took an encouraging 7th overall in the French GP later that month, which augured well for British hopes, with another home GP at Dodington Park on the horizon.

Davis fights to defend his title

Unfortunately there seemed to be a little dark cloud that tracked Davis in the GPs at Dodington. In race one he was really flying. He caught and passed Goss and was reeling in race leader Sylvain Geboers when his front tyre blew. Then in race two he battled his way through to second place again, but no sooner had he got there than he had to pull out as the bearing in the front hub disintegrated.

Further proof that he was really getting to grips with the CZ came at round three of the 250 British Championship at the Cotswold Scramble in July. He led both races, finishing a close 2nd to Goss in the first and going out of the second after being sidelined with carburettor trouble. Had he held on to win the second race he would have headed the standings with one

Davis passes fellow CZ man Harry Driessen, at the 1969 250 British GP at Dodington Park. (BH)

round to come, but as it was he was lying 4th, though just four points adrift of leader Wade.

Davis valiantly defended his crown in the final round at Tirley in late August, flying out of the gate and leading from start to finish with Goss 100 yards in arrears at the flag and Wade back in 3rd place. This left everything to play for in the final race and Malcolm soon passed ex-teammate Roberton for the lead. However, in the summer heat he was suffering with blistered hands and when Wade came through on a late charge he had no answer and Gloucestershire's resident Yorkshireman was the new Champion.

1970 The AJS years: Part 2

By late November, Davis had patched things up with AJS, re-signing to the Andover based company and making his racing return in the TV meeting at Naish Hill, where he finished a close 2nd to Arthur Browning in the 250 race.

Many people in the motocross world see the 1970 season as Malcolm's finest. There had been a lot of development done over the '69 season and the bikes were far more reliable than they had been back in '68 and in addition to contesting the 250 British Championship, Malcolm once again was given the opportunity to contest most of the 250 GPs. At 26 years old, he was also maturing into a smooth, consistent performer as he would demonstrate to British motocross fans nationwide during the early '70s.

Ambitious programme

At the end of March 1970, he was in fine form at Dodington Park, easily winning the final round of the 250 Grandstand Trophy from teammate Andy Roberton and after a consistent series he took the runner-up spot behind Bryan Goss.

A few weeks later, the 250 British Championship got underway at Nantwich. Despite being the pace-setter he came away from Hatherton Hall with just six points after enduring a troublesome front fork, which seized up in both races whilst he was leading. He did well just to salvage 2nd place to a rejuvenated Jeff Smith in race two.

Malcolm Davis

The following week Malcolm hit the GP trail, heading off to Spain, where history was about to be made, as Joel Robert scored the first ever GP win on a Japanese bike for Suzuki. But for British motocross fans the highlight was the performance of two of our best young riders, as Davis rode to a magnificent 5th overall, but was pipped for 4th by Bryan Wade, after falling in the opening laps of race two.

Untapped potential

The Spanish GP serves to demonstrate the potential that both British riders and manufacturers had during this period of the sport. But sadly, despite some flashes of brilliance from both Davis and Wade this was also the highlight of the GP season, as far too frequently the bikes were found wanting and within eight months both riders had made the permanent switch to foreign machines. Malcolm could only add points in France, from 9th overall, and 6th overall in Italy mid-season to finish the season on a disappointing tally of just 13 points.

After a two-month break, the British Championship resumed at Tilton in June, where Davis turned in what *MCN* reporter Mike Nicks referred to, as a *'powerful'* and *'immaculate'* performance. He stamped his authority on race one, comfortably winning from teammate Roberton, and overcame a stubborn challenge from Vic Allan in the second, eventually going on to lap everybody down to 6th place.

The Dodington jinx continues

A week later, Malcolm was making his annual pilgrimage to Dodington Park, for the British GP, hoping to improve on the disastrous luck of the previous two years that had seen him fail to finish a single race. Things started promisingly, as Malcolm was right on the pace in race one and was challenging Olle Petterson and Miroslav Halm for 4th place. But then disaster struck, as he caught his foot under the footrest, dislocating his ankle and tearing ligaments. Somehow he managed to ride on, despite the pain, to finish 10th in race one, but

Getting down to business. Davis dominated the 250 British Championship in 1970. Here he demonstrates the style that made him Champion at the final round at Beenham Park in October. (BH)

was then whisked away to hospital and sadly, his dream of winning his home GP in front of his fans was over for another year.

Incredibly, just two weeks later he made a return to racing, hastened no doubt by the proximity of the third round of the British Championship at Carlton Bank, Yorkshire. Shrugging off the injury, he majestically added two more race wins to stretch his championship lead to 13 points over teammate Roberton and Smith, with Wade being, the only man to bother Davis in either of the two races.

Dominant Davis regains title

At the at the end of July the venue for round four was Cuerden Park, where Davis marched on unchecked to record his 5th and 6th consecutive race wins in the championship and guarantee his second title with one round still to spare. No one had dominated a 250 season like this since Bickers in his heyday, though once again poor Bryan Wade suffered terribly as his Greeves seized up in both races.

Malcolm may have struggled to put points on the board in the World Championship, but in August he turned in another top class performance, racing to 2nd overall behind Husqvarna sensation Heikki Mikkola, the Finn who would go on to be a four-time World Champion, at the big international meeting at Laguiepie in the south of France. In doing so, he relegated Suzuki's Joel Robert to 3rd overall, the World Champion having picked up a puncture in the second of the three legs.

The final round of the 250 British Championship was played out at Beenham Park, Berkshire in mid-October, with the minor places still up for grabs. In a bizarre first race incident, Davis, who had led from the opening laps, slowed dramatically and then lay down his AJS in the final corner, reputedly to help teammate Roberton secure second place in the championship. A bemused Vic Allan took the win, whilst Davis jumped back on his bike to finish 3rd. Browning briefly led the second race before picking up an injury and allowing Davis through. But the champ was also out of luck on this occasion, as he suffered a broken rear shock, which left Vic Eastwood, who was making a comeback following a long

Davis on his way to victory with partner Bryan Wade, in the 100-Mile Scramble at Guildford in October 1970. (BH)

convalescence after breaking a leg, to win the race, his first British Championship success in two years.

To round off a spectacular season, Davis got together with his Gloucestershire neighbour Wade, who was now racing for Husqvarna, to tackle the 100-mile Scramble at Pirbright, Surrey in late October. This they did with great panache and were well rewarded for their efforts, as they headed home down the M4 £250 to the good.

Bultaco reunion

In 1971 after parting company with AJS, Malcolm signed to race for Bultaco again. In a deal that provided him with highly competitive trials and motocross bikes, one of his first commitments to the Spanish factory was to race the Bultaco Pursangs in a series of demonstration events in Africa that winter.

Ken Sedgley, a regular travelling companion to continental meetings, went with him on that trail-blazing adventure. "I remember riding in the Vic Brittain trial in early January and the weather was horrific, cold, wet and really miserable. We were about half way round and Malcolm said, "I'm not that bothered 'cause I'm off to Zambia on Tuesday." He went on to explain that he'd been asked to go out there to give a few demonstration rides. Well, a few sections later he said, "Why don't you come with me?", and I said, "You must be joking!" But the more I thought about it, the more it sounded like a good idea." After convincing his wife that it was a good opportunity, it was off to the doctor on Monday for Ken, to get all his vaccinations.

Whilst riding in Zambia, Malcolm and Ken were invited to take part in some further demonstration meetings in the former Rhodesia and in Durban, South Africa. So what had originally been planned as a couple of weeks away from the dire English winter, turned out to be five weeks travelling across the African continent. However, for Sedgley it was an experience to be relished. "It was a good trip all round, as we were provided with Bultacos to race and we were treated like royalty. After that first trip we got invited back four or five times, so we must have been doing something right! Malcolm was a great travelling companion, he was very easy going and a really nice bloke to be with."

Health issues

The break in the sun may have brought a welcome respite from the British winter, but on his return to the UK Malcolm was struggling against a mystery illness he appeared to have contracted on the trip.

At the opening round of the 250 British Championship at Nantwich in early April, Malcolm turned out despite running a temperature of 103°F. Peter Howdle in his report on the meeting for the *MCN* noted that, *'Davis hustled Wade for a couple of laps before nearly choking from a serious cough. His brother quickly whisked him home to bed.'*

Malcolm's efforts were also thwarted in round two, a week later at Brownrigg Fell near Penrith. Talking to Howdle he remarked, "I know my Bultaco is better than the AJS I rode last year, but this chest trouble has come at an awkward time." It certainly had and despite racing into the lead in race one, Malcolm had to stop to get assistance from a marshall before ignition trouble eliminated him. Things improved slightly in race two, as he chased Wade hard, but was forced to ease the pace again as another coughing fit came on. So, with just two rounds down, Wade had racked up four straight wins and 32 points, whilst Davis in contrast had scored just six and was languishing in joint fifth place with Alan Clough.

Malcolm makes his mark

However, following Wade's fifth consecutive win in his native Yorkshire at Carlton Bank in July, Davis, who had finished 2nd to Wade in the opening race, finally 'stopped the rot', winning the second, though only after Wade had taken one of his customary falls soon after passing Davis for the lead.

A fortnight later Malcolm showed his class as he took a double win in round four at Leighton Frome, though he could do nothing to stop Wade's march to the title; the Husqvarna man twice finishing as runner-up and amassing sufficient points to be crowned Champion for a second time. However, Wade, paid his close rival a compliment by confessing, "He was going so well today that I decided not to risk making a mistake."

Davis secured second place in the championship with a brace of runner-up spots in the final round at Stepaside, Pembrokeshire, where he chased Roberton home in race one. He then seemed to have the second race in the bag until his front brake cable broke allowing Wade through for his sixth win of the series, though he managed to hold off a charging Roberton to secure 2nd.

In a largely disappointing season by his standards, Malcolm found some form racing the big Bultaco in the 500 British Championship. In round four at Cuerden Park, in mid-August, Malcolm took the second championship race on the 360cc Bultaco, hitting the front on lap four and going unchallenged to the flag ahead of new Champion, John Banks, and Wade. Then in the final round at Tirley at the end of the month, he won the first race from Husqvarna's Wade and Roberton and finished 3rd behind Wade and Banks next time out to move up to finish 4th overall in the championship.

1972 From bad to worse

In 1972 Malcolm was plagued by further health problems that severely hampered his season, starting at the opening round of the 250 British Championship at Nantwich in March, where he was sidelined by blurred vision in the second race after finishing 4th in race one behind Roberton, Clayton and new teammate Browning.

Luck deserted him at the second round of the championship at the Cambridge GN, when after battling back from an early fall in race one he lost his chain on the final lap whilst putting race leader Wade under pressure. Things got worse in race two, when a collision with a fallen tail-ender whilst leading the race resulted in damaged forks and he was relegated to 6th place.

He slipped further out of contention at Hadleigh, Essex, in late-May, when he could only manage 4th place in race one after complaining of having difficulty in breathing.

Things picked up a little at the Cotswold Scramble at Stroud in early July, where he scored points in the 500 British Championship races with 5th and 4th place finishes, as Wade took a huge step towards the title, and added a win in the 250 race over Rob Taylor and AJS youngster Roger Harvey.

Later that month, he was close to his best for round four of the 250 Championship at the Rob Walker Trophy Scramble in late July. He finished the day as top-scorer from a 2nd place to Wade in race one, and a win next time out ahead of Maico's Rob Taylor and Wade. The points lifted him to 4th place in the title hunt, behind Roberton, Wade and Allan with one round still to come.

The Dodington GP jinx returned again in mid-August. After running in the top five in race one, he

Leaping the factory Bultaco in the final round of the 250 British Championship at Stepaside, Pembrokeshire in August 1971, where he twice finished runner-up. (RD)

Davis chases 500 British Champion John Banks, at the final round of the championship at Tirley in August 1971, where he was on top form, winning the first race and finishing 3rd in race two. (RD)

battled against a steering problem to eventually finish 7th. But he was robbed of an overall position, when his front wheel broke up in the second leg. Malcolm pitted, thinking he had a faulty spark plug, but within another lap he was thrown off the bike, as the front wheel caught on the forks. So, his unbelievable run of bad luck at this meeting continued.

In the final round of the 250 Championship at Beenham Park in October, he was sidelined by the recurring breathing problem, which at the time was incorrectly attributed to bronchitis, forcing him to retire from race one whilst leading.

1973

The comeback begins

Soon after this, Malcolm consulted a Harley Street specialist and in late October underwent corrective surgery, having a length of plastic tube inserted to replace a severely restricted airway to the lungs. Incredibly, just a few weeks later he won the 100-Mile Scramble at Pirbright, on this occasion paired with Bultaco teammate Allan, narrowly defeating the pairing of John Banks (CZ) and Ivan Miller (Husqvarna).

Following a season which was blighted by illness, Malcolm came back fit and strong in 1973. At round one of the 250 Championship, at Brownrigg Fell, Cumberland in April, he opened his campaign with intent, easily taking the first race on the boggy circuit from Andy Roberton. Peter Howdle, who was present, reported in the MCN that *Davis romped ahead, skipping through the black pudding with miraculous success.* He then finished third behind fellow title hopefuls Wade and Roberton in the second race after getting bogged down himself, to finish the day as joint championship leader with Roberton.

Historic Maybug

Round two came at Farleigh Castle, with what was to be the last 'Maybug Scramble' to be held at the famous Wiltshire circuit and Malcolm reserved his place in Farleigh Castle folklore, with a memorable double win. He dominated the first race from start to finish followed by Roberton and Allan, though you could have thrown the proverbial handkerchief over the three leaders early on, before Davis opened up a race winning seven second gap. In an exciting second race, Roberton led Allan and Wade, till the Nailsworth man slid off. Davis then passed Allan and Roberton in quick succession, though the race was far from over, as Davis later explained to Peter Howdle. *I twisted my foot in a rut. I let Andy through to shake my leg about. He thought I'd broken it until I blew him off again.* The startled Roberton had no answer to Davis, who rode on to record his second win of the day six seconds clear of his rival.

Though he never mounted a challenge for the 500 title, Malcolm enjoyed a profitable outing on the 400 Bultaco at the Favre-Leuba Motocross in Devon in mid-May, coming 2nd in both the British Championship races to claim the trophy provided by the Swiss watch company that sponsored the event. In the second race he had an intense battle with series leader, John Banks, until he caught a post and lost second gear on the Bultaco.

Sentimental win at Dodington

In mid-June the Harold Taylor International Motocross was staged at Dodington Park. Taylor, also known as the 'Colonel', was a leading ACU official and team manager for the Motocross and Trophée des Nations events from the inception of the MDN in 1947 through to 1967. He had died in September 1971 when attending the TDN in Holice, Czechoslovakia, having shared a lift out there with Malcolm and Bryan Wade. Davis considered Taylor a friend and as such, he was determined to win this event that was staged in memory of one of the sport's greatest characters. In the event, he did just that, not only taking the overall result, but also emphatically winning all three legs on the big Bultaco, to beat Wade and Eastwood.

A week later, Davis was riding in the third round of the 250 Championship at Tilton. In the first race he showed how he could fight for his points when it was required, coming through from sixth on the first lap to pass Allan for victory. Peter Howdle writing in the MCN waxed lyrical on the two-time Champion. *'His determination shining as brightly as the sun, Davis gained the lead at half distance'.* In race two, Roberton got the jump on his rival, taking off like a scalded cat. However, Davis stayed calm and collected and closed to within two seconds of the Welshman, but with the rear shocks over heating he throttled back to be sure of finishing. At this stage of the season it was a clear two-horse race between Davis and Roberton, the man from Gloucester, heading his Stroud neighbour 42 points to 35.

However, at the fourth round at the Cleveland GN held on a new circuit at Nether Silton near Thirsk, in mid-July, Davis faltered as Vic Allan dominated the day's racing, taking a fine double on the moors. At the close

Davis wrapped up his third 250 British Championship at West Stow Heath, Suffolk in July 1973. Here he leads '72 Champion Andy Roberton, who disputed the title until the final race. (BH)

of day, Roberton, who had twice out performed Davis, had closed the gap to just three points, with the final round a week later to decide which Gloucestershire town the trophy would be travelling back to.

Final showdown

West Stow Heath near Bury St. Edmunds, was the venue for the final round. The sandy, undulating Suffolk circuit was always taxing on riders and on this occasion soon sorted the men from the boys. In race one, determined to put the pressure on his rival, Davis took up an early lead ahead of Wade, Allan and Roberton. But the pack was soon shuffled, as Wade passed Davis for the lead and Roberton slipped past Allan. Davis and Roberton then indulged in some close combat until the diminutive Welshman took a tumble in the treacherous sand. Following a second fall, Jimmy Aird (Maico) pipped Roberton for 5th and the title was virtually guaranteed for Davis. In the final race of an enthralling season-long contest, it was Allan who shot to the front ahead of the title protagonists. With Allan out front, Davis knew that the title was his and poor Roberton, who had been in bed just the day before with a stomach bug, could no longer hold his rival, Davis, who rode on to take 2nd place in the race and his third British Championship.

With the Championship under his belt, Malcolm rounded off the year with some great rides. In August he took victory on his native Gloucestershire soil, winning the 250 race at Tirley, though he was less fortunate in the Tirley Championship, crashing out dramatically, whilst leading. The following month saw Malcolm on top form on the 125, taking both races at Wakes Colne, to close to within 12 points of the hitherto invincible Bryan Wade. A week later he was

Davis celebrates his third title with brother Tony, in the paddock at West Stow Heath. (BH)

back at Dodington Park, representing Britain again in the TDN and this time, he didn't disappoint. For once, with his trusty championship-winning 250 Bultaco, he managed to finish both races, coming 5th in race two and finishing the day as the best Brit.

Then in October, he took the final round of the 125 British Championship by storm, comfortably winning both races. However, it wasn't enough to catch Wade, who in twice shadowing his old rival to finish 2nd, became the first national 125 Champion. Davis might well have added the famous Beenham Jackpot, with its £100 purse, had the throttle cable not given out on the 400 after he had led the race for seven laps.

The 1973 championship-winning season was one of the most rewarding for Malcolm, and Tony Davis is convinced that despite the success of the double championship during the AJS years, Malcolm most enjoyed his time racing for Bultaco. *The best years for Malcolm were definitely the Bultaco years. He just loved the factory and they loved him. They would listen to him and take notice of whatever he said and Sr. Bulto was like a second father to us in many ways, especially to Malcolm.*

In-house rivalry

However, in 1974 Malcolm's toughest challenge came not from his Gloucestershire neighbours, Messrs Wade and Roberton, but from his Bultaco teammate, Vic Allan. The Scot, who had suffered several setbacks in his career, was determined to improve on his results over the past two seasons and desperately wanted to

At the 1974 250 British GP at Chalton in June 1974, Davis leads arch rival Vic Allan. (BH)

be Bultaco's number one rider. Malcolm, for his part, was in fine form that season and was one of a handful of riders to challenge the Surrey-based Scotsman, but he was no match for Allan, who, in my opinion, was quite simply hungrier for success.

In the 250 Championship, Malcolm put together a string of results that might well have won the title another season. He won the opening race at Nantwich, took four 2nd places, two 3rd places and was only outside the top three on one occasion when he took 5th place in the second race at Pickwick Lodge, Corsham in May. He failed to finish twice: in the second race at the Cumberland GN when the Bultaco's engine seized up whilst he was running 2nd and in the first race at the Cotswold Scramble in July, when the rear sub-frame broke after he had led the championship-deciding race. However, such was Allan's domination that he won eight of the 10 races to defeat his rival 64 points to 42, with another Bultaco runner, Ivan Miller, third on 37 points.

New venue, but the home GP jinx remains

There was also a last hurrah for Davis in the 250 British GP that had moved on to a new home at Chalton, Hampshire, though the change of venue did little to improve Davis' fortunes. Contrary to what its name might suggest, 'Ladies Mile' was a tough, unforgiving circuit, littered with flints. A crowd of 15,000 turned up to watch the spectacle and the British contingent were thrilled by the performances of Davis and Allan.

The Scotsman ran second to first race winner, Harry Everts, for several laps until a puncture dropped him to 5th, but Davis also performed heroically before his home GP jinx struck again. Malcolm led Allan for second place in race one, until the rear shocks over heated, causing him to slip back to 7th at the flag. Then early in race two he was struck on his left hand by a wayward flint, resulting in two broken fingers and a trip to the St. John Ambulance tent.

Biting off too much?

Malcolm had a very busy season in '74, contesting the 125, 250 and 500 Championships and he had the distinction of being the only rider to win championship races in each category that year. He added to his 250 win at Nantwich with victories on the opening day of the 500 Class at the Cambridge GN in April and the closing day of the 125s at Beenham Park in mid-October. Indeed for many riders this would have been an exceptional season, with 2nd in the 250 Championship, joint 4th in the 125s and 5th in the 500s, but by Malcolm's own high standards it didn't suffice.

I wondered whether, with Allan's ascendance to the undisputed number one at Bultaco, Malcolm had lost his competitive edge that season? Tony Davis is not of that opinion, echoing a comment Allan himself had previously made to me (see p254) *No, not at all. His first thought would have been, 'I'm a factory rider and I want to be number one and I'm going to go out there to win'. No, he never lost his competitive spirit and though he did go off the boil a bit in motocross, he remained a very competitive trials rider.*

By the mid-70s Davis, for whatever reason, was finding it hard to match the speed of the younger riders who were emerging in the new 'Top 35' series, such as teenager Graham Noyce, and Stuart Nunn and Ivan Miller who were in their early 20s, nor did he seem to weather the situation as well as his contemporaries such as Allan, Banks and Eastwood. To illustrate this, in the inaugural revamped British Championship in 1975, he finished the season with just 23 points, whilst winner Allan had amassed 116. He fared even worse the following season when his best race finish was 6th place in race one at the Cotswold Scramble in July.

Back to his roots

However, Malcolm never lost his enthusiasm for off-road motorcycling, returning to his first love, trials-riding, and winning the Western Centre Trials Championship in 1976, outpointing Tony and Mark Kemp. Tragically, it was whilst competing in a trial, the President's Trophy in Devon in October 1980, that he lost his life when he was struck by a car whilst on his way to the first group of sections. Ironically, Tony who had been by his side on so many occasions was absent, though his father, Les, had travelled down to Devon with him as he was the ACU steward for the trial which was a round of the British Championship.

Thus ended the career of an immensely talented motorcycle rider, who on his day was a match for any rider in the world. His brother, Tony, who so often sacrificed his own riding opportunities to selflessly help his kid brother, describes him as: *A great trials rider, but a brilliant scrambles rider,* and had this to add. *Joel Robert, who had a special relationship with Malcolm and is probably the best motocross rider ever, once said to me, "Malcolm is the fastest rider in the world downhill and what annoys me most is he doesn't look like he's going fast."*

30 years may have passed since Malcolm's death, but those who, like myself, were fortunate enough to see him racing at his best, will always remember him for his own impeccable, and as Joel Robert suggested, seemingly effortless style. He was pure gold.

Bryan Wade

Born to be Wild

Photo BH

Bryan Wade was one of a handful of highly talented young riders who emerged on to the motocross scene in the mid-60s. At 19 years old, he rode in his first Grand Prix in Spain, where he finished 7th overall. In 1968, armed with a works Greeeves, he showed great promise racing in the 250 GPs leading many of those involved in the sport to consider him a potential World Champion. A month after turning 23, he was the 250 British Champion and appeared to have the motocross world at his feet. As things turned out, he didn't do too badly, adding four more British Championships and becoming the only rider during that era to claim 125, 250 and 500cc titles. However, as Wade himself would admit he never really allowed himself a good crack at a world title.

Bryan Wade was born in August 1946 and grew up in a small village on the edge of Bowes Moor, on the borders of Yorkshire and Durham. A bright lad from a rural background, Bryan was educated at boarding school. However, his progress was hindered as he suffered from dyslexia and so he began to look elsewhere to make his mark in life.

His first experience on a motorbike was as a 14 year-old on a 125 BSA Bantam which his father, Len, bought him. Bryan then set about getting a grounding in off road riding in the company of a few of the local lads. *We started racing round the fields at home on the Bantam. Then my mates got all sorts of wonderful stuff, like side-valve BSAs with girder forks and rigid back ends! You wouldn't believe the hole you can dig when you land a 500cc hand-change BSA off a six foot jump. Mind you, bike and rider normally parted company!* It would seem that even from an early age, Wade, who would go on to gain notoriety for his antics both on and off the bike, enjoyed a strange affinity with terra firma!

Having learnt the basics on the Bantam and on reaching the age of 16, Bryan entered his first race at nearby Toft Hill on a thirty year-old rigid BSA. Needless to say he struggled and a replacement was soon sought. This materialised in the form of a 197 Francis-Barnett which, though a great improvement on the BSA, was still lacking in certain departments, not least speed! So Wade Snr, recognising the passion his son had for racing bikes and being happy with the progress he had made, rewarded him with a new MDS Greeves, whilst Bryan was still at school.

Special dispensation for scrambling!

Like so many riders of his generation, Bryan was a huge Dave Bickers fan and he drew inspiration from following his progress whilst at school. So, once on a pukka scrambler like that of his hero, his progress was quite spectacular as he notched up 10 race wins before leaving school. However, there were a few complications along the way. *Being at boarding school made it quite difficult, as you were only allowed four Sundays out each term. But the school gave me special leave as long as I was back before lights out. I remember coming back with a broken collarbone one day though and that didn't go down too well!*

But Bryan was getting some good results at this time and just a month after leaving school his father managed to persuade the organisers of the Thirsk International meeting, at nearby Boltby, to accept his entry. He didn't disappoint the organisers or his dad, finishing a creditable 13th overall and turning a few heads in the process. As school had proven to be so difficult for him, Bryan was just glad to be making progress and, as he still proudly recalls, on May 23 1964, his photo appeared in the *MCN* for the first time.

1964

Shortlived factory ride

1965

Someone who was quick to spot his talent early on was Ernie Wiffen, the Competition Chief at James. Wade takes up the story. *We met up with Ernie at the Earls Court Show in January 1965 and I was given a works ride for James.* However the glory of having a works ride as an 18 year-old was short lived, as Wade goes on to explain. *By July, I was back on a Greeves having snapped the James clean in half coming off a big jump.*

The Greeves in question was a new Challenger, purchased from local dealers Scott and Wallace in Guisborough, who were happy to give the talented teenager some support. On competitive machinery again, the results started to improve dramatically. Highlights during this period included 5th place, and the first of many British Championship points, in the 250 race at the Lancashire GN; 3rd in the Yorkshire GN, and an excellent joint 3rd overall in the 250 Class at the Thirsk International, behind winner John Griffiths, Ron Tate and tied with factory Dot man, Pat Lamper.

At this time in his career, he was already receiving a fair amount of media attention. Writing a profile of the young rider in the *MCN* in January 1966, Colin Hutchinson, who was very influential in Wade's early progress, hyped him as 'Britain's youngest professional scrambler'. At the time he was 19 years old and although he hadn't secured another works ride just yet, he had quit his day job as a car salesman.

1966

The Maverick

Even in those early days Wade stood out from the crowd, whether it was for his customised bike transporter, a 1960 3.8 litre Jaguar which featured a cut-away boot and a raised roof, or his distinctive crash helmet design, with an intricate weave of black sticky tape, which Wade had designed when his mother said she couldn't pick him out on the start line. It certainly worked and race-goers throughout the '60s and '70s never had any problem spotting Bryan Wade.

However, it was his spectacular style on the bikes which really got him noticed and led to him being

Bryan Wade

Wade making a nuisance of himself, as he chases fellow Yorkshireman Arthur Lampkin, at the Gloucester Grand National at Tirley in August 1967. (RD)

tagged 'Wild' Wade. *Yes, that was dear old Murray Walker on Grandstand, probably due to another one of my upside down antics. I always wanted to be at the front, but unfortunately I didn't have the brain, so I was off the bike a great deal of the time. But nine times out of ten I was rolling before I hit the ground and it got me noticed as a fighter.*

The fans loved it, the TV pundits lapped it up, and Bryan Wade was good press. In 1968, he told a *MCN* reporter 'The crowd love it when I get all crossed up in mid-air, so I do it. It gets me publicity and attention and that can help when you're arranging start money with organisers.' However, not all of his fellow competitors appreciated the style, especially if it would put a result in jeopardy. *Arthur Lampkin nearly slapped me round the head one day at a North v South meeting. I can still hear his voice. "Slow down you young bugger!" I'd whistled past him, and then four corners later ended up on my ear!*

Keeping good company

The fact was, that he was out there mixing it with the likes of Arthur Lampkin and he was learning all the time. Bryan told me that his father's philosophy had always been that to get to the top he had to get into the big meetings and ride against the top riders of the day. It's a fairly common philosophy, but many young kids are overawed by the experience and fall by the wayside, never to be seen again. This was not the case with Wade, who was never lacking in confidence, and a twist of fate meant that he would soon be very grateful for his father's forward thinking.

In March 1966 he was out of luck in the televised races at the BBC TV meeting at Brill, Buckinghamshire, but in one of the non-televised invitation races he finished 2nd behind fellow Greeves man Goss, but ahead of fellow youngster Keith Hickman, who was starting to make a name for himself on his Cheney BSA. Results such as this were being monitored by the Greeves competition department, who were constantly on the look out for young talent.

Wade gets a break

Then a week later, on the eve of the 250 Spanish GP, Greeves' factory rider Goss broke his collarbone racing at a Yeo Vale MCC meeting and the ACU were desperate to find a replacement rider, as Wade recalls. *They asked Greeves to find a rider, so Bill Brooker came on the phone. "Do you have an International Licence? Do you have a passport?" I said yes to both.* He could do so, thanks to his father's foresight and the help of Colin Hutchinson, who had pulled some strings to get him into the Thirsk International at Boltby. *Then he said. "You're riding in the Spanish GP. Be at the factory first thing tomorrow morning." then he hung up! I drove the old Jag through the night from Barnard Castle to Southend and slept outside the factory. They rebuilt my bike from front to back, and Bill, Freddy Mayes and I drove in an A55 all the way to Barcelona.*

The whole event was a great experience for the young rider. With the adrenalin pumping, he rode brilliantly in both legs, to finish an excellent 7th overall on his GP debut. He remembers being overwhelmed when he was approached in the paddock and given some invaluable advice from the man who would go on to regain the World Championship that season. *Torsten Hallman came over to me at the end of the meeting to congratulate me on my result. For me it was a big thrill that*

At the BBC Grandstand meeting at Leighton, Somerset in March 1966, Wade battles with fellow Greeves rider Dennis Smith. (CB)

he'd even noticed me! I showed him my hands which were badly blistered and I noticed that his appeared soft and unmarked which was staggering to me after what we'd just done. He put a hand on my shoulder and told me, "Don't fight the bike, guide it." That was probably the best advice I ever had in my career and years later I passed it on to every rider who came through my racing schools.

A handsome reward

For the next three months Wade received a lot of support from Greeves, before they offered him a full contract in June 1966, two months shy of his 20th birthday.

What does he remember of those early days at Greeves? *After my problems at school, I felt I had to prove myself at something and this was the first thing I was any good at. The problem was I had no interest in the bike, but luckily for me Bill Brooker soon realised this. He was extremely helpful and professional, indeed everybody at the factory was very friendly and seemed committed to making the best bike they could. But I remember Bert Greeves having some reservations about incorporating some new developments (not least of all telescopic forks), though I can understand this as his innovation had helped make Greeves the success story it was.*

At Greeves, Wade found himself in the company of, amongst others, Freddie Mayes and Arthur Browning, though to his great regret his childhood hero, Dave Bickers, had already departed to ride for CZ. *Dave Bickers was the guy I read about in the papers while at school, a fighter and a really nice guy too and I was fortunate that we became friends later in my career. Arthur and I got on really well, even though at that time he was beating me hands down. I think of him as one of the great characters I came to know in the sport. He was a great all-rounder and a few years later he even coached me on how to ride speedway, in readiness for Super 6 (A multi-discipline competition organised by road racer Phil Read). Freddie Mayes was a good guy, he was quiet, but he always got on with the job in hand.*

By March 1967, 'Wild' Wade was beginning to challenge the very best. Here on the 360 Greeves, he is battling with double World Champion Jeff Smith in the TV meeting at Hankom Bottom. (BH)

A move south reaps success

But back before the Greeves contract came along Bryan was considering a move south where he would be nearer most of the big meetings and felt he would face stiffer competition. Once again fate was to take a hand in proceedings, following a mid-week trip down to Dorset. *I'd come down to do the Weymouth Wednesday race and then had the Cotswold GN meeting at the weekend. I slept on the beach using my old Jag as a mobile home and I met some guys at the meeting who invited me to stay in Nailsworth, which was only a couple of miles away from the next race and I ended up staying there for a great many rewarding years.*

Over the next couple of years, Wade made good progress on the factory Greeves. A noteworthy success in 1966 came at the John Donnelly Memorial in Ireland in September, when he beat Bryan Goss on his Husqvarna by a winning margin of 10 seconds over the two legs. He was also selected to represent Great Britain for the first time in a BBC TV match race at Canada Heights, showing his mettle against the mighty Swedes. Then in 1967 he began to make his mark in both the British Championships and the BBC Grandstand series on the 250 and 360 Greeves.

At Clifton, Derbyshire in late January, he was selected for the Great Britain team in another BBC Match race, this time with Czechoslovakia. In the main event he was on good form finishing 3rd in both legs behind Bickers and Browning. He also split Bickers and Jeff Smith to take 2nd in one of the invitation races. In the Grandstand Trophy he would go on to produce some great rides, not least of all at Naish Hill, Wiltshire in February, where he won the 250 Trophy race and came 2nd in the 750s, splitting the factory BSAs of winner Vic Eastwood and John Banks. With such inspired form, he would go on to finish 4th in both the 250 and 750 Trophy series that winter.

1967

Calmly waiting to go to the startline at Hawkstone Park in March 1967, Wade is flanked by Dick Clayton (left) and Bill Gwynne (right). (RD)

Racing on one of his favourite circuits, Hawkstone Park, he was in sparkling form for the 500 British Championship meeting in March. Racing in exalted company, he was unlucky in the main event, crashing out whilst battling with former World Champion, Smith, but bounced back in the remaining races to take 2nd to Clough in the 250 race and 2nd in the 350 race behind Bickers.

Talent for all to see

At Wakes Colne in July he performed brilliantly in the 250 GP, exceeding all expectations as he raced to an excellent third place in the first leg behind World Champions Joel Robert and Victor Arbekov. However, in the second race he was involved in a first lap pile-up and although he rejoined the action he later crashed again and finally finished the race in 19th place and sadly out of the points.

Such form saw Bryan selected for the TDN at Holice, Czechoslovakia in August, along with Goss, Malcolm Davis and teammate Browning. After Goss'

win in the first qualifier, where Davis finished 5th, hopes were high for the British team in the final but they struggled with Goss finishing 10th, Davis 11th and Wade finding himself a little out of his depth in the face of the assembled talent.

It was around this time that I first saw Wade race, at Hintlesham Park near Ipswich in August, where he got in the points in the 250 British Championship race from 6th place and went on to win the Senior race on the twin-port 360 ahead of Banks on his factory BSA. He was right on the pace at that meeting and like so many race fanatics of the day I remember him for his vivid, all-out riding style.

Trying times

1968 was to prove to be a season of frustration for Wade, not least of all in the British Championships. He already had the reputation of being a crasher, but he'd also proven that he had the speed to run with the best. Bryan had a really torrid time in the 250 Championship,

1968

Ray Daniel captures Wade racing in the 500 British Championship at Hawkstone Park in March 1967, where again he battled with Jeff Smith.

In the first race of the 250 British GP at Wakes Colne in July 1967, Wade was in magnificent form as he raced to third place behind Joel Robert and Victor Arbekov. (BH)

where he was dogged by a combination of bad luck and injuries and after three rounds he had just three points to show for his efforts. Typical of his luck was round three at the Cleveland GN in his native Yorkshire in July, where he was plagued by a loosening petrol tank in both championship races. However, to prove what he was capable of he took the Grand National race, narrowly defeating new AJS recruit, Chris Horsfield.

Bureaucracy rules!

To exasperate his situation, Wade had his entry for the fourth round at Cureden Park controversially returned, the organisers refusing to accept it despite an appeal from Bert Greeves, who eloquently stated the case of a young rider who had been travelling across the continent representing his nation in the 250 GPs and not taking a holiday as some might assume.

Had the Lancs GN organisers been following the sport in the press, they would have been aware that Wade had indeed been taking in the 250 GPs, showing fine form in France and Holland, where he finished 7th overall at both rounds.

But trouble was in store for Wade at the next round in West Germany, where after being the surprise package in practice, qualifying 2nd, he would crash on the super-fast wooded circuit at Bilstein compounding his misery and breaking a wrist. *I was running fourth in the first race until the piston rings disappeared out of the exhaust port! I had to change engines between races and as I was on my own, Joel Robert's mechanic helped me out. The second race was on the line and ready to go when I blasted out of the pits and I came up behind the line of riders just as the gate dropped. I think I was about fifth into the first corner, but as we dived away into the pine*

Right, relaxing in the paddock of the 1967 500 British GP at Farleigh Castle, Wade does his Simon Templar (The Saint) impression! (MC)

Below, Synchronised Scrambling! Greeves teamsters Arthur Browning and Wade (right) do battle at Hintlesham Park in August 1967. (DK)

Champions all in a row! At the 1968 250 British GP at Dodington Park, Wade finished an excellent 5th overall. Here he is sandwiched between Freddie Mayes (Montesa) and fellow Greeves man, Vic Allan. (CB)

forest, both of my boots slipped off the footrests and I was laid full-length on the bike and disappeared into the trees like a bullet. I'd had to change boots, as a footrest had gone through one in the first race, and the new ones had no grip at all! Poor Dave Bickers, who was following Wade, was convinced he'd killed himself!

GP win slips through his hands

He returned to the GP circus for the Scandinavian leg of the championship, where he was out of luck in Finland when the Greeves' engine failed in both races. However, at Hedemora, Sweden, two days after his 22nd birthday, he turned in a brilliant performance, especially in race one, when he followed Robert and Malcolm Davis home for 3rd place. Then when Robert retired early in race two and Davis fell, he suddenly found himself as, to use today's vernacular, the 'virtual GP winner'. However, the excitement was too much for the inexperienced Wade who crashed where Davis had gone down, on a section of the track the officials had decided to water between races. I only had to stay where I was, but I hit a big rock and flew off and for some reason I couldn't will myself to get back into the race and go for it.

Then at the home GP at Dodington Park, Gloucestershire in August, he raced to a season's best result of 5th overall and second Brit home after Dave Bickers, who finished 3rd, to Robert and Hallman. Wade finished 4th in the first leg and came home 5th second time out, a result that would have gained far more media attention at the time had it not been for the sterling efforts of Malcolm Davis (see p156).

Though he hadn't exactly 'blazed' the GP trail, he had proven to himself, and many others, that he could compete at the highest level. *My dad was right, mixing with the big guys brought a familiarity, but not contempt. It brought an inner strength and from very early on I realised that these guys were not the super humans I'd read about, they were just like me, only better at the job.* This realisation was very important for Wade's psyche.

1969

Against the odds
1969 was to be a turning point in his career. By then he had already established himself at Greeves and now had a helper and a mechanic on hand wherever he rode. *I would arrive at the races in a car with my riding gear and a helper. He would take care of getting my bike into the box early, so I'd get first pick on the line and he would also take care of signalling, which gave my mechanic a breather. It worked really well.*

I'm sure many old-school riders who had ridden their bikes to and from meetings and had had to remove the lights and then refit them after a long day's racing would have scoffed at this, but with hindsight it seems to me that Wade was in fact casting the mould for the professional rider of the '70s and '80s. Bryan, who loved to play mind games with the opposition, feels it gave him a psychological edge when he went to the start line. *It was very important to me. Arriving in a car, help running around sorting stuff out and my own mechanic. You'd be surprised how many people can get beaten before the race even starts!*

However, despite the help, as the 250 British Championship got underway in March, Wade looked far from being a contender. In the first round at Tilton, he took just three points from 4th place in race one, fighting through the field from 15th on the opening lap to pip Andy Roberton on the last and things soured when he was disqualified from race two for allegedly cutting the course. Things got worse in round two at Nantwich later that month, when he added just two points from finishing 5th in race two. The meeting was dominated by the 'old guard' as Messrs Clough, Smith and Bickers finished in that order in both races and Wade found himself lying 8th in the championship, as teammate Vic Allan and Clough shared the lead.

The tide changes
Things improved from there on though, with his fortune changing at Hadleigh, Essex in May. Wade won the opening race after catching and passing Goss on the last lap for a narrow victory. No doubt eager to impress the Greeves top brass, the Thundersley factory lying just 3 miles away from the circuit, he then stormed into the lead in race two and looked to be on for a double win. But in the closing laps he tired allowing Clough, Bickers and Allan to come through as he finished 4th at the flag. However, the points moved him up to 4th in the table behind Clough, Allan and Davis.

With series leader Clough absent from the fourth round at the Cotswold Scramble at Nympsfield in early July (see p119), the championship was thrown wide open. In race one after a poor start Wade picked off riders lap by lap, though there was nothing he could do to catch runaway leaders Goss and Davis. In race two he followed Davis initially, until the Gloucester rider's CZ went off song and Wade moved to the front to win comfortably from teammate Browning and Bickers.

Tumultuous Tirley
Though Wade was coming into his best form yet, no one rider had stamped his authority on the championship. As a result, when the riders made their way to Gloucestershire for the final round at Tirley in late August, no less than six riders were still in contention. They were Bickers, Allan, Davis, Goss, Clough and Wade, with just seven points separating championship leader Wade and 6th place Bickers. To add extra spice to the situation, Wade and Davis, were racing on 'home soil', so the scene was set for a memorable afternoon's racing.

When the gate dropped at the start of the first race at Tirley, the atmosphere was electric. Davis rode a blinder in the first leg, getting the start and pulling comfortably away from the rest of the field. In contrast, Wade could only finish third behind Husqvarna's Bryan Goss, who chased Davis all the way to the flag. This meant that going into the final race of the series Wade and Davis were level pegging on 31 points, whilst Goss, who was only a further point adrift, was also eyeing the silverware.

I wondered how Wade had felt going to the line for that all-or-nothing final race of the series? *I was focused and excited, as was everyone in the team. Remember, I didn't have the bike to worry about; that was all down to Bill and the boys in the comp shop. It was a real turning point for me. Every time my dad had come to watch me race since I had moved south, I would have some problem. But my parents were there to see me win and I wasn't going to disappoint them. Dad shook my hand before the race and then disappeared into the crowd. Then between races I bumped into Malcolm and he showed me his hands, which were covered in blisters.*

The title is up for grabs
Tension was high. Who would win? When the race got underway, Goss was the first to crack, overshooting

In October 1969, Wade took the 380 Griffon to 5th place in the final race of the 500 British Championship at Builth Wells, but the new 250 British Champion is pictured here on his way to victory in the 250 race. (RD)

the first corner, whilst Wade, who was poorly placed at the start, kept his nerve and worked steadily through the pack. *I kept thinking of Malcolm's hands as I saw him in the distance in the second race.* Then, as the race neared the half-way stage, Wade swept past Davis into the lead. *I smiled at him as I passed him on the top straight and he just shook his head, he was done.* Davis faded towards the end and was passed by former AJS teammate Roberton, leaving Wade to ride unchallenged to the chequered flag and his first national title.

It was celebrated in style, as Wade's fans shouldered him to the podium, where he received his trophy, and a kiss from Miss World! The win ended a three-year drought for Greeves, who hadn't had a major title win since Freddie Mayes had been 250 Champion in 1966. It was also excellent publicity for the new 'Griffon' and led a euphoric Competition Chief, Bill Brooker, to tell the waiting journalists, "Now he can have a go at the World Championship next year. He certainly deserves it."

Wade described his '69 250cc bike as 'a dream', that was until he was reunited with it a few years later in Switzerland, where he did a demo lap at the MDN. *It was like a bad dream, terrible, and I thought to myself, "However did I make this thing fly."* He also acknowledges that the 380cc twin-port was more to his taste. *For my riding style it was great. Having that extra power I was pulling broadsides and wheelies everywhere!*

The highs and lows of a British Champion

1970

In 1970, Greeves had high hopes for their young Champion and true to their word they announced that Wade, seen by many at the time as a potential World

Champion, in the company of Bill Brooker would contest the 250 World Championship. Wade was also confident and hoped to retain his British Championship and to make his mark on the GP scene, having shown his potential two years earlier. However, what should have been a great season for the man from Nailsworth turned into one of great frustration as the Greeves repeatedly let him down.

Things started brightly as Wade raced to victory in the opening race of the British Championship at Nantwich in early April, but after three falls in race two he found himself out of the points. Then just a fortnight later came one of the highlights of a memorable career, as he raced to 4th overall in the season-opening GP in Spain, a performance that warranted a front page photo on the *MCN*. Wade was sensational in the first race chasing the factory Suzukis of Robert, Sylvain Geboers and Olle Petterson, before overhauling the Swede mid-race. In the second leg he recovered from a poor start to once again pass Petterson for 6th place to finish level overall with Davis, beating his countryman by two seconds on aggregate time.

It was a great start for the 23 year-old, but if Wade had entertained thoughts of emulating his childhood hero, Bickers, he would soon come to realise that it needed a lot more than just talent to lift a world title. At the French round the following weekend the Greeves broke down twice in the closing stages of each leg, to deny him another excellent overall result. Then in Belgium having proved his speed again by qualifying 6th fastest, he was eliminated with further mechanical problems.

Mixing it with the GP stars

At the Italian GP at the end of May, he led the world for two laps until he crashed, but bravely fought back from a lowly 28th to finish 11th. He was also right on the pace in race two holding second place to Geboers for the opening six laps. He slipped to third, but then was cruelly ruled out with a rear tyre puncture. A week later he finished both races in Russia, being credited with 9th overall, which earned him two championship points, though there was a lot of confusion amongst the lap scorers and many felt he should have been 6th overall.

At the end of June after a break of some eleven weeks the British Championship resumed at Tilton, Leicestershire, in what for Bryan was a completely wasted opportunity. The Greeves that Wade rode at that meeting featured an experimental frame with new head angles and, incredibly, it would appear that the first time he rode it was in the first championship race. Wade persevered on the bike till mid-race distance, though by that time he was already outside the point scoring positions. After the race he told *MCN*'s Mike Nicks *'It was unrideable. The bike just kept trying to slide away from me on the corners.'*

Frustrated Wade speaks out

A week later it was the home round of the World Championship at Dodington Park, with British fans looking to Wade and Davis to provide a challenge to the world's best. Poor Wade's GP lasted just a matter of yards, when broken piston rings put him out on the first lap. In anger he spoke out about the British effort.

In the Spring of 1970, Wade in company with Bill Brooker set off to conquer Europe. Here they are pictured with Ray Taylor, who worked in the Comp Shop, outside the Greeves factory at Thundersley, Essex. (Photo supplied by Bill Brooker)

'You can't expect English riders to stay on English bikes when they keep breaking down. Something has to change drastically. I want to move on'. his words appearing on the cover of the *MCN* on July 1st under a dramatic headline: *'THE BRITISH EFFORT WAS PATHETIC'– WADE'*. Ironically, on the eve of the British GP the Spanish manufacturer, Montesa, had approached Wade, who at the time was contracted to Greeves until the end of the year.

The relationship with Greeves deteriorated rapidly as the bike let him down again in successive British Championship rounds at Carlton Bank and Cuerden Park. In Yorkshire the engine seized up in race one as he was disputing the lead with Davis and in race two it mysteriously lost power as he challenged the same rider for the lead, though after slipping to fourth he recovered to finish the race in 2nd place. At the Lancs GN things were worse still as *MCN*'s Mike Nicks witnessed. *'The only man fast enough to challenge the Davis-AJS combination for the title, his works Greeves seized in both races.'* At the time Wade told Nicks, *'It's so frustrating the bike is really good while it lasts'.*

Maybe Wade was too outspoken in his criticism of the Greeves, as its seems the rift between the two parties had grown too deep for it to be repaired, but too many breakdowns over the season had left him frustrated with a situation that he feels could easily have been resolved. *The problems Greeves were experiencing with rings going out the exhaust port and the like were down to, for want of a better expression, 'poor metal'. I asked them, "Why not get special pistons or whatever we need made up?" I was getting so close to the front guys in the GPs and I couldn't understand why they couldn't change the 'soft' bits for better quality stuff on my GP bike.*

A new venture

After suffering so much disappointment, few were surprised when it was announced that Greeves and Wade were to part company. At the time Wade had already embarked on a new, parallel, profession when he decided to enter the restaurant business. In partnership with an old friend from his Barnard Castle days, Jim Hannaway, he opened the 'Wade-In' in Nailsworth, with Hannaway acting as manager. In an interview for *MCN* in June 1971 he told the reporter: *'I've wanted to work for myself since I left school. I fancied a night club or a motel but never a motorcycle shop… When I landed works support from Greeves I decided to take the plunge'.*

No turning back

It's ironic that no sooner had he got his restaurant up and running than the factory support disappeared. Wade is adamant that a new contract with Greeves was never on the table and it would appear that Greeves wanted him out. *Before my contract was up, Derry Preston Cobb told me they couldn't afford to keep me on and that he wanted me to go to Husky and had already talked to Brian Leask* (the Husqvarna importer).

Whatever the reasons for the split, for Wade the old proverb, 'Every cloud has a silver lining', certainly came true, as Leask was more than happy to sign him up and once on the Huskies he went from strength to strength. Wade signed with Leask in August 1970, making his debut in front of 30,000 motocross fans at the International meeting at Laguiepie in the south of France, though it wasn't a happy occasion as bike problems and a fall meant he failed to finish any of the three legs.

The start of a fruitful relationship

But within a few weeks he was repaying the faith Leask had invested in him, bagging a brace of 4th places in the final round of the 250 British Championship at Beenham Park, tellingly the first time he'd managed to finish two championship races on the same day all season. Then the following weekend, after focussing on the 250 Championship all season, he rode to a memorable double victory at the final round of the 500 British Championship at Builth Wells, where he was simply too strong for Vic Allan and the new Champion, Bryan Goss.

What does Wade remember of the switch to the Swedish bikes? *The move to Husky came at just the right time for many reasons. Brian was fantastic, he gave me 100% support and Ray* (Barber), *my mechanic, was amazing. The bikes were always perfect, I'd ride them into the ground in the first race and by the time the second race came around they were as new again.*

In his first full season on the Swedish marque in 1971, Wade recaptured his 250 crown after, as he put it, *Giving it back to Malcolm Davis* in 1970, and pushed John Banks all the way in the 500 Class. Ironically, though, after having been 'let go' of by BSA, Banks clinched the title, his third, on the ex-Arne Kring factory Husqvarna.

Winning run

In the 250 Class he was clearly the in-form rider again. At the opening round at Nantwich in April, he took a brace of very solid wins. With one of his main

Another good day for Wade at Builth Wells in October 1970, as he races the 400 Husqvarna to a double win in the final round of the 500 British Championship. (RD)

Wade partnered AJS' Malcolm Davis to victory in the 100-Mile Scramble at Guildford in late November 1970. Here he turns on the style on the Ray Barber prepared Husky. (BH)

title rivals, Malcolm Davis, struggling in vain against a virus, Wade won both races ahead of Andy Roberton, having his first outing on the 250 BSA, the two of them being in a race of their own and lapping the entire field in race two.

In round two at Brownrigg Fell in Cumberland, he added two more race wins against a rather poor field, with only Malcolm Davis showing that he had the pace to worry Wade. But the Gloucestershire motorcycle dealer was still being plagued by health problems and after briefly leading race one, he was forced to retire when the ignition failed on his Bultaco, leaving Wade to ride on to take the race at a stroll. In race two the reigning Champion shot after Wade after deposing Dick Clayton, but a coughing fit as the race entered it's final third caused Davis to slow and Wade rode in to the flag unchallenged once more.

So Wade had won the first five races in the championship before a spill in the second race of the third round at Carlton Bank, in his native Yorkshire, saw the chance to clinch his second title slip through his hands, as Davis ended the winning run. However, he had two rounds in hand and needed just one to regain the title from the man who was still his closest rival, Malcolm Davis.

Just Champion

In the fourth round at Leighton, Somerset in August, Davis was the star of the show, winning both races, but Wade kept his cool, raced to two second places and bagged enough points to put himself in an unassailable position. For the second time in three seasons, he was the 250 British Champion.

Out front! At the Cotswold Scramble in 1971, Wade won the second race of the 500 British Championship round on his spare bike. Cecil Bailey caught him entertaining the crowd with a massive wheelie ...

Though deadly rivals out on the track, Wade had a lot of respect for Davis. *Malcolm was a great rider and a very nice guy too. He could be a bit ruthless on the track, we had our moments as you do, but that's all part of racing and it was all left on the track.*

Outside bet for the double

With a bit more luck and a little more patience, he might well have landed the double in 1971. At the first round of the 500 British Championship at Hawkstone Park in March, he finished second to Banks in the first race then crashed twice, early on in the second. Then in the mud at Farleigh Castle in late May, he led the first leg before he caught the back wheel of Arthur Browning's Greeves and slid off. He remounted to finish second, but was plagued by a whiskered plug in the second race.

At Nympsfield in July, in front of his many fans, he won the second leg, after being eliminated from the first when the big-end gave out as he was chasing championship leader Banks hard. Wade was then cruelly robbed of victory at the Lancs Grand National in August, when his plug whiskered again, leaving Banks to clinch the title with the final round still to come.

However, Wade showed his class in the final round at Tirley in late August. In the first race he took the start and soon opened up what appeared to be a race-winning lead, but he allowed Davis, Banks and Roberton to close him down and Davis powered ahead on one of the climbs. Banks then retired and Wade held off Roberton to claim 2nd place. He made no mistakes in race two, leading from start to finish to seal the runner-up spot in the championship and although he finished a distant second to Banks in the final standings, for the

... and with his stylish cornering technique.

first time he had emerged as a serious contender for the 500 crown.

Unfulfilled promise

But despite his successes, this was a difficult period in his career. He was now on a fast, competitive machine, had a good team to back him up and was getting great results to prove it. But, as he himself told me, *I had taken my eye off the ball.* The restaurant and night club were taking up much more of his time and, with hindsight, he could see that he was trying to do too much. *It was great fun. I became friendly with all of the Radio 1 DJ's, but going into business killed any chance I had of being World Champion.*

Things were definitely not going well for him in the GPs and after a succession of setbacks, culminating in a broken down-tube on the alloy-framed, six-speed 250, he decided to pull out. An interview in the *MCN* in June 1971 caught him in sombre mood. '*I get a kick from racing but I regard motocross as a money making pastime. I pulled out of the 250cc World Championship because I was losing money. I was £40 in the red after Spain, Switzerland, Poland and West Germany.*'

However, it wasn't just about the money, as Wade recently admitted to me. *I pulled out of the World Championship because I blew it mentally; my mind set was well off target and you need to be totally focused. I think you have to have two or three years in that company and to be truthful I didn't mix it enough at International level. With hindsight I should have gone to live in Belgium and got really stuck into the international racing scene. I certainly had the pace, but maybe my head wasn't in the right place. I think the frustration was with myself; I had taken a fork in the road of life and had committed myself to business. There was no going back; I would have let so many people down. I'd split myself between racing and the restaurant and couldn't do both at the level needed. What do they say, 'Jack of all trades, but master of none?'*

After finishing 8th in the opening leg of the 1971 250 British GP at Dodington Park in August, Wade's luck ran out in the second race when the Husqvarna's engined seized up on the second lap. (RD)

1972

Wade's double shot!

But by now Wade had learnt to 'roll with the punches', both physically and psychologically, and he bounced back in 1972, again coming very close to that elusive 250/500 double. The season was dominated by the rivalry between the Husqvarna riders Wade and, his close friend and frequent travelling companion, Andy Roberton. They really were a class apart from the rest, winning 15 of the 20 championship races between them. For his part, Wade showed great consistency only failing to finish two championship races all season, the first coming in the opening race of the 250 series at Nantwich, where he caught a post and ripped the gear lever off. The other came in the final race of the 500 Championship when, having won the title, he decided to pull out as he was nursing an injured back.

Hadleigh headache and Beenham bruising

Wade was in good form on the 250 and after a disappointing opening round at Nantwich where he scored just three points, he picked up a double win at the Cambridge GN in Roberton's absence, to move in front of the man from Stroud, though the next round at Hadleigh, Essex would prove to be his Achilles heel. Despite finishing both races he scored just one point, whilst Roberton scored another maximum. However, Wade regained some momentum at the Rob Walker Scramble in late September winning the first race and finishing 3rd behind Davis and Rob Taylor in the second as Roberton faltered.

As a result going into the final round at Beenham Park, the Welshman led Wade by just four points and the title chase seemed to be between the two Husqvarna riders. However, Bultaco mounted Vic Allan, who was returning to top form after breaking his leg whilst on GP duty for BSA in Italy, had other ideas. Two second places saw Roberton win his British title, whilst a double win for the Scot, meant that he snatched the runner-up spot from a rather subdued Wade by just two points.

Out-front all season

However, Wade arguably saved his best riding for the 500 Class, where he headed the standings from round one at Frome in April, scoring a resounding double win, whilst his rivals struggled, Maico's Rob Taylor finishing as second highest points scorer on the day. At round two at Farleigh Castle in May, Wade and Roberton won a race apiece, with Roberton moving to 2nd in the points classification.

Three-time Champion John Banks had been getting used to the different power characteristics, not to mention the left-hand gear change, of his new CZ, but at Tilton in June, he stepped up his effort with a double win, which moved him to within six points of the leader, Wade. The Husqvarna men had mixed fortunes. An off-key Wade still managed to score eight points, but Roberton's challenge faded after a day marred by mechanical problems. A week later Roberton and Wade took a win each at the Cotswold Scramble at Nympsfield, though Roberton went out of race two with a broken throttle cable whilst chasing race leader Vic Eastwood. There was little change in the title hunt though, with Wade adding nine points, whilst Banks and Roberton added eight apiece to hold their positions.

History repeats itself at Tirley

So, as with his first 250 Championship win in 1969, the final, deciding, round of the 500 Championship would be at Tirley, some 22 miles from Wade's Gloucestershire home in Nailsworth. However, this time around Wade knew that a win in the first race would be enough to see him crowned Champion. Local hero Malcolm Davis led the first race until the gearbox on his Bultaco seized up, leaving Wade in front and seemingly on his way to the title. However, fate was at hand again, as first Banks had to pull out when his gear lever got damaged and then Wade picked up a rear wheel puncture and was soon caught and passed by Roberton and former Greeves teammate, Dick Clayton. Vic Eastwood on the AJS also caught and passed him on the last lap, but he managed to make it to the finish to gain the all important points that made him British Champion. The newly crowned Champion valiantly went to the line for the second encounter, but after sliding off early in the race he decided to rest, maybe quite literally, on his laurels.

Sublime Wade

This really was a 'purple patch' in Wade's career with back-to-back title wins, so was this Bryan Wade racing at his very best? *I would think so, the Husky days were hot and I'd put my frustration behind me. I'd got on the ACU grading list for the 500s, but had chosen not to do the GPs. I'd cleared my mind and I decided just to go out and enjoy this 'purple patch'. It was great and it seemed so easy too. I'm sure that if I'd not started the business, I could have carried the form over into the GPs, but we'll never know.*

A fourth place finish in the first race at Tirley in August was enough to see Wade crowned 1972 500 British Champion. (CB)

Impressive as Wade's form had been there was still more to come the following season, when he would face a new challenge.

Although the FIM would only bestow World Championship status on 125 racing in 1975, the ACU ushered in the new category in 1973. Of course, there had been a European Championship for some time prior to that and the big European manufacturers such as Bultaco, CZ and Husqvarna soon entered the market, aware of the huge potential it had, not least of all for the schoolboy scene which was blossoming in the UK at the time and where the previously ubiquitous BSA Bantams were no longer quite the ticket.

Wade was one of the established stars who decided to have a crack at the new title and was joined by, amongst others, Malcolm Davis and Vic Allan (both Bultaco), Dave Bickers and Stuart Nunn (both CZ), Dick Clayton, Ivan Miller and Roger Harvey (all on Husqvarna), Les Lloyd (Suzuki) and a certain 16 year-old from Eastleigh on a Zundapp-powered Rickman, Graham Noyce.

No lack of ambition

That year, Wade ambitiously contested the 125, 250 and 500 British Championships. From the opening round at Hawkstone Park in March, Wade, Davis and Allan established themselves as the main protagonists for the 125 title. On a track he just loved to race, Wade stamped his authority on the series, comfortably winning both legs from Davis, whilst Allan pushed his fellow Bultaco rider all the way in the second leg. In the 500s, Wade won an enthralling first race, winning over the crowd as he wrestled the new 460cc Husky home with a flat rear tyre, beating John Banks on the Cheney BSA by a machine's length. However, after his Herculean efforts in the first race, he only lasted a few laps in the second, prompting Banks to comment "He had too much on his plate."

Wade dominated the first half of the 125 series with five race wins and a second place, including another fine double at Hadleigh, Essex in May. There, Allan, who was recovering from an ankle injury he picked up whilst at the 250 Italian GP (see p254) which caused him to

Sponsor Brian Leask (right) supplies the bubbly for the new Champion and his mechanic, Ray Barber, in the Paddock at Tirley. (CB)

miss the second round, put up the most resistance, but Wade was still clearly the man to beat.

Out of luck in the 250s ...

In the 250 Championship, he won the second race at the Cumberland GN at Brownrigg Fell in April before suffering an uncharacteristic run of four races without a finish. After adding a measly three points at round four at Nether Silton, the new home of the Cleveland GN, in July, Wade went to the last round at Bury St. Edmunds to try and help Roberton retain his 250 Championship, though the odds were stacked in Malcolm Davis' favour. Wade won the first 250 race ahead of Davis though Roberton struggled and could only manage 5th place. Wade then abandoned race two after twisting a knee to finish the series in 4th place though a long way adrift of new Champion Davis, Roberton and Allan.

... and no match for 500 King, Banks...

In the 500 campaign, Wade won the first race at round two in North Devon and came 4th in race two to make up ground on Banks, though the Bury St. Edmunds man dominated the third round at Builth Wells, taking a double win and stretching his lead over Wade to 10 points. But it was in the fourth round at Frome that the title slipped away from Wade as he suffered a day to forget. At the close of racing, he had failed to add a single point to his tally, after a sticking throttle eliminated him in race one and a recurring knee injury forced him to retire from the second whilst leading. Meanwhile Banks recorded his fifth and sixth race wins of the series and now had an unassailable lead. With one round still to go at Wakes Colne, Banks was Champion again for the fourth time.

I was among the crowds that gathered at Wakes Colne in September, for another 125/500 double-header, hoping to see local hero John Banks dominate the 500s and Wade clinch the 125s. However, it was not to be. Wade faltered, allowing Davis, who recorded a double win, to close to within 12 points, with 16 points still at stake in the final round at Beenham Park in October. Meanwhile, newly crowned 500 Champion

Above, Wade began the defence of his 500 crown at Hawkstone Park in March 1973. Ray Daniel caught Wade, on the 460 Husky, and John Banks, on the Cheney BSA, side-by-side at the height of their epic battle in race one. Below, Wade didn't have too much luck on the 250 in 1973, but he won the penultimate race of the British Championship at West Stow Heath, Suffolk in July. (BH)

Banks also had a 'poor day at the office', but the day was still memorable for me, as I saw future World Champion, Graham Noyce ride for the first time. He was impressive too, with an excellent 3rd place finish in the second 125 race to back up his 5th from race one.

… but he secures a unique hat-trick

The 125 series culminated at Beenham Park in October, where Wade knew a 2nd place finish would see him crowned Champion and the first rider to win all three titles. In the event that is exactly what he did, following 250 Champion Davis home in both races and doing no more than was necessary to outpoint his long-time rival, 67 points to 59, with Yamaha's Roger Harvey a distant 3rd in the series.

At the season's close, perhaps John Banks' words following the first 125/500 round at Hawkstone Park had proved to be prophetic, perhaps Wade had been too ambitious. *Oh yes, my plate was overflowing! I had the equipment, I was in, or coming to my peak and I was going after everything. It could have come off, but John was right, if I had left the 125 alone maybe I could have got another 500 title. But if we had pulled it off, wow what a story! Remember I had made a decision not to do the GPs, so why not try and grab something a bit different? It didn't come off, but we tried and had a great time in the process. In the end I came away as the only rider to win all three championships.*

High-profile move

Wade's fifth and final British Championship win would come in 1974, when he retained his 125 title. By then he had made the switch to the Beamish Suzuki camp, a move that had attracted a lot of media attention with the four-time British Champion racing the World Championship winning marque. *Graham Beamish offered me basically the same deal I had had with Brian Leask and again I received wonderful back up. Graham was a very professional man, I had a tremendous amount of respect for him. He treated me like a superstar and on the Suzuki I thought we could still mix it at the top.*

This was certainly true on the little bike, where his performances were nothing short of sensational. Wade

In October 1974, Wade won Suzuki's first, and his last, British Championship, as he retained his 125 title in style at Beenham Park. (CB)

won the first four races of the series, though there was a notable absence of established stars competing in the second year of the 125 series, with Suzuki teammate Terry Dyer emerging as his early challenger before he got injured.

Champion for the fifth time

However, Wade tasted a rare defeat in the first race of round three at Wakes Colne in September, when he was pushed into 3rd by race winner Roger Harvey and Davis, who rode in selected rounds. However, from there on he reeled off three more race wins, with Graham Noyce, now at liberty to race a Maico following a protracted legal dispute with Husqvarna, pushing him for the wins at West Stow Heath, Suffolk in late September, where Wade retained his title with one round still to go.

At Beenham Park a fortnight later, he fell on the first lap of race one and fought his way back to 6th at the flag, with Davis taking the win ahead of Noyce. Then, just to prove that he really was the 125 'King', he won the final race beating Noyce and Bultaco's Les Lloyd. Over the season, he had won eight of the ten championship races, had finished in the points in every race and amassed 69 points, an enormous 45-point advantage over the runner-up, who tellingly, was Noyce.

Although Wade was dominant on the 125, he really struggled in the 250 Championship, where he failed to score a single point. At the final round at the Cleveland GN in his native Yorkshire in mid-July, *MCN*'s Brian Crichton noted that '*His* (Vic Allan's) *early challenger was Bryan Wade at last showing the aggressive form which has eluded him all season.*'

Waning motivation

His time at Suzuki wasn't as successful as it might have been, given that he was 28 years old and arguably should have been in his prime as a motocrosser. I remember watching him race during this period, and it seemed to me that although he could still get great starts, the spark seemed to be missing from his racing and all too frequently he'd slip back through the field.

The 400 Suzuki was never Wade's favourite ride. Here he is pictured at round one of the new British Championship at Matchams Park in March 1975. (CB)

Was he by now perhaps tiring of the scene? Yes, I think you're on the right track. I'd been at the sharp end for a while, been there, done that, got the t-shirt and yes, the stamina probably was on the decline, driven down by a number of things; fading interest, the big Suzuki wasn't an easy bike to ride, plus there were new guys coming through with more hunger: eventually it happens to us all. I still enjoyed the rush. But yes, things were starting to slow.

Wade would race in the Top 35 series until the end of the seventies, though he rarely troubled the top riders during that period. Having said that, he has a vivid memory of racing in the British Championship at Hawkstone Park, where he decided one of Graham Noyce's passing manouveurs was just too close for comfort. In the first race, after getting the start and leading for three laps, he was passed by Noyce when he was least expecting it, as he came down off the hill. He was forced out of the first race when he crashed at the top of the infamous hill, but boldly took to the line for race two. *I can remember it like it was yesterday. I led again, and the same scenario panned out, though this time Noyce passed me on the fast jump on the straight. I wasn't going slowly at this point, but Graham was alongside me with his footrest at the same level as my head. The thought that went through my mind this time, was that I'd had enough, the fight was not there anymore.*

However, as you've probably ascertained by now, Wade is an eternal optimist and a new venture in his life would prove to be very rewarding as his riding career began to wind down.

Discovery in the face of a new challenge

In the mid-70s Bryan Wade started his 'Train with Wade' riding schools which turned out to be more successful than he could ever have imagined. *To my surprise, I found I could teach. I could take the whole racing thing apart and I knew what the guy's were going through. In its way, it gave me as much pleasure as winning my five championships. We had some schoolboys that went on to great things, such as Dave Watson and Rob Andrews* (Both went on to be stars of the British Championships and were GP contenders). *I have to say, that if it hadn't been for Hawkstone Park and the amazing people at the Salop MC, who backed me 100% and gave me a tremendous amount of help, we wouldn't have been able to accomplish a fifth of what we did.*

After a brief spell on a Hewitt Maico, Wade saw out his racing days in 1979 on a KTM provided by Hereford dealer, Gordon Jones. Some 14 years after he had registered his first points in the British Championship whilst racing at the Lancashire GN at Cureden Park, Wade scored his last at Cadders Hill, Norfolk in August 1979, when he notched two 10th place finishes before bowing out of competition at the close of the 1979 season.

The Wild Man of Borneo

Today Bryan is working with motorcycles again. Once more, fate was to take a hand in proceedings, as whilst attending the F1 GP at Sepang, Malaysia, Wade met up with an old friend, Terry Mills, who invited him to spend time with him in Kota Kinabalu, Borneo. *He had a couple of bikes and we went out for a day's ride. It was a fantastic place for biking, great roads, no traffic, also amazing gravel trails that took you through the rainforest and I said, "People would pay to do this." and that was how it all started.*

Wade and Mills now run 'Borneo Biking Adventures'. Bryan takes groups of tourists out into the wilds of Borneo on 650 Aprilia Pegaso bikes and still manages to do a fair amount of off-road riding.

Life is good

Wade is incredibly enthusiastic about what he is now doing and told me that he is grateful that the road of life has taken yet another turn. This reminded me of the lyric in that old song the Hollies sang all those years ago:

> The road is long
> With many a winding turn
> That leads us to who knows where
> Who knows where

For Bryan it's taken him on what he refers to as a 'great adventure'. As he told me: *Fate is a fantastic thing, I love it. A charmed life I've led!*

Bryan Goss

From Grasstrack Hopeful to Scrambling Champion

Photo RD

Throughout his long career in motocross Bryan Goss was known to most of us as 'Badger', though for me the characteristics he possessed were more akin to those of a pedigree terrier. He was a prolific race winner and anyone who ever watched him race will remember him for his tenacious, doggedly determined riding style, which saw him fight all the way down to the chequered flag. Despite starting out in the late '50s, when big four-strokes still ruled the roost, Goss was a two-stroke specialist and after many years racing two-fifties, as very few others could, ironically his only British Championship came in the 500 Class in 1970, which he won as a privateer.

Bryan Goss was born in September 1940 and grew up in the small Dorset village of Yetminster, which by a happy coincidence was also home to the grasstrack great, Lew Coffin. Indeed it was thanks largely to Coffin's influence that Goss acquired his nickname as he explains. *I was always badgering Lew to let me have a ride on his bikes and one day one of the village lads called me 'Badger' and it just stuck after that.*

Coffin was to become Badger's mentor in the early days, taking an interest in the youngster and getting him started on the grass with a 197cc Villiers-powered special. Bryan flirted with grass tracking until an accident in his first season of racing left him with a broken leg. He was out for a year and by the time he was ready to make a comeback he had decided he wanted to try his hand at scrambling. *Lew wasn't very happy about it, but we stayed friends and he helped prepare my bikes.*

1958/60 **The switch to scrambling**

Badger's first appearances in local scrambles were on a 197cc Greeves in 1958 and following a few early successes, such as his win in the 350 race at Bulbarrow Hill, Dorest, 'Pops' Sharp, father of top West Country scramblers Triss and Bryan, put his own 250 Greeves at the disposal of the youngster.

However, Coffin was keen to see his young protégé get the support he felt he warranted and in late 1959 he took him along to the Bristol Road, Gloucester, premises of Cotton Motorcycles to meet the directors, Monty Denley and Pat Onions. Although neither had heard of Goss at the time, they made him a promise that if he proved to be worthy of their support, they'd back him 100%.

The Cotton years

Goss bought himself a 250 at cost price, taking to the Gloucester-built bike immediately and winning five races under difficult conditions at the Somerset GN. In the light of such success, the Cotton management proved true to their word and a factory bike was soon on its way to Dorset. They also gave him a job working in the factory, though that didn't quite pan out as expected. *I had to prepare my own bike and put the cam in wrong once. On race day it broke and so I rode a Dot for the day. When I got to the factory on Monday morning they gave me the sack! But I went back again after a bit and Fluff Brown prepared the bikes for me and did an excellent job.*

Goss enjoyed some good seasons on Cotton especially when racing against the big four-strokes in the all-comers races. As he told me, *In the South Western Centre, you had the Rickmans (Don and Derek), the Sharps, (Triss and Bryan) the Jarmans (Paul and Neil), Benny Crew and Len Sanders, all of them riding 500s and me on my 250.*

A youthful Bryan Goss poses with his trophies for the camera. (Photographer unknown)

1961

By March 1961 Badger and the Cotton were headline material in the *MCN*: 'WATCH THAT COTTON GO! Goss and Rickman star at Bulbarrow.' Ace photographer Gordon Francis, who also wrote the report, had this to say about Goss. *'Leaping, sliding and forcing the Cotton along at an incredible speed he outpaced all of the star-studded entry with the exception of Don Rickman and his Métisse'.* Goss beat Triss Sharp on a factory Greeves and Dave Wootten, also on a Cotton, to take the 250 race and fended off John Clayton on a 500 AJS before chasing Rickman home in the eight-lap Premier Riders race.

In May of that season, Tirley, Gloucestershire was the scene for Goss' first win in the 250 ACU Star competition. In a closely disputed race he beat Arthur Lampkin, who would go on to take the ACU Star that season. *As Lampkin came down the hill, I was going up the other side and I thought he was going to catch me. But I pushed on a bit and everything worked out.* The win was a timely one, as he took victory under the watchful eye of Cotton's top brass, who must have been suitably impressed.

The move to Greeves

1962

However, by the time the 1962 season kicked off, speculation was rife about who the young truck driver from the West Country would be racing for. In February, he was unbeaten at the Somerton MCC's meeting at Stoford racing a Cotton, but within a few weeks he was out on a factory Greeves following what for him was a dream move. *It was everyone's ambition to*

20 year-old Goss flies the factory Cotton downhill at Tirley in 1961. (BC)

ride for Greeves, it was the cream at that time. I spoke to Derry Preston Cobb one day and told him that I'd like to ride for Greeves. To Goss' surprise, Preston Cobb expressed an interest in helping him and a short time later they met up in Southampton, where he was offered a £25 retainer to ride for Greeves that season. *That was the happiest day of my life and from that day on I rode my heart out for that man, Derry Preston Cobb.*

Goss still holds Preston Cobb in great esteem. *I loved that man. I went down to the factory one day and was greeted by Cobby. "Hello Badge. You're my favourite."* He said. Well, I had to get into his invalid car and go for a ride, and he went up to the top of this hill and down again in this thing with a tuned scrambles engine in it with Alpha big-end and all! He frightened me to death, but you daren't show it. He was a super man.*

At Chard in March, Goss was already repaying the trust his new bosses had shown him, winning four of the day's finals and to illustrate just how well he was riding at that time, at the Wessex Scramble at Glastonbury in April, he twice beat Arthur Lampkin, who was leading the 250 World Championship, taking both the 250 and 350 races.

Goss 'Badgers' Bickers

At Greeves, Badger went from strength to strength, soon becoming virtually invincible in the South of England, establishing himself as one of the top challengers to 250 'Kingpin', Dave Bickers, who when I interviewed him referred to Badger as being "a thorn in my side." Goss told me *That's one of the nicest things I've ever heard. He never would have admitted it at the time. We were friends off the track and used to travel together, but when we were on the start-line we were rivals, though through it all we always respected one another.* After so many years, he seemed genuinely touched by this and proud of the compliment his old friend and rival had paid him.

As Britain came grinding to a halt in the big freeze up of 1963, Goss was going about business as usual, showing well at the Beaulieu TV meeting, where he chased World Champion Torsten Hallman and Bickers home in the 250 race. Then at Larkstone, near Stratford upon Avon, he emerged victorious in three races during the two-day TV meeting in March, taking both 250 races before adding Sunday's Unlimited race.

ACU Star

As the season wore on, Goss would represent the main threat to Bickers' supremacy in the 250 ACU Star. At the Wessex Scramble at Glastonbury in April, he was in devastating form winning the Lightweight race and the 250 ACU Star race, albeit in the absence of Smith, Bickers and Lampkin. Goss took the Star race after beating off a spirited Chris Horsfield on the works James. Horsfield managed to get the James ahead of Goss' Greeves on the last lap, but after leading for almost the entire race, Goss wasn't about to roll over and in a thrilling finale, he fought back and repassed Horsfield to finish 25 yards clear at the flag.

More points followed in the ACU Star at the second round at Cuerden Park, where he consolidated his lead in the competition with 2nd to surprise man of the meeting, Yorkshireman Norman Crooks on his Dot. However, the race was more a war of attrition than a great spectacle of off-road racing, as Bickers, Joe Johnson, Pat Lamper and John Griffiths were all sidelined and Goss must have been more than happy just to head home with another six points in the bag.

Out of luck

After the Lancashire round, Goss had 14 points, whilst Bickers had yet to open his account. However, from there on the Coddenham Flyer took control, scoring three straight wins and notching 24 points. But had it not been for some seriously bad luck Goss may well have been crowned British Champion in 1963.

Due to injury he was unfortunate enough to miss the penultimate round at Shrubland Park on August Bank Holiday Monday through injury, where Bickers and the Husky prevailed. Then, after making the long trip from Dorset to the North Yorkshire moors for the final round at Boltby in October, Goss picked up a puncture on the opening lap of the Star race and could not continue. In contrast, Bickers, who had led Goss by a single point going into the last round, dominated the race to win comfortably from John Griffiths and Alan Clough to secure his third ACU Driver's Star, though Goss still captured the runner-up spot.

Although disappointed with the outcome in the ACU Star contest, Goss' season wasn't over yet and he hit a rich vein of form in the inaugural BBC Grandstand Trophy series. He finished as runner-up to the seemingly invincible Bickers-Husqvarna combination at Beeston, Winchester and Newport, which moved him up to second place in the points reckoning. He also finished as runner-up at Naish Hill in the last televised meeting of '63, though this time to Arthur Lampkin, following a rare slip from Bickers in the tricky conditions. At this

Doing the winning in the two-day TV meeting at Larkstone near Stratford-on-Avon in March 1963. (MC)

juncture Goss was lying 2nd in the Grandstand Trophy which would continue into 1964.

TV capers

Though perhaps not as well remembered as Smith, Lampkin and Bickers were for their TV exploits, Badger always put a lot of effort into the TV races. *The only good thing about them was that you knew they didn't restart them! I was down at Hankom Bottom (Winchester) one day and I looked across and Bickers was away. He was watching the TV guy giving the starter the go-ahead, and he was gone! So after that I did the same.*

Goss had a disappointing start to the 1964 season and the Grandstand Trophy series. After missing the Tweseldown round and finishing out of the points at Clifton, Alan Clough edged past him into 2nd place in the series and a 4th place at Builth Wells behind Bickers, Clough and Smith saw him slip further behind.

However he bounced back at Wakefield in early February, despite spending the previous night in his car. Though hardly the ideal preparation for a big race, it didn't seem to hinder his form too much, as he raced to his first big win of the year, putting one over Arthur Lampkin in his native Yorkshire in the process. It is interesting to note that Badger achieved some success on the ill-fated Starmaker-engined 24ME, winning at Wakefield and leading the field for two laps at the final round at Cuerden Park, before bowing to teammates Bickers, who had returned to the fold after his sojourn on the Husqvarna, and Clough, on their new Challenger models.

Goss fondly remembers the affect that those televised scrambles had on the people in his village. *At that time I had a 'wolf whistle' on my truck, and when I got home on a Saturday night I'd see all the lights on because a lot of the villagers would wait to hear my whistle*

Typical of the duels that took place across the country in the late '50s and early '60s, Privateer Jim Holt (500 Maverick, left) leaps side-by-side with Goss on the factory Greeves at Hadleigh, Essex in June 1963. (MR)

Goss never gave anything less than 100% when he rode. Here he is captured racing the much maligned ME Greeves in the Kiwi Scramble at Tidworth, Hants on Easter Sunday 1964. (CB)

to announce that I was safely home. It was wonderful. On a Sunday if I was walking through the village, people would come up and shake my hand and pat me on the back and say "Well done Badger."

1964 certainly wasn't Goss' best season in the ACU Star competition, as he failed to mount any challenge to Bickers, though mechanical and electrical problems severely hampered him along the way. At the final round at Farleigh Castle in October, for example, he got a great start in the Star race and chased Bickers for more than half the race, only to be eliminated by a whiskered plug.

Doing the business

However, he may also, to borrow a footballing metaphor, have taken one eye off the ball, as he opened his first shop in Yeovil that year, with Derry Preston Cobb travelling down from Essex to perform the traditional cutting of the tape in the opening ceremony.

However, he was in good form when the 250 World Championship came to Cadwell Park, Lincolnshire in July. In the first race he chased home World Champion Torsten Hallman on the Husqvarna to finish 4th and only lost out to Greeves teammate Malcolm Davis, for the final podium place on overall time, after finishing a weary 6th in the second race.

Badger did find some form as the season drew to a close, outsprinting Jeff Smith to take 2nd behind Alan Clough in the Grandstand Trophy at Hatherton Hall, Nantwich, in November and splitting Bickers and Smith at his local round at Leighton. Then he went one better at Caerleon, South Wales, where he finally got the better of Bickers. With his confidence returning, Goss sprinted away from the rest of the field while Bickers had to battle his way through on a borrowed bike, after his own had seized up in practice.

1965

Seduced by a beautiful Swede

Having struggled to find his form for most of the previous season, Goss took control of his own destiny in 1965, relinquishing his works Greeves and buying himself a 250 Husqvarna from Jeff Smith, though it was a decision he didn't take lightly. *I had some great times at Greeves, I used to take the bikes down there and I'd arrive early in the morning and walk around the factory while they were stripping my bikes down. You'd go round the back and there'd be an old boy in the foundry. He'd have a pot of hot aluminium and he'd pour it out and make 10 cylinders for the day. Wonderful!*

When I first went there, Greeves were the best bikes and over the years they had the pick of the riders. Bickers. Clough, Browning, Davis, even Joel Robert! You had to be on them. Anyway one day I was up at the BSA factory, I was friendly with Jeff and used to go up there from time to time, and he had just bought himself a couple of Huskies. (See p55) Well when I saw the bike I knew I had to have it even though he wanted a lot of money for it.

His first big test on the Swedish lightweight came at the Hants GN in April, in the first round of the ACU Star contest. Bickers, who always went well at the Hants, stormed away at the start followed by Don Rickman on the Bultaco Métisse and Goss. Goss clung on to Rickman and when the local man slid off Goss moved up to 2nd place, which he held to the flag. At this time, having only had the Husqvarna for a few weeks

In November 1964, Goss is pictured on an early Challenger at the BBC Grandstand meeting at Leighton, Somerset. (CB)

In his first season on the Swedish Husqvarna, Goss is captured by the lens of Cecil Bailey, racing at one of his favourite tracks; Bulbarrow Hill, in his native Dorset.

Goss' name was being linked with a move to Bultaco, curiously enough in a deal with the Rickmans.

The following week saw the country's leading quarter-litre exponents heading to Elsworth, Cambridgeshire, for round two of the ACU Star. Goss showed his grit and determination battling back to finish 5th, behind a Greeves quartet of Bickers, Clough, Griffiths and Mayes, after a couple of tumbles had dropped him well down the field.

Prolific winners

The Goss-Husky combination was soon a winning one, especially in the South and South West of the country and Badger was soon recouping his outlay. At the Maybug Scramble at Farleigh Castle, he was just too fast for Don Rickman on the Bultaco Métisse, beating him by 20 seconds. At this time, the deal with the Rickmans still hadn't gone through and maybe it was this encounter that persuaded him to stick with what he had, especially as he was now receiving some help with parts from the Swedish concern.

Goss was obviously enjoying his racing at this time, travelling north to Kineveton in mid-June, to compete in an evening meeting where a win and two 2nd places saw him take the Derbyshire Motocross ahead of Bickers and the consistent Triumph factory runner, Roy Peplow. The following day he was racing closer to home at the Bridport Club's meeting at Chilcombe Hill, where although a little jaded from his long drive, he was still too good for the opposition winning the 250, Lightweight and Dorset GN races.

And the wins just kept on coming. *'MASSACRE AT BOLTBY!'* read the headline in the *MCN* following the North v South team contest in August, where Badger was in devastating form, winning three of the team races. Then at the prestigious Experts GN meeting at Larkstone, Warwickshire, he won his first 250 ACU Star race on a Husky, finishing some 34 seconds ahead of Dave Bickers, before repeating the performance to take the overall in the 250 Motocross. Goss was really enjoying his day out in the Cotswolds and set a diabolical pace in both races, notching up a race time that was some 10 seconds faster than Bickers winning time in the first 500 race on the new 360cc Greeves.

Unfortunately, bad luck prevented Goss from ending the ACU Star contest on a winning note at the final round at Cuerden Park in August. He was leading Clough by 20 seconds when a sheared fixing key on the magneto brought his race to a premature end on the 13th lap of 18. However, he still out-pointed race winner Clough to finish as runner-up to five-time winner Bickers and his form in the last two rounds suggested that he was now a good match for Bickers.

A psychological edge

Once on the Husky Goss finally seemed to have the confidence and the belief that he could beat Bickers. *There was something about Bickers, he was so dedicated and he always had the best. I beat him a few times on the Greeves too, but it was harder then. But the Husky was lighter and handled better and when I got it, I felt I had the legs on him. He knew I could beat him, and I knew I could beat him and a lot of it was just psychological then.*

His performance in the TV meeting at Farleigh Castle at the end of October serves as a good indication of this new-found self-belief. Goss really had the measure of his long-term rival, Bickers, winning the 250 race from the Greeves of Bickers, Browning and Mayes and being first 250 home in the TV Invitation. Indeed the only riders to get the better of him all day were Andy Lee on a very potent Matchless Métisse and, the then 500 World Champion, Jeff Smith.

Lured back to Greeves

Given his success on the Husvarna, Goss' next move confounded many in the sport, as he re-signed to Greeves. With Bickers being linked with a move to CZ, Greeves were probably keen to find a replacement and Goss readily admits that the Husky didn't always suit him. *I didn't like it on muddy rutted circuits and I'd tried Bickers' bike at Swanley and I really liked it. Money had a lot to do with it too, as I'd spent £500 on the Husky, which was a lot of money in those days.* So December 1965 found Goss back on the Essex-built machines and despite having to give second best to Chris Horsfield, who was now campaigning a 250 CZ, he must have been thrilled to beat Dave Bickers in one of his last rides for Greeves in front of the TV cameras at Belmont near Durham.

The 1966 season got underway with TV drama at Nantwich, as the BBC cameras caught Badger re-signing to Greeves between races, when Competition Chief Bill Brooker, presented him with a contract. Looking on this with cynical hindsight, one might conclude that this was a well-timed piece of theatrics, probably dreamt up by Greeves' Derry Preston Cobb,

1966

to show the nation that although they had lost the services of Bickers they had lured Goss back to the fold and that everything was hunky-dory.

He soon hit peak form in the Grandstand TV series, winning back-to-back rounds at Jewell's Hill, Kent, in truly atrocious conditions in February and then closer to home at Leighton, Somerset, later the same month. Goss prevailed over teammate Mayes and Jerry Scott, who was racing a 250 Cheney BSA, after Bickers had taken an early exit when his new CZ shipped its chain. The series culminated at Brill, Buckinghamshire a week later, when TV viewers watched Bickers clinch his third straight Grandstand Trophy, winning the 250 race after a great dice with fellow CZ man, Horsfield. Goss finished 3rd in the race for 4th in the series, behind Bickers, Horsfield and Clough, who edged him out by just a single point. However, he made amends in the TV Invitaion, thrilling the TV punters as he withstood the pressure of Scott and Smith to take a fine win.

Temporarily sidelined

However, fate dealt Goss a cruel blow, when on the eve of the Spanish 250 GP in mid-March, racing just a few miles from his home at a Yeo Vale Club meeting, he crashed heavily breaking a collarbone. When he returned to action he had also returned to Husqvarna and at Witham Park Farm near Frome in late June, he proved too fast for Bultaco mounted Malcolm Davis and ex-Greeves teammate, Clough, winning both legs of the 250 Motocross, before taking on and beating the

Back on a Greeves, Goss cleans up at the Len Heath Trophy Scramble at Tweseldown in February 1966. (CB)

Larking around with Dave Bickers in the paddock at Leighton in March 1966. (RD)

500 Motocross winner, Don Rickman on his Triumph Métisse, to confirm his status as man of the meeting.

1966 and all that!

This was the start of a real 'purple patch' for Goss over the summer of '66, when, like the England football team, he did his share of collecting silverware. At Wakes Colne in July, he was on top of his game being one of only two men to better Dave Bickers, who was also enjoying some of the best form of his career, the other being Vic Eastwood. In the 250 British Championship round, Goss led Bickers for seven laps until a broken rear shock absorber ruled him out. But a win in the second leg of the 250 K&L Cup redressed the balance and he wrapped things up with a morale boosting win over Eastwood and Bickers in the Barn Garage Trophy.

Then in August, the Staffordshire Motocross caught him in winning mood. On the day Goss and his Husky were just too good for the Greeves of factory riders Browning, Mayes and Wade, the CZ of Horsfield and the works BSA of John Banks, as he took all three legs of the main event and the All-comers race, and all this achieved on a two-fifty.

Conditions for racing at Herringfleet Hills, near Lowestoft, in September may have been stormy, but the month started brightly for Badger, as he won the St. Nicholas' GN from local man John Banks and Arthur Browning and collected his trophy from Britain's oldest woman, 107 year-old Ada Rowe. And from there on things just got better, as a week later at Brands Hatch, he recorded what was undoubtedly the biggest win of his career.

The weakest link?

Sunday September 11th 1966 marked Bryan Winston Goss' 26th birthday and by coincidence it was also the day that the Trophée des Nations team race came to the Kent circuit. However, things started badly for Goss when team manager Harold Taylor called a meeting on the eve of the event. *I'd been going well in practice and I was flabbergasted when he said. "Goss, you're the weak link of the team and I'm putting you on the second row." Well, I didn't sleep very well after that and when I went to the line*

Goss snatches the lead from his good friend Freddie Mayes, on his way to victory in the Staffordshire Moto Cross in August 1966. (RD)

the next day I rode right to the end of the second row, so I could get a good run at the first corner. I had nobody in front of me and I kept it flat out over the jump, did a nose dive, but found myself fourth round the first bend and then went into the lead and won it.

The circuit, which was fast, wide and grassy, was perfectly suited to Badger's riding style and, stung into action by Taylor's words, Goss soon passed Don Rickman for the lead and was never headed again all afternoon, racing to victory in both legs against the cream of Europe's 250 racers. In the first leg he came home 12 seconds ahead of two-time European Champion Bickers and two-time World Champion Torsten Hallman, whilst second time out the winning margin was a massive 23 seconds over 1964 World Champion Joel Robert, with Hallman third again.

Where do you go from totally dominating the world's best quarter–litre motocross riders? Well, Badger jumped in his car and drove to Wakes Colne for the Daily Express International Motocross, where he continued his winning ways. He was on the crest of a wave and crushed the opposition in the 250 Motocross, winning all three legs and leading for 38 of the 39 laps! Husqvarna factory rider Olle Petterson finished 2nd overall while local man Pete Smith, on a Bultaco Métisse, enjoyed one of the best results of his career taking the last step on the podium.

Too tough a call

The 1966 season caught Goss in arguably the best form of his life, though the accident, and resulting early season lay-off, meant that once again, he was unable to challenge for the top spot in the British Championship. That honour fell to close friend Freddie Mayes, but after missing the opening rounds at Nantwich and the Hants GN, Goss won two of the three remaining

A birthday Goss will never forget! On the day that he turned 26, he won both races at the Trophée des Nations meeting at Brands Hatch, Kent despite starting from the second row of the start line. (RD)

rounds, including a dramatic victory in the final race at Builth Wells (see pp95-96), to finish 4th in the series just one point adrift of Clough.

1967 held a lot of promise for Goss' and a clean sweep in muddy going at Steart Hill, Sparkford in Somerset in late February, over a field that featured Greeves works riders Browning, Wade and Davis and the Villiers-Métisse pairing of Mayes and Roberton, suggested it could be his best season yet,

TV Drama

The following week, Goss and Bickers put on a fantastic show in front of the BBC cameras at Hankom Bottom. They went at it hammer and tongs in the 250 race with Bickers leading for the first three laps until Goss hustled his way to the front. There he stayed until a missed gear allowed the 'Television King' back into the lead, which he stubbornly held on to until the flag. Then in the 750 race Goss wheeled out his new 360cc Husky and once again thrilled the armchair viewers in a spectacular and dramatic duel with his long term adversary. This time Goss was setting a diabolical pace and it was all Bickers could do just to stay with him. But then Badger's luck deserted him, when the petrol cap came off, soaking him from head to foot and although this didn't seem to deter him unduly, Bickers had now drawn alongside him and as they went into the last lap the unfortunate West Countryman slid off his Husky allowing Bickers to ride on unchallenged to the flag.

But although there were some great wins along the way, such as at Boltby in the North v South match race, where once again he dominated the racing, and wins in the 250 British Championship at the Cleveland GN meeting in July, where he outpaced Champion to be, Alan Clough and the final round at Cadwell Park in October, when nobody could get near him, Goss didn't live up to expectation in 1967.

As the season drew to a close, Goss was indulging in his own version of musical chairs. In October it was announced in the motor cycle press that he had signed to race for AJS, replacing Freddie Mayes, and at the Player's Winternational meeting at Horton Common, Dorset later that month, he scored a debut win in the 250 race. But, just two weeks later he had quit AJS and was back on a Husky at Canada Heights for the Grandstand Trophy, as Malcolm Davis and Wigan's Dick Clayton made their debuts on AJS.

The Coombes' Husqvarnas

After a long lay-off in 1968, when Davis would become 250 British Champion on the AJS, Goss bounced back in 1969 with a brace of Husqvarnas supplied by Bridport garage owner John Coombes and prepared by Triss Sharp, who like his father before him, had come to Badger's aid. *That man is unbelievable. If you could have seen his workshop, it was cleaner than most people's kitchens! Triss Sharp's my man. If he prepared your bike, you could guarantee it was right.*

With such confidence in his bikes, Goss soon demonstrated that he had lost none of his thirst for winning, as he dominated the racing at Tweseldown near Aldershot at the end of January, taking four races including the final round of the Tweseldown Championship. He

Locked in combat. Neither Dave Bickers (left) nor Goss gave any quarter in the 250 Trophy race at the BBC Grandstand meeting at Hankom Bottom in March 1967. (CB)

was simply too good for the likes of Greeves' factory rider Dick Clayton and leading CZ privateer Norman Messenger, though the market gardener from Clacton ran out winner of the winter championship.

Goss had mixed fortunes in the opening rounds of the 250 British Championship, winning race two at the opening round at Tilton, Leicestershire, in March after failing to finish in the opener. And it was a case of 'bad day at the office' at round two at Nantwich, Cheshire, when Goss left Hatherton Hall with no points to show for his long drive north.

In late April Goss switched his attention to the 500 British Championship, opening his account at round two at Wakes Colne, where he turned in a spirited performance finishing 2nd to the irrepressible John Banks in the first race and backing it up with a solid 3rd behind Banks and Alan Clough in race two.

Crowd pleaser

Given such form, arguably the best ride of Badger's season was ironically one in which he didn't appear on the list of winners. In the 250 British GP at Dodington Park at the end of June, Goss thrilled the spectators as he took an excellent 3rd in race one, beaten only by the works CZs of Sylvain Geboers and Jiri Stodulka. However, Lady Luck turned her back on Goss, when he was involved in a pile-up involving fellow Brits Clough and Roberton on the opening lap of race two and by the time he had returned to the racing he found himself running last. However, urged on by the partisan crowd, he was at his most determined, battling throughout the race to pull back to 11th at the flag and claim a magnificent 6th place overall.

Goss enjoyed a fruitful trip to Nympsfield in July for the Cotswold Scramble, where in addition to winning the Cotswold Trophy he took a win and a 5th place in the 250 British Championship races to climb to 3rd place in the general classification behind new leader Wade, and Clough, and was within striking distance with just one round to go.

Over enthusiastic

He went on to finish 3rd in the 250 British Championship, which went right down to the wire and was eventually won by Greeves' Bryan Wade. Goss finished 2nd to Malcolm Davis in race one, which meant that he went to the start line lying just a single point adrift of Davis and Wade. However, in his haste to make a good start, Badger overdid things running wide on a corner on the first lap, whilst pursuing Davis and Andy Roberton, and eventually finishing a lowly 6th.

After missing the 500 British Championship round at Beenham Park through injury, Goss returned for the final round at Builth Wells in mid-October, where he became the only man to beat John Banks in the championship all season, winning the final race to climb to 4th in the overall standings. However, earlier that same afternoon, he had been out of luck in the ninth race of the series, going out with a whiskered plug whilst comfortably leading the Bury St. Edmunds rider.

As an eventful season came to a close, there was little in the opening rounds of the Grandstand Trophy series to suggest Goss might challenge for a trophy. 5th place in the 250 race at the opening round at Naish Hill, was followed by 4th at Caerleon, in late December, as Arthur Browning and Jimmy Aird did the winning to round off the year.

Goss lifts TV Trophy watched by millions

However, 1970 would prove to be Goss' most successful season and armed with his John Coombes' Husqvarnas, he got off to a flying start, lifting his first major trophy when he clinched the 250 Grandstand series at Dodington Park in late March. However, it wasn't all plain-sailing, as Goss claimed just one 250 race, at Canada Heights in February, where he went on to complete a rare 250 -750 BBC double before adding the Invitation race for good measure. However, with

1970

They're at it again! With petrol spilling from his tank, Goss refuses to yield to the pressure from Bickers in the 500 Grandstand Trophy race at the Hankom Bottom meeting (BH)

Goss pushes on relentlessly in the second leg of the 1969 250 British GP at Dodington Park, where his efforts were rewarded with sixth overall. (BH)

2nd place finishes at Hadleigh, Essex and Leighton near Frome, he knew that a single point from the final round would make him Champion.

Although nearest rival Malcolm Davis won the final 250 race at Dodington from AJS teammate Roberton, 5th place was enough to win Goss the prestigious Grandstand trophy. He finished three points clear of Davis with Greeves' Arthur Browning 3rd. To cap another good day, he went on to win the invitation race in addition to the final 750 race which moved him up to 4th place in the final standings of the 750 Trophy, just a point adrift of Vic Allan.

After 12 years in the sport, Goss had finally won a major title and it is one that he's still very proud of today. *We had a surveyor come out to the house a few years ago and when he saw the name, he asked. "Do you know Badger Goss?" When I told him it was me, he said, "I used to watch you on telly." So I took him round the house, showed him my Grandstand trophy and he forgot all about surveying the house!*

Come in N° 46, your time is up!

Ironically, after so many seasons in the top three as a 250 rider, Badger's only British title came on a 500. This happened in what was to be his final season on Husqvarna, riding the Coombes-owned, Sharp-prepared bikes, and they were sharp! Bryan was in superb form that season and exuded a confidence that showed he had truly matured as a rider.

However, he made a 'false start' at the Cambridge GN at Elsworth, at the end of March, where the muddy going proved not to be to his liking. He crashed several times in the opening race and then pulled out of race two after ramming the back wheel of Vic Eastwood and left for Dorset with no points on the board.

But the main talking point following the opening round was the injury John Banks had picked up; BSA's Champion had torn ligaments in a knee and would be sidelined for most of the season. Ever the opportunist, Goss then shifted his attention to the 500 British Championship and, as a result, was the runaway victor, racking up double the points total of runner-up, Vic Allan.

Turning point

Goss had great form all year, and took fellow Husky riders Clough and Eastwood to the cleaners in the Senior race at the Wessex Scramble at Glastonbury in April. The following month he moved up a gear, dominating the second round of the 500 British Championship at Wakes Colne in May and winning both races. *Fred Mayes gave me a confidence boost at Halstead in 1970, when he told me. "You'll just push off and leave them tomorrow Badge." Which I did, and I went on to become British Champion.*

He won the first race easily from Clough and Hickman, though he didn't have it all his own way in race two. BSA's Dave Nicoll led at the start, but Goss soon caught and passed him whilst Allan, who had been sidelined in race one, stormed back to pressure Goss in the closing stages, though he couldn't get close enough to catch him. When the dust had settled there was a tantalising three-way tie for the championship lead between Goss and the BSA teamsters, Nicoll and Hickman.

Badger seized the momentum in round three, when he had another great day out, at the Cotswold Scramble. He took another impressive double in the British Championship races with AJS' Andy Roberton twice finishing as runner-up on his 370. In the first race, Goss was so dominant that he was lapping back markers after just four laps and eased away from Roberton at the front, whilst race two was a Goss benefit as he led from start to finish. Of his closest rivals, only Hickman added

Out front! A fantastic Ray Daniel study captures a determined Goss on his way to winning the Wessex Scramble in April 1970 ahead of Husqvarna teammates Alan Clough and Vic Eastwood.

The newly crowned British Champion is pictured racing in the Kidston Scramble at Builth Wells in October 1970. (RD)

points, but he finished the day 10 points adrift of Goss. He also retained the Cotswold Trophy when he passed the hapless Roberton on the final corner (see p227).

Rampant Goss is champ

Goss sealed the title at Tirley in late August, with the final round at Builth Wells still to come. Once again he dominated the meeting taking his tally of race wins to six. However, he had to endure several false starts in race one and as a result the Husky suffered with clutch slip throughout forcing him to make an impromptu clutch replacement between races. In the second race he stayed out of trouble by finishing well clear of the scrap for second between Clough and Davis, with the AJS man finally prevailing.

Wily Badger bags International win

With the championship done and dusted, Badger put on a great show at the Halstead International at Wakes Colne in September, which I was privileged enough to witness. In confident mood, he finished 2nd behind the 250 Suzuki of Sylvain Geboers in the first of three legs and turned the table in the second, when the Belgian fell on the first lap whilst trying to stay with the West Country ace. Then with victory in his grasp, he rode a cagey race in the final encounter finishing 3rd which was enough to edge out Geboers, whilst fellow West Countryman, Rob Taylor, finished an excellent 3rd overall.

In the final round of the 500 British Championship at Builth Wells in October, Goss started as the red-hot favourite, but nursing a sore shoulder, following a fall at the Inter-Centre meeting the previous weekend, he struggled to 3rd in race one and had to pull out of the second, whilst Husqvarna new recruit, Bryan Wade, tellingly recorded his first wins in the 500 Championship.

Surprise move

Often labelled as being 'unpredictable' in the past, Goss had found the consistency he'd previously been lacking, though as the 1971 season dawned Bryan Goss

1971

For the 1971 season Goss moved on to race for Maico. Here we have a nice shot of him launching the West German machine downhill in the 500 British Championship round at the Cotswold Scramble in July. (RD)

the man, was as unpredictable as ever. Having won two major trophies on the Swedish Husqvarna, he raised a few eyebrows when he announced his decision to ride for Maico in the coming season. But another of Badger's qualities was his ability to spot a good bike when he saw one. *People like Adolf Weil and Willi Bauer were going really well on them and they were damn good bikes. Back in the '60s, I'd desperately wanted to import Husky's, but I couldn't afford to at the time and I lost out to Leasky (Brian Leask). I could have kicked myself then, but really I'm glad I didn't get it, knowing what I went on to do with Maico.*

I remember watching Badger at Hadleigh, Essex at the traditional Bank Holiday Monday meeting in 1971. In his first season on Maicos, he was keen to prove that he was still a force to be reckoned with and he won both 250 races in style from former Greeves teamsters, Arthur Browning and John Pease. But the reigning 500 Champion didn't enjoy the same success on the big bike and remembers the meeting for an entirely different reason.

Shocking moment

After a poor start and a lowly 6th place in the first 750 race, Badger was keen to make amends in the second. However, things didn't turn out that way. Soon after the start, young Eastern Centre expert Ken Atkinson went down leaving Badger no way of avoiding him. *He came off right in front of me and all I could think about was what had happened to poor old Jerry Scott (Killed in a racing accident under similar circumstances). I saw him there on the ground and started to brake, but I knew that if I*

Always keen to promote the bikes he was selling, Goss racing the radially-finned Maico leads Bultaco mounted Malcolm Davis at Builth Wells in 1972. (RD)

braked hard it would put more pressure on his neck. So, I opened the bike up, but it was too late and I rode right over his neck. I stopped and rode back and I thought for sure he was dead.

Given the situation, Atkinson could be considered lucky, I suppose, escaping with just a dislocated shoulder. But Badger, who is a sensitive soul, was too upset by the incident to take to the line for the re-start and returned to the pits.

Come August and the 30 year-old Goss turned in a vintage performance on the 250 in the British GP at Dodington Park. He twice finished 7th, despite a lack of competition at this, the highest level, to finish as the best home rider taking 6th overall.

By 1972 Badger had some 14 years of top flight competition under his belt and felt ready to dedicate more time to building his business selling Maicos. He still rode as many of the 500 British Championship rounds as he could, his best finish being 3rd in the second race at Farleigh Castle in May, but he was also investing a lot of time and energy in his top runner Rob Taylor, who finished 4th in the championship.

Sound business ruse

He also used every opportunity he had to promote the West German marque and at the 250 GP at Dodington Park in August, in a calculated gamble stepped down to the support races. However, he ran out winner in three of these, bringing Maico some welcome publicity as he let the *MCN* reporter know: '*I've sold 164 Maicos already this year*'.

Over the winter months he also put on a good show for the armchair sport addicts, performing brilliantly in the ITV World of Sport meetings at Cadwell Park. Being a shrewd businessman he knew that if he got out there and got the Maicos some screen time, the orders would flood in come the spring, as they duly did.

One of his last big wins came in March 1974, when he retained the massive Patchquick Trophy in March and had his name etched on it for a record fourth time. He finished 2nd to Andy Roberton in the first race, but won an exciting second leg by capitalising on Roberton's bad luck when he clashed with a fallen rider and broke the sub-frame of his 460 Husky.

The Maico investment pays off

After establishing himself as Maico's leading rider in Britain, Goss became the official importer and remained so during the marque's 'Golden' period. After the pioneering efforts of Weil, riders such as Bauer, Ake Jonsson and Vic Eastwood rode them to great effect in the GP's and teenage stars Graham Noyce and Neil Hudson were both Maico mounted as they shot to world prominence. As a result, the popularity of the bikes just snowballed. *We sold over a thousand bikes a year, for three straight years. Everyone had (or wanted) a Maico back then. You could buy a standard bike, take it straight out of the crate and win on it. It was a beautiful machine.*

Reflections

Looking back over his career, Goss feels privileged to have been one of a band of riders who were lucky enough to compete in scrambling in Britain during its heyday. *We had some excellent riders in the South-Western Centre in those days and then you'd roll up at the nationals and TV meetings and they'd all be there, the Lampkins, Bickers, Smith and Clough and your stomach would just turn over. So every weekend you had a hard scramble, and they were hard!*

He also got to do his fair share of travelling in Europe and still holds fond memories of those adventures. *I once raced in Leningrad in front of a crowd they said was 200,000! We practised on the Friday and Saturday and people camped out there all weekend in an area three times the size of Glastonbury. That was an education!*

A West Country boy at heart

But despite such experiences, one gets the impression that he was never happier than when he was racing in his native West Country. *Even local meetings at Bulbarrow (Hill) drew between 8,000 and 12,000 people. In those days the crowds loved to see us dicing it up and they'd run from one side of the track to the other to see us charging up and down the hills. The atmosphere, you can't buy that and I lived through it all. Wonderful!*

It was wonderful and Badger was a wonderful rider. Anyone who was lucky enough to see him on top form, as he frequently was, would attest to that, but he is, and I'm sure he will remain to his dying day, also a real character, and the sport of motocross was all the richer for the contributions of Bryan 'Badger' Goss.

Andy Roberton

The Little Man with a Big Talent

Photo RD

Andy Roberton burst onto the motocross scene in a big way in the mid-60s making an instant, and what was to prove lasting, impact. In 1967, aged just 19, he was the best home rider in his very first Grand Prix at Wakes Colne, Essex, finishing 6th and scoring points into the bargain. This marked his arrival on the scene and for the next 14 years he was prominent in the British Championships and was one of Britain's best Grand Prix runners. His only British Championship win came in 1972, during his third spell on Swedish Husqvarna machinery, when he was arguably at his best. However, Andy, like a good wine, matured with age and during the late '70s was still a force to be reckoned with.

1965/6

Andy Roberton was born in the Welsh border town of Knighton, in March 1948, to a Welsh father and English mother and it was in the hills surrounding the small rural town that he rode his first motorcycle, a BSA Bantam, at the age of 12. However, he spent his formative years in Stroud, Gloucestershire, where he joined the local Stroud Valley MCC as a mad-keen 16 year-old.

His first race meeting was a closed to club event at nearby Morehouse Farm. This was a low-key affair and Andy rode his bike, a Triumph Tiger Cub that also doubled as his regular form of transport, to the event. Although not a resounding success he did well enough, finishing all of his races, but more importantly he had whet his appetite for the sport.

Making his presence felt

Though just 5' 4" tall, as a youth Andy was strong and possessed a lot of natural ability on the bike. His talent was obvious from the start of his career and once on a competitive machine, a 250cc Bultaco Métisse, he was soon making headway as *MCN* reporter Jack Parkin, who saw him race at the Longleat Motocross in June 1965, noted, describing his performance in the Junior Unlimited race as '*an outstanding victory*', adding that Roberton and his Bultaco were, '*head and shoulders above the big 500s*'.

Renowned two-stroke tuner Fluff Brown was also quick to spot Andy's potential and recalls the first time he encountered Roberton as a raw teenager. *I remember it was a very muddy meeting and this unknown lad just rode past all of us as if we were standing still. I knew there and then that he was going to be something special.*

Cotton factory ride

Following that first meeting, Fluff decided to sponsor the youngster on one of his own bikes, before the Cotton factory, where Brown was working at the time, stepped in and offered him a works ride. Andy was quick to demonstrate his potential riding at a higher level, beating

Racing the 250 Bultaco Metisse, a fresh faced Roberton competes in the Len Heath Trophy Scramble at Tweseldown in February 1966. (CB)

Later in 1966 Roberton is pictured racing the factory Cotton. (RD)

Greeves' Malcolm Davis to win the Whiteway Unlimited final at Cirencester in August 1966.

Then in October, he headed off to his native Wales for the Kidston Scramble at Builth Wells, where the stars of the day were gathered for a round of the 250 ACU Star. Although he didn't feature in the results in the Star race, his confidence was boosted when he finished 6th in the supporting 250 race, in company with winner Bryan Goss, Arthur Browning, Alan Clough, Chris Horsfield, and Ken Sedgley.

CZ investment

As the season wore on he was looking for a competitive edge and after trying Dave Bickers' CZ at a TV meeting, he decided to buy himself a 250 from the former European Champion. At the time CZs were in great demand and it didn't come cheap, so Andy set himself the ambitious target during the winter of 1966/67, of winning the Tweseldown Championship, with its £50 prize money, to try and recoup some of his investment.

As well as attracting the attention of the leading factories of the day, Roberton was also receiving the plaudits of the motorcycle press, including the venerable Ralph Venables, who, in a profile of the rising star, referred to him as being 'Cast in the Bickers mould'. A compliment indeed!

Andy rode consistently well that winter, sticking to his task and clinching the championship at Tweseldown in early February 1967, where the 18 year-old out-pointed Greeves' Roger Snoad. His moment of glory came in the Len Heath Trophy Race which served as the fourth round of the championship. Roberton got a great start and led for two laps until Greeves' young gun, Bryan Wade, who had won both of the 750 races on his 360, stormed through to the front. But Wade's luck ran out when he picked up a rear wheel puncture allowing Roberton to slip through and take the win, though the

Roberton makes his debut on the Métisse-framed Norton-Villiers at the BBC Grandstand meeting at Naish Hill in February 1967. (RD)

gritty Yorkshireman rode on to a hard-earned 2nd place finish. Roberton and Wade later became great friends and near neighbours following Wade's move south in search of more competitive racing.

Norton-Villiers deal

Roberton's performances on the CZ didn't go unnoticed and less than a week after clinching the Tweseldown Championship he was signed up by Norton-Villiers, who were developing a motocrosser and were looking for a second development rider, having already contracted Freddie Mayes who switched from Greeves following his British Championship success.

The project was led by former road-racer Peter Inchley, with assistance from Fluff Brown, and was based in Andover, Hampshire, where Andy had relocated. Inchley and Brown were experimenting with different frames in which to house the Mark 2 Starmaker engine and had bought a batch of 'Petite' Métisse frames from Rickman. Andy made his debut on the Métisse framed bike at Naish Hill, Wiltshire, in front of the BBC TV cameras, where he finished an excellent 4th place in his very first 250 Grandstand Trophy race.

Fluff Brown recalls that despite such a promising start, it wasn't to be a fairy tale relationship. *Andy didn't get on so well with the Métisse framed bike and he was disappointed with his results. So I built up a bike using the Y4 engine* (a development of the Starmaker that would go on to power the AJS Stormers of the late '60s and early '70s) *in a Cotton frame and he soon returned to his winning ways.*

Sensational GP debut

On the new Cotton-framed model Roberton was unlucky not to take his, and Norton-Villiers', first British Championship win at the Cotswold Scramble in June, where a shipped chain robbed him of a potential victory. However, at the 250 GP at Wakes Colne in

Roberton made a sensational GP debut when he took the Cotton-framed (and badged) Norton-Villiers to a magnificent 6th overall, and best home rider, at the British round of the World Championship at Wakes Colne in July 1967. (BH)

July, he was the surprise package as he emerged as the only Brit to get amongst the points, as Gavin Trippe reflecting on the poor showing by the home contingent observed in the MCN – 'The day was saved, however, by an outstanding ride in both legs by Villiers' young hope, Andy Roberton. Despite being nervous in this, his first big race, Andy scratched with the best to earn his first championship point for sixth place overall'.

In the first leg he fought through the field from a lowly 16th on lap one to take the flag just behind the vastly experienced Alan Clough in 8th place. Race two looked even more promising when he slotted into 4th place in the opening laps, behind a triumvirate of World Champions, Joel Robert, Torsten Hallman and Victor Arbekov. Unfortunately the pace and race distance finally took its toll and he slipped back to eventually finish in 7th place.

Czech mate

But, before the season was out Andy had returned to CZ and at the North v South match race at Boltby in August, he was in sensational form ending up as the day's second highest points scorer after finishing 5th, 2nd and 2nd again in his three races. He couldn't match the all-conquering Bryan Goss, but he outpointed more experienced riders in the form of Malcolm Davis, the Lampkin brothers, Mick Andrews and Bryan Wade and all this accomplished on a 250.

Indeed Roberton's improvement in form over the year was so marked that he gained selection to represent Britain for the first time, in the Trophée des Nations at Holice, Czechoslovakia, later that same month, joining Goss, Davis, Wade and Arthur Browning. In a new format, there were two qualifying heats and a final and although Goss won his qualifier, the British

During his second spell on CZ, Roberton hounds the newly crowned 250 British Champion, Alan Clough, at the Lincolnshire Grand National at Cadwell Park in October 1967. (RD)

team failed to perform to its ability in the final. Amidst all the excitement of his first ride as a team member, Roberton crashed heavily and suffered concussion. Talking to Peter Howdle in the *MCN* in August 1971, he recalled: *'It was only my second motocross abroad and I shot over this jump much too fast. I was lucky I didn't write myself off. I was just too young. What do you know when you're 18 or 19?'*

The Husqvarna link up

After starting the 1968 season on CZ, Andy was offered a ride with Husqvarna importer Brian Leask, making his debut in the Grandstand Trophy series at Naish Hill, Wiltshire, in February, where he took the 360 to 3rd place in the 750 race. This marked the beginning of a long, and largely successful, relationship for Roberton and Leask.

Roberton soon looked at home on the Husqvarna and after finishing level on points with Don Rickman in the opening round of the 250 British Championship at Penrith in April, Peter Howdle, writing in the *MCN* was prompted to tip the youngster as his favourite to take the championship.

Trouble in store

Andy had a very promising season on the Husqvarnas and might well have seriously challenged Malcolm Davis for the 250 British Championship had it not been for a moment of over indulgence at Carlton Bank, Yorkshire, mid-season. Point's leader Don Rickman had to withdraw from the meeting when his

A great action photo catches Roberton racing a Husqvarna in the 1968 Hants Grand International. (RD)

Brian Holder caught Roberton racing in the 500cc British Championship round at Wakes Colne in June 1968, above; and below, having one of his first rides in the BBC Grandstand series on the AJS at Clifton in December of the same year

wife was taken ill, opening the door to the youngster who was holding 2nd place in the standings at the time. However, he was forced to retire from race one when the magneto key sheared, though worse was to come. In race two, whilst pushing on hard, he took a heavy fall resulting in a broken collarbone which effectively ended his push for the title.

Although he was back for round four at Cuerden Park in August, the reliability of the little Husky was found wanting again, as the engine seized up in race two following a solid 3rd place finish in race one behind Davis and Greeves' Arthur Browning. However, the 5 points gained in Lancashire left him with an outside chance of snatching the title from new leader Malcolm Davis and Rickman at the final round at Nantwich, Cheshire in October.

However, that all went pear-shaped when his plug cap broke as he was chasing leader Alan Clough in race one. There was some consolation though, as he managed to finish 2nd to Clough in race two, to clinch 3rd place in the championship, just three points adrift of runner-up Rickman.

AJS step in

As a result of his strong showing over the season, Roberton was rewarded with a contract from AJS with immediate effect, meaning that he would have a winter of TV scrambling to become accustomed to the new bikes, before joining new 250 Champion Davis, in a twin pronged assault on the 250 British Championship and the 250 GPs in 1969.

The AJS had grown out of the Norton-Villiers project that Andy had been involved with back in 1967 and he made a promising return with 5th place in the non-televised invitation race at the opening round of the 1968/69 Grandstand Trophy series at Dodington Park and built on that a fortnight later, at Cadders Hill, Lyng, where he was in the points with 6th place in the 250 race.

Trying times

Roberton had two seasons on the AJS which resulted in some real highs and lows. Much was expected of Andy in 1969 though all too often the bike, which was still in a developmental phase, let him down. In that year's 250 British Championship he regularly struggled to get the bike home in both races, only really hitting his stride in the dramatic final round at Tirley, Glouctershire in late August. However, by that time Davis, who had experienced an especially torrid chain of events, had ironically been sacked by AJS. This left Andy as the factory's number one rider with support coming from recently contracted Jimmy Aird.

Despite a poor run of results in the British Championship, Roberton showed great form at the start of the GP season. Racing in just his third GP, he caused a sensation when he finished an unofficial 3rd overall at the opening round in Spain in April. Sadly the result didn't stand, as the lap scorers, who couldn't identify the riders who were caked in mud, relegated him to 6th overall. Andy recently explained to me that the meeting was run under blue skies, but the organisers had created two mud holes by watering the track to make the racing more interesting for the local dignitaries in the grandstand! In race one he battled through the field from a lowly 14th in the opening laps to a magnificent 4th at the flag, though the race officials eventually credited him with 5th. In the second encounter he once again showed his mettle coming back from 11th on the opening lap to finish 6th, before being officially demoted to 8th place.

Poor Andy must have had mixed feelings as he left the circuit at Sabbadell, naturally disappointed to have lost out on what he and AJS' Peter Inchley believed was a legitimate 3rd overall, but at the same time happy to have won points in the first GP of the year. However, he went on to score more points in the Swiss GP the following weekend, briefly led the world in the opening race in Holland and recorded his season's best result in Czechoslovakia, where he finished 4th overall behind Sylvain Geboers, home rider Karel Konecny and Olle Petterson to score 8 points.

Going out on a high

Roberton and AJS enjoyed their best spell as the season drew to a close, turning in their best performance of the championship at the dramatic final round at Tirley, Gloucestershire. Here he finished 4th in the first race and improved to 2nd behind new Champion Wade, in race two to finish 8th in a very closely contested championship.

Arguably his best performance of the year came on the 370 AJS though. At the penultimate round of the 500 British Championship at Beenham Park, Berkshire in October, Roberton turned many heads as he challenged the seemingly invincible, John Banks. In the first race, he actually caught and passed the BSA man

Out front! At Beenham Park in October 1969, Roberton stuns the British Champion, John Banks, as he moves into the lead in race one of the 500 British Championship, racing the 370 AJS. (BH)

and although Banks was strong enough to fight back to the front, Roberton chased him all the way to the flag. In race two he fought back from an average start to finish 4th just behind Wade, but passing Chris Horsfield, Clayton and Keith Hickman on the way.

Stateside trip

At the season's close, Roberton and Swede Bengt Arne Bonn travelled to the USA with Peter Inchley to promote the British marque by racing the 370s in the Inter-Am series. *We just did the West Coast meetings in California and Seattle, racing at Saddleback Park and Carlsbad and all those tracks and we got some quite good results considering the best of the Europeans were there.* Roberton did well in such celebrated company finishing 3rd, 4th and 5th from the five meetings he competed in.

For the 1970 season the AJS bikes were much improved and this was reflected in the results. Encouraged by Andy's showings on the 370, AJS had him contest the 500 British Championship in addition to supporting Malcolm Davis, who had returned to the team, in the 250s. He also had a busy GP schedule participating in rounds of both the 250 and 500 World Championships getting entries where he could, as he had failed to make the ACU's grading list for either category.

Promising form

As the season got underway he was in fine form, finishing 2nd overall behind the 500 World Champion, Bengt Aberg, in the muddy three-leg Lydden Motocross in Kent in March. After finishing 3rd in the opening leg and 4th in race two, he finished with a morale boosting win ahead of Aberg and Hickman.

Later in the month he showed that he could be a real threat in the 500 British Championship, when he finished 3rd in the opening race at Elsworth, behind BSA teammates John Banks and Dave Nicoll. In the 2nd race, despite battling throughout, he could only finish 7th, just outside the points.

His attentions then switched to the 250 British Championship at Nantwich in April, where he finished

2nd to Champion Wade in race one and 4th in race two behind veteran Jeff Smith, teammate Davis and Dick Clayton. At the close of the day's racing Roberton was lying second, three points adrift of Smith.

Roberton rockets to podium in Swiss GP

However, despite showing such promise on the domestic front, it was to be on the international scene that Andy made the biggest impact, sending out shockwaves in the motocross world when he took the unproven AJS to an unprecedented 3rd overall in the 500 Swiss GP at Payerne in April, arguably the best ride of his career. In a brilliant display of riding in the first leg, Roberton caught and challenged the man who would go on to become Champion, Aberg, though passing him was another matter entirely, as the AJS couldn't match the factory Husqvarna for speed and they finished in that order. Then he was involved in a first-lap crash in the second race and had to fight back from 25th place to eventually finish 8th to tie on points with second race winner Friedrichs, though Roberton got the nod for 3rd overall by virtue of a quicker aggregate time.

Then in a busy spell at the end of April, he took 8th place in race two at the 250 Belgian GP. He then switched to the 500s for the Dutch GP in May, where he set the fastest time in practice but crashed heavily whilst lying sixth in the first race, and had to pull out as he was feeling dizzy. He bravely went out for the second leg, but crashed again and decided to call it a day.

In the points

Back on the domestic front he showed a vast improvement over the previous season, as he scored freely in both championships. In the 250s he enjoyed a season long tussle with a rejuvenated Smith whilst in the 500 Class he was one of the few riders to challenge Bryan Goss, who was running amuck in John Banks' absence.

One of the highlights of the season came at the third round of the 500 Championship at Nympsfield, Gloucestershire in July, where the local man thrilled the crowd, as he took on championship leader Bryan Goss. Having twice finished runner-up to the popular West Countryman in the championship races, he was outmanoeuvred by Goss in the Cotswold Scramble with its £50 purse. The two were locked in combat, with Roberton holding a slender lead as they entered the last lap. With the crowd on their toes, both riders took the same line up the final hill and Roberton, expecting Goss to come around the outside, deliberately ran wide. But the older, more experienced rider had anticipated this, breaking hard and accelerating through on the inside as they exited the corner to win by a tyre's width.

As the championship season came to a close, he had a good day at Beenham Park, one of his happy hunting grounds, at the final round of the 250 British Championship, when he sealed 2nd in the final standings following a brace of second place finishes, albeit in the absence of rival Jeff Smith, who was racing in America. Unfortunately though, he failed to add to his points tally in the final round of the 500 British Championship at Builth Wells. With Goss the runaway winner, Roberton finished just seven points adrift of runner-up Vic Allan, but in 5th place for the championship.

A ride that typified the roller coaster element of his AJS career came in Sweden in September, where Andy was the best of the home riders in a disastrous Trophée des Nations at Knutsdorp. After finishing 2nd in his heat behind factory Suzuki factory runner Sylvain Geboers, his luck ran out in the final when his throttle cable broke when he was lying sixth.

BSA new boy

In 1971 BSA, who had been following Roberton's progress with interest, stepped in to sign Andy, who joined Grand Prix regulars John Banks, Jeff Smith, Keith Hickman, Dave Nicoll and fellow new signing Vic Allan.

As he got used to the power characteristics of the Small Heath four-stroke, so the results improved. In March he enjoyed a good fight at the Battle of Newbury which BSA dominated. He finished fifth in race one behind his teammates Banks, Allan, Hickman and Smith, who finished in that order. In race two Roberton and fellow new boy Allan fought it out with Bryan Wade on the big Husky, with Allan taking the verdict ahead of Roberton after Wade took a tumble. Sadly, Roberton was sidelined in race three, when his BSA ran out of sparks two laps from home.

British Championship success

A week later as the 500 British Championship kicked-off at Hawkstone Park, all eyes were on Allan who had emerged victorious at Newbury, but it was Roberton who sprang a surprise. He took a promising 5th in race one behind Banks, Wade, Allan and an in-form Alan Clarke from Sheffield on a 400 Husqvarna,

On the factory BSA in 1971, Roberton fights for the lead at the Battle of Newbury with teammate Vic Allan, whilst Husqvarna's Bryan Wade follows closely. (CB)

but in race two he was flying and caught teammate Banks when the Bury St. Edmunds man found himself with no rear brake. Roberton raced clear to victory, his first in the British Championships, oblivious of the drama unfolding behind him as Banks' BSA gave up the ghost and he had to push in to the line. Andy finished the day as runner-up to Banks, just two points adrift of the two-time British Champion.

One of Andy's most memorable days on the BSA came at the 500 British GP at Farleigh Castle in July, though sadly it would be his only GP on the Armoury Road bike. A brilliant performance earned him 6th overall, though he wasn't awarded the points as he was on the ACU's 250 grading list. In race one he held off three-time World Champion Paul Friedrichs until the closing laps, when he slipped back to 4th though he still found the energy to fight off a late charge from Belgium's Jaak Van Velthoven. In race two he found the pace a little too hot to handle, but rode to a well deserved 8th place in very good company.

BSA close Competition Department

The downside of all of this, of course, was that on the Monday after the GP, the entire BSA team received telegrams informing them that their services were no longer required. Roberton soon found a ride though. *BSA gave me the option of hanging on to my bikes until the end of the season, but as soon as Brian Leask* (of Husqvarna) *heard what had happened he rang up and offered me a ride.*

Roberton renewed his acquaintance with the Swedish bikes, racing them for the first time in three years at the third round of the 250 British Championship at Carlton Bank, Yorkshire, where it soon seemed as if he'd never been on anything else, as he racked up a brace of 3rd places in the championship races.

At the 500 British GP at Farleigh Castle in July 1971, Roberton turned in a brilliant performance racing to a magnificent 4th place in the first leg and finishing the day in 6th place overall. (RD)

At the Beenham Jackpot Scramble in October 1971, a startled Phil Neville is passed on either side by Roberton, now on a Husqvarna, (left) and Bryan Goss (Maico). (CB)

Roberton cedes to Banks

When the 500 British Championship resumed at Cuerden Park, Lancashire in August, John Banks also went to the startline on a Husqvarna, the difference being that Roberton lined up on a pretty much standard 400, whilst Banks was armed with the ex-Arne Kring factory bike. After leading Banks early on in race one, Roberton came home in 2nd to keep a slim hope of catching the East Anglian alive. However, in race two, it was Malcolm Davis who did the winning, whilst Roberton's title ambitions ended as his engine lost power mid-race and Banks secured his third 500 British Championship by finishing ahead of Wade.

The final round saw Wade and Roberton go head-to-head at Tirley, Gloucestershire, to decide who would finish runner-up to Banks and the local riders thrilled their fans with Davis, Wade and Roberton filling the first three places in race one. Then Wade shot to the front in race two, whilst Roberton, in his attempt to stay with his rival, out braked himself and fell. Despite fighting back from 10th to 4th behind Banks and Davis the damage had been done and Wade secured the runner-up spot by winning the race.

In the form of his life

Roberton, had many successful seasons, but he enjoyed a real 'purple patch' in 1972, when after concentrating his efforts on the 500 Championship the previous year, he had a real crack at both the 250 and 500 Championships enjoying a thrilling season-long battle with his friend, rival and frequent travelling companion, Bryan Wade.

Roberton kicked off his 250 Championship campaign in style, winning both races at the opening round at Nantwich in March, fighting back from an early crash in race one to finish ahead of Dick Clayton and Arthur

1972

Browning and then passing Malcolm Davis for the lead, as the Gloucester man was troubled with blurred vision in race two. In contrast, Wade hit a post in race one and lost his gear lever then struggled in race two and left Cheshire with just three points to his credit.

Following a disappointing start to his 500 campaign at Frome in mid-April, Roberton's season came alive over the May Bank Holiday weekend when he was in majestic form. At round two of the 500 Championship at the Maybug Scramble at Farleigh Castle, on the Sunday, Wade deposed early leader Goss in race one, whilst Roberton fought to make up places, eventually moving into 2nd place after 20 minutes. With the clock ticking down he closed in on Wade, though his rival still had something in reserve and was a comfortable winner at the flag. Next time out, however, Roberton seized control after passing fast-gating Goss and riding to a comfortable victory, whilst Wade could only finish 4th behind Banks and Goss.

Championship winning style

The following day the intrepid duo drove up to Southend for the 250 round at Hadleigh, where Roberton was in scintillating form winning both races and establishing himself as the favourite for the title. For the second consecutive round his closest challenger was not Wade, but comeback man Vic Allan who also moved into 2nd place in the championship as an under par Wade could only add a single point, despite finishing both races. Ironically though, Wade managed to take both legs of the 750 event and the Invitation race too.

There then followed a brief respite from the British Championships, as the focus switched to the British 500 GP, which once again was staged at Farleigh Castle. However, it was the usual suspects, Wade and Roberton, who proved to be Britain's best in the GP too, as they bettered the more experienced Eastwood and Banks. Wade raced to 6th in race two, one place ahead of Roberton, as they finished 7th and 8th overall.

A lot has been made in other publications of Britain's inability to produce top-flight GP riders during the late '60s and early '70s, but the efforts of Roberton and Wade can be put into perspective when you realise that they were on fairly standard Husqvarnas, whilst the riders they followed home in race two at Farleigh, Ake Jonsson (Maico), Jaak Van Velthoven (Yamaha), Roger De Coster (Suzuki), Adolf Weil (Maico) and Gerrit Wolsink (Husqvarna) were all racing full factory bikes. Not such a bad performance after all!

Wade closes in

After the excitement of the GP, it was on to Frome for the Rob Walker Scramble that hosted round four of the 250 Championship, where Wade closed to within 4 points of his rival with a win and a 3rd. Roberton suffered plug trouble in race one, before fighting back to finish 3rd, though once again he went out of race two with throttle cable problems, leading *MCN*s Peter Howdle to write: 'ROBERTON'S JINX LEAVES HIM IN DILEMMA'. The dilemma in question was whether to stay and try to wrap up the 250 British Championship, or to go to the USA to contest the Trans-AMA series. Roberton was obviously keen to experience the US series again, with far better start money and the chance to race against the world's top riders and was frustrated that the last round of the national championship would not be run until early October.

To consolidate his growing status as Britain's leading 250 star, Roberton was the best Brit in the 250 GP at Dodington Park in August, where he finished 6th overall. On a day that was unkind to British riders, Roberton gave the home fans something to cheer about, as he raced to 6th place in race one and finished 9th next time out behind Malcolm Davis and Sweden's Torlief Hansen.

Roberton is tops at Tirley

In contrast to the protracted 250 series, the 500 Championship reached its conclusion at Tirley in August, where Wade, with a seven point lead over John Banks and 15 over Roberton, was the clear favourite to lift the crown. But Roberton, who was never anything

Friends reunited! The author caught Roberton and Wade catching up on old times in the paddock at the North Devon Classic meeting at Combe Martin in August 2009.

less than 100% committed, turned in a tremendous display of riding to take both races and overhaul Banks for second place in the championship.

It was all the more remarkable given that he looped the Husqvarna on the first lap of race one, and fought back from last to first in a little over half an hour. In a dramatic race, Banks also had to fight back after being left on the line only to go out when the bike kept jumping out of gear. All of this left Wade sitting pretty behind his teammate, until he picked up a rear wheel puncture in the closing laps. Dick Clayton and Eastwood both passed him before the flag, but he held on to finish 4th, which was enough to clinch the championship. However, Roberton's work was not finished, and he took the last race of the championship by storm, whilst local hero Davis overpowered Banks and decided 2nd place in the championship in favour of Roberton.

Beenham or Bust

So, with one championship decided, Wade and Roberton travelled up to Beenham Park in early October for one final curtain call and while Wade was entertaining thoughts of doing the 250/500 double, for Roberton, who had passed up the opportunity to contest the Trans-AMA series in order to try to claim his first national title, the task ahead was simple; finish in front of Wade and the title would be his. However, Vic Allan, who had steadily improved all season, also believed that he still had a shot at his first British title, which guaranteed a very interesting day's racing.

A three-way battle developed in the first race with Davis leading Roberton and Allan, until he was forced to slow with breathing problems. Wade, who was having gear selection problems, never recovered from a poor start and could finish no higher than 4th. But to keep things interesting Allan eased past Roberton to take the win with Roberton taking a comfortable 2nd ahead of Davis.

Champion at last!

By finishing 2nd Roberton had an unassailable lead and was the new Champion. He finished his campaign with another 2nd behind Allan, whilst Wade slipped to 3rd in the race and also in the championship. In a long, tough season Roberton prevailed and was a worthy Champion. One might hypothesise that had he been supplied with superior throttle cables, he might well have been a double-Champion in 1972. However, he wasn't, but for many he was the man of the season and if British Championship wins are totted up, he shaded Wade with eight wins to seven and also accumulated more points from the two series; 93 to 86.

Roberton always gave 100% when he was selected to represent Britain. Here he forces on through the sand at the 1972 Motocross des Nations at Norg, Holland. (RD)

At the final round of the 1972 250 British Championship at Beenham Park in October, Roberton leads the man he deposed for the title, Malcolm Davis (Bultaco). (CB)

1973

It is often said that retaining a championship is always more difficult than winning it. That would appear to have been the situation for Roberton, as his 1973 season saw him struggle to get the results he was capable of.

Ironically, whilst racing in the USA as British Champion, Husqvarana asked him to go and live and race for them there. Even though he was quite keen on the idea it never materialised, but he did get a factory 250 on which to contest the 250 World Championship. Sadly, for Andy, though he now had the machinery, the form was missing.

Battling till the last lap

In the 250 British Championship he made a brave attempt to retain his title, only going down to Malcolm Davis in the final round at West Stow Heath in July. He found himself joint leader with Davis after round one at the Cumberland GN in April and was runner-up to the Bultaco man at Farleigh Castle in May, before winning round three at Tilton in late June. From there on the battle for the title was a straight contest between the two Gloucestershire residents.

Roberton closed to within three points after round four at Nether Silton on the North Yorkshire moors, but on the eve of the final round he was troubled by a stomach virus, which left him tired and far from his best. To make matters worse when race one got underway he crashed into Jimmy Aird which left him with a huge mountain to climb if he were to retain his title. However, he dug in and managed to claw himself up to third behind Davis, but just as he was challenging his rival for second place he fell in the deep sand and slipped back, eventually finishing a shattered 5th. Davis meanwhile, with a comfortable 2nd behind Wade, was the new Champ.

The deep sand of the West Stow Heath circuit proved to be the undoing of Roberton, as his hopes of retaining his title slipped away in the final round of the 1973 250 British Championship. (BH)

Feature race success

Curiously, it would appear that Andy had trouble finishing races in the 500 Championship, but found consolation in the feature races. He was out of luck at round four at Frome, in late July, when he failed to add to his points total, though he took the big race of the day, the Rob Walker Trophy, from Vic Allan and Suzuki youngster, Terry Dyer. Then in the final round at Wakes Colne in September, where he was forced to retire in race one he bounced back with 2nd behind Maico mounted Eastwood in the final race of the championship. Having finished 5th in the championship behind Banks, Wade, Eastwood and Bob Wright he continued the trend by taking the Essex GN ahead of Banks and Eastwood.

The GP season was very disappointing as he slumped to 23rd at the season's close, the highlight being a visit to Leningrad for the Russian GP, as he told Peter Howdle in the *MCN* in December, as he reflected on the season: *It was the first time I have been to Russia and the size of the crowd was unbelievable. I have never seen so many spectators.* Roberton finished a soilid 10th in race one, before winning a race-long duel with hard-riding home favourite Leonid Shinkarenko, to claim fifth place and six very deserving points.

Reliability issues

The 1974 season was Roberton's last on a Husqvarna and despite some good results he only scored in half of the races counting towards the 250 Championship

Andy Roberton

Roberton struggled on the 1974 factory Husqvarna, in what for him was a hugely disappointing season. (RD)

as the Swedish bike began to lose its competitive edge. Vic Allan was the runaway winner having the title sewn up at the Cotswold Scramble in late June, with one round still to go. Andy, who had finished 2nd to the new champ in race one, was well placed behind Kiwi, Ivan Miller in the second when the throttle jammed open sending Andy cart-wheeling down the track. He eventually finished the season in 4th behind a Bultaco trio of Allan, Davis and Miller, though had the Husky been more reliable, he might well have challenged Davis for the runner-up spot.

It was a similar story in the 500 Championship, with Andy's best day coming at Tilton in June, where he took 2nd place to Maico's Vic Eastwood in race one and followed that up with 3rd behind Banks and Allan next time out. Over the season, Allan was even more dominant than in the 250 Class, leaving Eastwood, Banks and Roberton to dispute the runner-up spot. This was decided at the final round at Tirley in August, where despite taking a double victory Banks lost out in a three way tie, which saw Eastwood pip him and Roberton demoted to 4th for the season.

Success in the new Championship

Andy raced on at the highest level for many years in the top 35 British Championship on three different machines. Having trailed three Bultaco riders home in the 1974 250 Championship, Roberton joined 1974 double-Champion Vic Allan and former 250 Champion Malcolm Davis on Bultaco for 1975 and as the new look championship got underway at Matcham's Park, in March, it was Roberton who left with the championship lead.

Andy jokes that, *I won the first round and the last and did nothing in-between*. Though not strictly true, Roberton did save his best till last winning the final round at West Stow Heath in late September. He raced his 360 Bultaco to 5th in the first race, then having ridden shot-gun for teammate Allan throughout the second race, he slipped by on the last lap to take victory and 5th place in the final standings.

1975

1975 started brightly for Roberton, when he won the opening round of the new style British Championship at Matchams Park, Ringwood in March. Here he leads fellow Bultaco rider Vic Allan, who would go on to win the Championship. (CB)

1976/7

The move to Montesa

In 1976 he signed to race Montesa for the UK importer Jim Sandiford, joining promising youngster Pete Mathia, on what were essentially production bikes, to contest the British Championship. Andy took quite a while to find his form on the Barcelona built bikes, but finished the championship in style, taking 20 points from the penultimate round at Beenham Park before, for the second season running, saving his best championship performance of the year till the last round. At Chalton, Hampshire, in October, he finished 6th in race one but improved to 2nd in the final race to earn himself the number seven plate for 1977.

Golden years

If 1976 had been a little disappointing for Roberton, 1977 was sensational. A factory Montesa supplied by Sandiford gave him a competitive edge and Andy considers it to be his best season ever.

His form improved dramatically on the factory bike, as he raced to 2nd overall in the British Championship, beaten only by Maico king-pin, Graham Noyce. He rode consistently well all season, but emerged as winner of round three at Kilmartin, Scotland, by virtue of a second race win after he and Noyce had finished with a win and a 3rd place apiece. Andy continued to add points and eventually secured second place in the championship at the final round at Chalton, in late October. Although Roberton could only add six points to his tally from 5th in the first race, his main rival, Neil Hudson, endured an even worse day, with only 7th in race two to show for his efforts.

However, Andy's season wasn't just about the British Championship and at Farleigh Castle in early

Andy Roberton

July, like so many times before, he ran out as the Best Brit overall with two solid performances seeing him finish 5th and 7th, though sadly there were no points available, as once again he was a listed 250 GP rider.

Further testament to Andy's form in 1977 came in his selection for both the Trophée and Motocross des Nations teams where Britain finished 3rd in both events, with Andy playing his part by finishing in both events and scoring valuable points.

He maintained his form the following season when he finished a magnificent 3rd in the championship behind the young lions of British motocross, Graham Noyce and Neil Hudson. He opened with 2nd overall to Hudson at Stepaside, South Wales with two hard earned 2nd places. Hudson, who went on to become 250 World Champion in 1981 paid Roberton a fine tribute when he told me. "I'd go away and win 250 GPs, then I'd come home and Andy Roberton would take me apart in the British Championship."

Yamaha snap up Andy

As his career at top level began to wind down, Andy was signed to race Yamaha for the importers, Mitsui, in the 1979 season. However, on what was essentially a production bike, he struggled to be competitive, the highpoint of his British Championship coming at the second round at Asham Woods, Frome, in April, where he finished 3rd overall behind Noyce and Maico's Vaughan Semmens. In a largely disappointing season, he went on to finish 14th in the series.

In stark contrast to the previous season, at 32 years old, 1980 was a huge success for Roberton. The season didn't begin brilliantly, though he was regularly getting in the points. But with top runners Noyce, Hudson and Dave Thorpe all sidelined over the course of the season, he finished runner-up to Maico mounted East Anglian, Geoff Mayes, racing a factory 465cc Yamaha, courtesy of Neil Hudson. Hudson was at the centre of a protracted contract wrangle between Maico and

1979/80

Roberton had some great years racing Montesas for importer Jim Sandiford. Here he is pictured racing the 360 at Brighton in September 1977. (BH)

Yamaha and when the courts found in favour of the West German factory, Andy was offered his GP bikes.

The highpoint of Roberton's season came at round four at Howe Hills, Northallerton, in July, where he blew away all the young guns, including Paul Hunt, Dave Watson, Steve Beamish and Mayes, winning both races in style and prompting *MCN* reporter Paul Fowler to declare: '*WELSH WIZARD ROBERTON WEAVES A SPELL!*'

Still winning today!

Although he quit championship level racing in the early '80s, Andy has remained very active over the years, featuring prominently in Pre-65 racing for many years and today he is one of the leading riders in the British Classic Scramble Championship, having been Champion in 2007 and 2008 and only missing out on a hat-trick of wins in 2009 by a few points.

It's ironic to me though that his success should come on a Cheney BSA, as the renowned frame-builder Eric Cheney had desperately wanted to sign Andy to race his machines in the GPs following John Banks' move to CCM. As he told Peter Howdle in February 1974. "If I can get Andy, I'll make him a Champion in six months. Andy is the only other rider I regard as a potential Grand Prix winner."

British four-stroke fans can only speculate as to what might have happened if Cheney had managed to coax him away from Husqvarna, but anybody who has seen Andy ride the Cheney BSA today, can be in little doubt that he would have given it 100% and would have been a formidable GP runner.

Roberton is still a force to be reckoned with today, as one of the leading lights in the classic scrambles scene. He is pictured racing a Cheney BSA at the North Devon Classic meeting in August 2009. (IB)

Vic Allan

The Highlander Who Rewrote History

Photo RD

A quick look in the record books would show Vic Allan to be one of the most successful riders in the British Championships. He wrote his name there with his unique double 250-500cc success in 1974, followed by victory in the new-look Top 35 Championship a year later. But record books never tell the whole story and throughout his long career Vic experienced some real highs and lows. But through it all he never lost sight of his goals and after each setback he always seemed to bounce back stronger than ever.

Vic Allan was born in 1945 and grew up in the small Aberdeenshire village of Garlogie, where his parents ran a pub which had about 15 acres of land with it. The pub also had a football team and it was on the football field, in company with brother Robbie, the older of the two by four years, that he learnt to ride a motor cycle. *I started riding when I was nine on a 1913 Levis and Robbie used to push me hard. Later on he had a rigid DMW and we'd go out to a scrambles track and ride across ditches and whatever and I'd fall off all over the place. It was hard going, but by the time I was 12 or 13 I was starting to go pretty quick.*

Racing at 14

Vic's first competition came when he was just 14 years old. *A neighbour, Gordon Morrison, had entered to ride in a meeting at Tain* (in the north of Scotland), *but couldn't make it. So I rode under his name and with his licence. I think I finished 4th, but there were only about eight riding and one guy complained that I'd been riding too fast!* It was a fairly inauspicious beginning, but the young Scot had been launched into what would ultimately be a very successful career in scrambling.

However, next time out, by then all of 15, Vic managed to break a leg. After such a setback many youngsters would have been put off racing for life. But Vic was made of tougher stuff and was raring to go again the following season, by which time he was legal and above board!

Racing on a regular basis in Scotland required a lot of commitment. *Robbie and I would go to meetings together and for us, up in Aberdeen, we'd sometimes have to go 200 miles to a meeting using old vans with trailers or pick ups. They were amazing days really, great fun and never a hassle never an effort, 'cause you just wanted to do it.*

Success north of the border

Growing up in a small village, playing football for the pub side, Vic had grown into a fit, robust teenager. Five feet six inches tall and 12 stone in his prime, he had plenty of natural strength and stamina. On the racetracks he made rapid progress soon establishing himself as one of the leading contenders for the Scottish Championships. As an 18 year-old, he narrowly missed out on success, but made amends the following year, 1964, by taking the 250 title riding a Dot and the 500 class on an ex-Bill Gwynne Matchless Métisse. It was all change in 1965, as he repeated the feat, though this time using a Greeves and a Triumph Métisse, thus firmly establishing himself as Scotland's top scrambler.

Grand Prix baptism

He also got his first taste of Grand Prix racing that summer, when he made the long trip south for the 250 British GP at Glastonbury, which turned out to be quite an adventure. *There was great excitement, I was a Grand Prix rider off to do a GP and we left Scotland with six of us in a van. We stopped off at the Dot factory so they could do some work on the bike and went on into Blackpool, to make a bit of a holiday of it. When we eventually got to Glastonbury, I started talking to the guy on the gate and he turns to his mate and says, "I think the Russians have arrived." It was magic!*

When he eventually made it to the start line, Vic turned in an encouraging performance in the first leg. *I remember riding round on the last lap, I'd been lapped and I had no idea of where I was, or how I was doing. But I turned around and saw a Union Jack and I thought I'd better pull over and let the rider past. Well, when I finished they said, "That was Freddie Mayes and he only passed you on the last lap!"*

By the mid-60s, Vic had a wife and young family to support and faced the difficult decision of staying put in Scotland or heading south in search of fame and fortune. Reflecting on his dilemma in an interview with *MCN* in 1969, Vic said, *I knew that if I wanted to do anything at all in scrambling, I had to move south. In Aberdeen, I couldn't hope to get to all the big British meetings, London was about 500 miles away for instance.*

Scottish raiding party

On the back of his Scottish Championship form, Vic was growing in confidence and in April 1966 he ventured south for a morale boosting victory in the Cumberland GN, where he beat off Greeves works riders Bryan Wade and Arthur Browning. He also won an invitation race from Wade and finished 2nd in the Junior GN when the young Yorkshireman finally managed to turn the tables. *At that time Wadie was starting to crack on in the TV races and I had a fair old run with him and I knew then that I had a fair bit of pace and I wouldn't be disgraced down south. I've always been the type of person to make sure that I can make myself an under dog and not say, "Oh I can do this or that", but once I had got confidence in myself I felt that I had a good chance to do well, though I would never say that to anyone.*

Vic Allan

Allan flies the Comerfords Greeves at the 1967 250 British GP at Wakes Colne in July 1967. (BH)

This newfound confidence allied to the support of his brother Robbie, who had enjoyed a brief spell in the early '60s working at the Greeves factory and racing at weekends, galvanised Allan into making his decision.

Chancing his arm south of the border

So he moved the family south and with the help of fellow Scot, Jock Wilson, secured a job with Comerfords, London's leading off-road motorcycle dealers. It wasn't an easy time though and there was a lot of soul searching for the young migrant. Initially Vic worked in the comp shop under the tutelage of Reg May and raced a Comerfords Greeves at the weekends. *When I came down it was hard going. From dominating everything in Scotland, all of a sudden I was going to Centre races and not being able to win them. But Roy East, the Australian, was there and all the New Zealanders, Graeme Stapleton, Dave Burns and all those boys, and we were working together and riding together at weekends and it was just a good crack!*

Though Vic found it difficult adjusting, he never forgot his reasons for coming south and though at times lacking in self-belief, he was blessed with another attribute. *The one thing I can't explain, even today, is the determination I had, I would never give up, it didn't matter what I did, playing table-tennis or anything, I just had to win.*

His determination was allied to an overriding desire to jump on his bike, which served the young Scot well. *You were working during the week, so you couldn't practice then, not like riders today. But for me, come the weekend, the desire to ride was so strong, I couldn't wait to get on the bike to ride it on Sunday.*

Progressing nicely

Allan made steady progress throughout the 1967 season, getting in the points in the final round of the BBC Grandstand series at Builth Wells in March and being placed in national meetings at Hawkstone Park, Bootle and Nantwich, before winning his first points in the 250 ACU Star competition at Carlton Bank, Yorkshire in July, with 5th place behind Bryan Goss, Alan Clough, Freddie Mayes and Browning.

By November 1967, Allan, on a 360cc Comerfords Greeves, was mixing it with the best riders in the country. Here he chases Dave Bickers at the Player's Winternational meeting at West Stow Heath. (BH)

The people at Thundersley were keeping tabs on young Vic, who with an early production 360 added to his stable was steadily improving. At the Rob Walker Trophy meeting at Longleat, Wiltshire, in August, he was on top form, the only rider to beat him all day being local man Rob Taylor who took the 250 race on his Husqvarna. He also won the prestigious Kaj Bornebusch Trophy at Oxenbourne Farm in October that year and a week later showed well in the opening round of the Player's Winternational series at West Stow Heath, Suffolk, his best result coming in the up to 1000cc race, where he finished 3rd behind the factory BSAs of local man Banks, and Vic Eastwood.

Greeves support

Impressed with such form, Greeves stepped in with an offer to pay his expenses for the televised races. This was fortuitous, because Comerfords weren't very happy at the time, as with an increasingly busy racing schedule he needed to take more time off work. *That was in the winter of '67 when I had some real good rides and they offered me a full contract the following year. I think I signed for £50! But they gave me bikes and paid my travelling expenses and any prize money I won, I got to keep and that was it. Wadie and Browning were there before me and John Pease. He (Pease) was a very good rider, but he was a quiet lad and he seemed happy just working in the*

Allan is pictured at Wakes Colne again, this time racing in the 500 British Championship round in June 1968. (BH)

Allan had a good day in front of the BBC cameras at Clifton, Derbyshire in December 1968. Here he is pictured 'setting the pace' on the pre-production 380 Greeves Griffon. (BH)

factory. Though he would never have voiced his opinion at the time, that was never enough for Vic, who was quietly ambitious. *I wanted to do the GPs and that meant finishing in the top two in the British Championships, because then you were guaranteed a place as a Grand Prix rider.*

Enjoying some support from Greeves, Vic started the 1968 season in confident mood, picking up points in the 250 Grandstand Trophy series at Naish Hill in February and at the final round at Caerleon in March. However, as a factory Greeves' rider the 250 British Championship was still the main priority.

Showing promise

As a contender, he put together an encouraging campaign, picking up points in the opening round at Penrith, Cumberland in April and finishing as second highest points scorer behind fellow Scot Jimmy Aird in round three at Carlton Bank, Yorkshire, in July. After finishing 2nd in race one behind Chris Horsfield on a factory AJS, he was leading the second race when he picked up a puncture four laps from the end, gifting Aird his first British Championship win, though he struggled on to a well-earned 4th place at the flag.

His performance in Yorkshire moved him up to joint 4th in the title standings, though that would be the high point for the season. Allan then took a break from the pressures of the British Championship, visiting Dodington Park for the 250 British GP in August, where he was in inspired form, finishing 6th and 7th in the two legs, to end the day in 6th overall and net his first World Championship point. He was also the third best Briton, after Bickers, who finished 3rd and teammate Wade in 5th.

Back in the British Championship, he added points at Cuerden Park, Lancashire, with 5th in race one and 3rd next time out, though he was leap-frogged in the points standing by Greeves teammate Browning to lie 5th with one round to go.

Knee injury halts title ambitions

At the Halstead International meeting in late September, he rode an experimental, 390cc Griffon to an excellent 3rd place behind Adolf Weil (Maico) and

The Flying Scotsmen! Jimmy Aird on the factory AJS takes to the air alongside Allan on the works Greeves. (RD)

John Banks in the first of three legs, but could play no further part in the meeting after catching a knee on a course marking post in the second. The injury sidelined him for several weeks and he aggravated it in a fall in race one of the final round of the championship at Nantwich, Cheshire, in late October. As a result, he slipped to 6th place in the final championship standings, as Freddie Mayes, who added three points at Nantwich, pipped him by a single point.

In *1969 Allan* had a second string to his bow, as armed with the 380cc Griffon he was now also a serious contender for the 500 British Championship. He began the season brightly in the Grandstand Trophy series, winning the up to 1000 supporting race at Canada Heights in January and appearing to be on course for his first win in the 250 series at Caerleon, South Wales, in February, until he was caught and passed by a flying Malcolm Davis, on his AJS, on the last lap.

British Championship contender

With such form over the winter, Allan was seen as having an outside chance in the 250 British Championship and he got off to a great start in the opening round organised by the Leicester Query Club at Tilton. Allan took 3rd place in race one and 2nd in race two behind Bryan Goss, to finish the day second on points to Davis. Things looked even more promising following a steady ride at Nantwich in round two, which saw him emerge as joint leader in the championship with Alan Clough.

But from there on in, he didn't have the best of times. He took 3rd behind Clough and Bickers in race two at Hadleigh, Essex, after his chain had broken in the first race as he challenged Davis for 4th place. Then at the Cotswold Scramble, he added just two points from 5th place in race one and he was simply out of sorts at the final round at Tirley, where he rode hard all day only to finish both races in 7th place and out of the points. Fellow Greeves man Wade was crowned Champion and Vic finished 6th for the second year running.

Taking on the might of BSA

But if the 250 series had been disappointing his 500 campaign more than compensated for it. He got off on the right foot in the opening round at Brownrigg Fell, Cumberland, where he split the factory BSAs of John Banks and Keith Hickman in the first race and finished 3rd behind a rampant Banks and BSA Métisse mounted Horsfield, in race two. He went on to match this performance in rounds three and four, at Cureden Park and Beenham Park, and did well enough to finish the season second to runaway winner, John Banks, despite missing the final round at Builth Wells whilst promoting the Griffon in the USA, racing in the Inter-Am series.

His best performance in the championship had come at Beenham Park in mid-October. The previous day, he had finished runner-up to teammate Wade in three races at the ITV meeting at Brill, before eventually turning the tables in the TV All-Stars race. However, the Greeves teamsters had twice beaten the seemingly invincible Banks. This must have boosted Allan's confidence for the championship races, but he nearly didn't make it as the Greeves was misfiring on the start line. When he did get going he was well down

Enjoying a day out on the South Downs at Clayton near Brighton in April 1969, Allan drifts the 380 Greeves. (BH)

With the trademark 'Allan clan' tartan now added to his helmet, Vic led 500 British Champion John Banks for most of the second championship race at Beenham Park in October 1969. (BH)

and had to fight the whole race through to eventually finish 3rd behind Banks and Andy Roberton. But it was a different story in race two, when he took the start and led Banks for 21 of the 24 laps, before the BSA man overhauled the tiring Scot.

Gaining experience overseas

Allan also gained some valuable International experience in 1969. In June he took in the 250 French and British GPs, showing his potential, but being let down by the unreliable Greeves. After exiting the first leg in France with ignition trouble, he bounced back with an impressive 4th in race two behind Joel Robert, Sylvain Geboers and Heikki Mikkola. Then at Dodington Park, he had the chance to show British fans his GP credentials. However, he was plagued by problems when the Greeves' engine seized up in both races. In race two, he had the fans on their toes, as he was actually leading Geboers when the Greeves nipped up for a second time as he dived into a fast corner.

However, in August he was making headlines when he took victory in an international meeting at Remelard in northern France: '*ALLAN BEATS WORLD STARS IN FRANCE*' reported *MCN*. The stars included a Swedish quartet of Sten Lundin, Gunnar Nilsson, Jan Johansson and Arne Kring, but Allan took the first leg ahead of teammate Browning and Lundin; finished 2nd behind Nilsson in the next, after edging out Lundin; and took a comfortable 4th in the third leg won by Browning, who finished as runner-up overall.

The American experience was also one that Vic enjoyed. He rode consistently well, scoring several 2nd places, before finishing the series with 4th overall at Saddleback Park, California, behind the dominant Swedes, Kring, Aberg and Jonsson, and taking 6th place in the series. Although not on a par with the Swedes, he edged out Dave Bickers and finished ahead of Belgian superstars Roger DeCoster and Joel Robert.

1970 would turn out to be Allan's last season on Greeves, but more importantly it marked his coming

Out Front! At the 1969 250 British GP at Dodington Park, the Greeves let Allan down, but not before he'd forced his way into the lead in the second leg. (BH)

of age as a rider of real pedigree, not just in the UK, but also on the race-tracks of Europe, where he would contest the 500 GPs.

TV star is front page news

But as always, the season kicked off with the 'more mundane' TV races, where Vic was in great form. He had his picture on the cover of MCN of 14th January, after winning the opening round of the ITV World of Sport series at Hawkstone Park, though an anonymous, but clearly biased, journalist reported that: *the chubby Scot never won a race – but his two second places were enough to give him a four-point lead in the series over BSA's John Banks, who won a total of three races.* Banks and Allan fought a hard campaign that would only be resolved at the final round at Morestead Down, near Winchester at the beginning of April.

He was also in sparkling form in the Grandstand Trophy series, dominating the racing at Leighton near Frome, on Saturday 14th March, with wins in both the 250 and 750 classes. In the 250s he beat points leader Goss and Davis, whilst in the 750s he headed home the BSAs of Nicoll, who clinched the title, and Banks. With his confidence boosted, he then caught a ferry bound for Holland and the following day's St. Anthonis classic.

Dutch delight

The consistency Allan was now showing helped him to a famous victory in Holland, where he surprised many of the sports established stars in spite of only getting in four laps of practice. In the two-leg motocross event, he finished 2nd to Swede Bengt Aberg in the opener, but beat established sand masters, Pierre Karsmakers and Jef Teuwissen. Then in race two, he finished 4th behind Jaak Van Velthoven, De Coster and Gerrit Wolsink to take the overall result from Van Velthoven and De Coster.

Busy holiday period

Two weeks after his stunning success in Holland, Vic, along with many of his contemporaries, embarked on a three-day motocross fest over the Easter period. First up was a trip to Hampshire, for the Hants Grand International at Matcham's Park, Ringwood, on Good Friday, where he furthered his reputation

Vic Allan, resplendent in tweed and tartan, is pictured sharing a joke with Derry Preston Cobb (in chair) and Bill Brooker at the Greeves factory. (Photo supplied by Bill Brooker)

in the world of international motocross, performing heroically to take 3rd overall behind the Belgians Geboers and Teuwissen.

In the first leg he finished 4th, on the back wheel of Teuwissen, as Aberg beat Geboers to take first blood. In race two, GP regulars Geboers, Banks and Aberg finished in that order, as Allan slipped to 4th place in the closing stages. A dramatic final race saw De Coster lead from start to finish, whilst Aberg withdrew mid-race, leading the partisan ten thousand strong crowd to believe that Allan, who was lying second, could actually win it. However, Geboers who was flying through the field after being left on the line, denied the plucky Scot his chance, when he rode into 4th place, to take the trophy for the second time in three years and demote Allan to 3rd overall.

The following day, the Grandstand series reached its conclusion at Dodington Park, where Vic experienced a day to forget, being unplaced in both the 250 and 750 races. As a result he was demoted to 4th overall in the 250s but hung on to 3rd in the larger capacity behind BSA teamsters Nicoll and Banks.

Then on Easter Sunday he drove up to Cambridgeshire for the opening round of the 500 British Championship at Elsworth. Although Allan would go on to finish as runner-up in the championship he had a disappointing day at Elsworth, his best result being 7th place in race one, which wasn't good enough to secure him any points.

Bike problems prove costly

In early April the outcome of the ITV World of Sport series was decided at Winchester in what was to prove to be an anti-climatic meeting. Things started very badly for the Scotsman and only got worse! *I was going round in practice when all of a sudden a huge rock came up and smacked me right in the mouth. My lip split open and I had to go to hospital to have it stitched up and didn't know if I'd get back in time. Anyway, I got a good start and was second and after about three laps I was away from Banksy and I was following Badger and I knew I'd be alright if I just stayed there and then the bike just stopped dead. I couldn't believe it! I was heartbroken as I was about to win my first major trophy. It was just a wire that attached to the coil that had popped off and after that they always taped them on. Greeves were very good though and paid me the bonus as if I'd won it.*

However, he bounced back from the disappointment to enjoy his most successful season yet. Again the 500 British Championship was his main objective and had the Greeves shown more reliability, he might well have pushed Bryan Goss in the title hunt. As it was he found it very difficult to finish both races, but took a 2nd place at Wakes Colne, 3rd at Nympsfield and another 3rd at Tirley. However, the Greeves held together in the final round at Builth Wells, where he twice finished runner-up to ex-teammate Bryan Wade, who had switched to Husqvarna.

Running with the best

It was a similar story in the 500 GPs, though sadly for Allan, at that time, unlike the British Championships, riders still had to finish two legs to pick up championship points. In the curtain raiser in Switzerland in April, he led the world in the opening race, but two falls eventually relegated him to 12th at the flag. Then two weeks later in Austria he took a confidence building 8th overall after finishing an impressive 4th in race two behind Paul Friedrichs, Bengt Aberg and Arne Kring.

A barren spell followed, but the long trip to Czechoslovakia in mid-June paid dividends; here he was rewarded with 6th overall after finishing 8th in race one and 7th in race two. He also got an overall finish in East Germany in late July, but saved his best for the last round in Luxembourg, where he managed 5th overall, to finish the season as the best British rider, in 12th overall with a total of 18 points.

This was a pretty good performance from the 25 year-old making his debut in the tough 12 round series that was packed into five months and I put it to Vic that had all his finishes counted he might have done better still. *Yeah, but having said that I still feel it's the way it should be. You've got to prove something and you've got to make your bike last, it was like that. But it made a big difference to me that year, I had some cracking rides, but the bike always broke so I never got the overalls to get in the points.*

Outstanding in Motocross des Nations

In September he represented Britain in the MDN at Maggiora, Italy, where he turned in a sensational performance to finish as the second best individual rider. After riding to a strong 6th place in the first leg, the bike held together for once and he finished 2nd to Czech star Jiri Stodulka in the second, though

Making an impression on the factory BSA, Allan leads fellow BSA new boy, Andy Roberton, on his way to victory in the 1971 Battle of Newbury Scramble. (CB)

A week after his success at Newbury, Allan is pictured on the BSA at the opening round of the 1971 500 British Championship at Hawkstone Park in March. (RD)

Allan scored a memorable double win at the final round of the 1972 250 British Championship at Beenham Park in October to overhaul Bryan Wade for second place overall in the series. Here he puts Champion-to-be, Andy Roberton, under pressure. (CB)

1971

Joy and pain

In 1971 Allan was contracted to BSA to join Messrs Banks, Nicoll and Hickman on the GP team and it was a move that did wonders for his confidence. He had always respected and admired Jeff Smith and it would seem that the respect was mutual. *Jeff always gave me good write-ups in his columns, saying that I was a young rider who was very strong and one to watch out for in the GPs, which was a real boost for me.*

Allan took to the BSA very quickly, winning a race on his debut at the Jeff Smith Trophy meeting in the Isle of Man just six days after signing to the Small Heath factory. But it was at the Battle of Newbury in March

unfortunately, teammates Nicoll, Hickman, Roberton and Goss couldn't match his efforts and the British team slumped to a lowly 4th place finish.

that he really made his mark, winning overall from teammates Smith, Banks and Hickman and showing such promise that many felt he could challenge for the British Championship.

At the opening round at Hawkstone Park the following weekend, he finished a fine 3rd in race one, behind Banks, who had fully recovered from his knee injury of the previous season, and Wade. Then in race two he held second place for over half race distance, until the battery on the BSA died.

Allan took another big win at Elsworth in April, when he took the Cambridge GN race ahead of Hickman and Banks. But sadly, for the public at least, the anticipated Banks-Allan confrontation never really came to fruition, as the Scotsman's season came to an abrupt and premature end at the Italian GP in April, when he crashed heavily on the hard packed circuit and broke his right thigh.

Ray Daniel catches Allan in action on the 400 Bultaco with forward action kick-start.

1972

Back to Comerfords

Vic endured a long, difficult recuperation, though he drew encouragement from his good friend Vic Eastwood, who had suffered a similar lay-off previously. The 1972 season saw Allan come back in style. He returned to the fold at Comerfords, who by that time were the Bultaco importers and therefore Allan was pitched straight back into the 250 British Championship, though neither party had especially high hopes for the season.

The comeback began in earnest at round two of the championship at the Cambridge GN, where he twice finished runner-up to Champion Wade in muddy conditions. Then on the Spring Bank Holiday Monday at Hadleigh, Essex, in late May, Allan moved up to second in the title race with 3rd and 2nd places leaving him 10 points adrift of Roberton, but two ahead of Wade.

Allan scoops the jackpot at Beenham

In the later rounds, Vic had mixed fortunes. He took 4th place in race one at the Rob Walker Trophy at Frome in August, following a race-long battle with championship leader Roberton, but was out of luck in the second race, going out with a puncture at mid-distance whilst lying 3rd behind Wade and Rob Taylor. But he was on top form come the final round at Beenham Park in October, scoring a memorable double to pip Wade for the runner-up spot in the championship behind Roberton.

Allan also rode a few of the 500 British Championship rounds and at Tilton, he had a run out on an ex-works 500 BSA, finishing 4th in race two and chasing reigning 500 Champion, John Banks, home in the Tilton Chase. Then at the Cotswold Scramble at Nympsfield in July, he switched to a 400 Husqvarna, once again finishing 4th, though he was unplaced in race two when he slid off to avoid hitting a prone John Banks and lost his front brake in the resulting melée.

Come the season's close and he hit fine form in the winter ITV meetings at Cadwell Park, Lincolnshire, where, armed with a new 400 Bultaco, he rode consistently well. He took a memorable win in the Castrol Trophy race there in mid-November, with a narrow win over Bryan Goss, who he hounded for the full race distance, and John Banks.

Another break in Italy

After such a solid comeback, 1973 held great promise for the Scotsman, but a freak accident whilst practicing at the Italian GP left him with a broken ankle and threatened to wreck his season. *I didn't even fall off the bike, I just caught my foot on a rock and I twisted it and that was that.*

It was a huge blow for Allan, coming so soon after the broken leg, and Peter Howdle reflecting on Allan's 250 GP season the following season noted: *'Italy, where previous visits yielded a broken leg and broken ankle, was a dead loss for Vic. Mercifully, perhaps, his car broke down in France and he never got there.'*

Back with an ambitious goal

As a result of the injury, when the 250 British Championship got underway at Penrith, Cumberland in late April, Vic was still absent. But when he did eventually take to the line in the championship, he went there with a definite goal in mind. *I wanted to get back my status as a top rider in Britain. The GPs were not a priority for me, which was wrong really; my only priority was to be 250 British Champion.*

Allan opened his account with a brace of 3rd place finishes in round two at the Maybug Scramble at Farleigh Castle, where fellow Bultaco rider Malcolm Davis staked his claim on the title with a fine double win. A thrilling meeting at Tilton in June saw Davis extend his lead over Roberton, though Allan with 2nd and 3rd place finishes gained a point on the Welshman.

Intense rivalry

Although they both rode for Bultaco, Vic Allan and Malcolm Davis were never especially close. *He (Davis) was always the opposition and I was resentful that he was able to get stuff that I couldn't. I felt that with what I'd done I deserved more backing from Bultaco. He was their status rider and he had factory support. When you're on the same make of bike, the last thing you want is to get beat by your teammate, because it proves you're not as good as him.*

Allan's best showing in the championship came at the Cleveland GN, held on a new course at Silton near Thirsk, in July, where he scored a stunning double win over Roberton, before adding the GN race to cap a great day out. He was in a class of his own on the fast moorland track, leading both championship races from start to finish. When *MCN*'s Norrie Whyte caught up with him after the racing Vic told him: *'I've never had it that easy for years. I couldn't understand where the rest were.'*

Finishing on a high

The final round came at West Stow Heath, near Bury St. Edmunds in late July, where he rode conservatively in the first race to help Bultaco teammate Malcolm Davis in his effort to clinch his third British title. But in the second race Roberton needed nothing less than a win. So with his mother, down from Scotland looking on, Vic rode away from the field to win by the proverbial 'country mile'. *I was winning everything at the start of the year and with the speed I had at the end of the season I know that if I hadn't broken my ankle I probably would have been Champion in 1973.*

That year Bultaco also had Allan and Davis contest the inaugural 125 British Championship. Allan had a decent day's racing in the double-header 125 and 500 championship rounds held at Hawkstone Park, in March, with a 3rd place in race two of the 500s and 6th and 3rd in the 125 races, as Bryan Wade took maximum points with two faultless rides. At Hadleigh near Southend in late May he twice finished runner-up to Wade, who had really taken to racing the 125 and was running away with the championship. In contrast, Allan, who weighed in at 12 stone, was never truly comfortable on the 125 and finished a distant third in the final standings behind teammate Davis and Champion Wade.

Vic rounded off the season in style, winning Britain's oldest scramble, the Southern Scott, at Tweseldown in November. After he and Vic Eastwood had taken a win and a 2nd place apiece, the overall result was decided on the second race result which Allan had won. He also had some inspired race wins in the ITV World Of Sport meetings at Lydden, Kent and was good enough to beat newly crowned 500 British Champion John Banks on no less than four occasions, racing his 250 Bultaco against Banks' 500 Cheney BSA.

Vic Allan

The Two Vics, Allan and Eastwood, in close company at Tweseldown in November 1973. Allan holds Eastwood in the highest regard, the Kentishman having shown him a lot of moral support when he broke his leg in 1971. (CB)

The Year of the Scotsman

This kind of form gave Allan renewed self-confidence as he started the 1974 season, and he got a further lift when he won a muddy Battle of Newbury in March, repeating his success of three years earlier on the factory BSA. After finishing 2nd to Maico's Eastwood in the first leg, he won the remaining races to beat Andy Roberton and Stuart Nunn for the overall win.

The first British Championship action of the year came at round one of the 250 series at Hatherton Hall, Cheshire, where Vic had to settle for eight points from a second race win, after the factory Bultaco had uncharacteristically seized up in race one. His great rival, Malcolm Davis, stole a march in the title hunt with a win and a 2nd to put him six points clear of the Scot.

Plenty in his Easter basket

Next up was a double bill weekend, as the 500 British Championship kicked-off at the Cambridge GN at Elsworth on Easter Sunday, followed by round two of the 250 series the following day, some 250 miles away in Penrith, and for Allan it was a dream weekend as he took three of the four championship races, thereby setting the tone for the season.

At Elsworth, a trio of Bultaco riders, Allan, Davis and New Zealander, Ivan Miller, dominated the racing with Andy Roberton the only rider to get amongst them. Roberton may have run Allan closer in the first race, had he not stalled the big Husky, but the second race was a Bultaco benefit, with Davis winning ahead of Allan, who had suffered a poor start and had to fight his way back through the field, whilst Miller took third.

The following day at Brownrigg Fell, Allan had John Banks' share of the luck, as the East Anglian, on the unfashionable Ossa, presented his credentials as a surprise, but serious, challenger for the 250 title. In the first race, following a good start, Banks moved up to challenge Allan, but just as he seemed poised to snatch the lead, he lost a footrest and had to retire, leaving Allan to ride on unchallenged to the flag. Race two was a different story, with Banks 'aceing' the start and Allan down in seventh. However, Allan moved up rapidly and closed in on Banks, who after holding a 25 second lead had lost ground when his exhaust was damaged on a rock. Allan eventually passed the four-time British Champion as he struggled up the hill on the last lap.

After such an eventful weekend Allan, for the first time, allowed himself to consider the possibility of doing the 250-500 double, something even Dave Bickers had failed to achieve.

Glastonbury eye-opener

To make April 1974 an even more memorable month for Allan, he romped to another double in the 500 British Championship at Glastonbury. Allan chased Rob Taylor and his very rapid Maico for most of the first race, before Taylor was hampered by loosening handlebars. Allan took the win from fellow Scot Aird, on a 500 CCM and Miller. The second race saw a similar pattern with Taylor leading again, before being afflicted with the same technical problem. Meanwhile Banks was up front on the CCM and Allan took nine laps to hit the front, though once there he eased away from the Champion, to claim his second win of the day. And what of the hapless Taylor? Well after riding out of the second championship race he came out to win the Wessex Senior race ahead of Aird and Davis.

Allan recalls the Glastonbury meeting as being a watershed in his season. *I remember as we came off the start line John (Banks) on the CCM was away, but once I'd caught him I was so full of confidence that I passed him where you would never have dreamt of passing him, motoring round the outside of him on a fast right hander. When I did that and had won the race, I said to myself, "I'm going to win this championship." It just gave me so much confidence 'cause he was still the man to beat.*

In control

May found Allan at Pickwick Lodge Farm, Wiltshire, the new home of the Maybug Scramble, for round three of the 250 British Championship and his amazing run of form continued as he scored another maximum. In both races he came from behind in a calm, assured fashion, reminiscent of Jeff Smith at his best, biding his time before seizing control and taking care of business. After three rounds he held a comfortable 12 point lead over his closest challenger, reigning Champion Davis, with fellow Bultaco man Miller holding on to third.

It had to happen somewhere though and at Tilton, Leicestershire in June, the winning streak came to an end, as Eastwood and Banks did the winning in the 500 series, though Allan, with 3rd in the first race behind Eastwood and Roberton and 2nd in race two actually extended his lead in the championship, as teammate Davis had a poor day and failed to add to his points tally. Roberton was now Allan's closest challenger, though he only had 20 points to Allan's 40.

Luck deserts him in the GP

With his confidence sky-high, Allan shifted his attention to the 250 GP, being held for the first time at Chalton, Hampshire in June. A tough track littered with flints drew much criticism and led to a high drop-out rate due to punctures. But in an exciting opening leg, the British Bultaco duo of Davis and Allan thrilled the 15,000 strong crowd, as they chased Kawasaki factory runner Torlisef Hansen. But Davis' luck ran out when his rear shocks seized up mid-race and he faded to finish 7th. Belgian Harry Everts then took up the lead shadowed by Allan, who seemed poised for a win until he picked up a puncture, though he battled on to eventually finish 5th. Allan experienced further disappointment in race two when his throttle cable jammed whilst he was well placed again.

250 Champion

Vic took the first half of the historical double, when he wrapped up the 250 title at the penultimate round at Nympsfield at the end of June. Reigning Champion Davis, racing just a few miles from his home in Gloucester, took the challenge to Allan, leading the first race until the rear subframe of his Bultaco broke, effectively handing the title to his Scottish teammate and rival. In the second race Allan was closing down Miller and Roberton, when his chain tensioner caught on the ground in a corner fetching his chain off. However, with Davis having to fight back from an early tumble and only finishing 3rd the title was guaranteed for Allan.

With the pressure off, Allan rode to two more brilliant wins at the Cleveland GN, at Hunters Hill Farm, Nether Silton, later that month. In the first race Miller, who was enjoying a 'purple patch', led the first race until the last five laps when a lapse in concentration allowed Davis and Allan through, with the Scot confident enough to wait until the last lap before slipping past his rival for the win. In the second race, Allan seized

The new Champion leads the old, as Allan heads Malcolm Davis at the penultimate round of the 1974 250 British Championship at Nympsfield, to take the first part of his historic double. (CB)

control from the start and was never headed, riding on to finish comfortably ahead of Roberton, who put up the only resistance to the Bultaco onslaught.

Double Champion

Then in August, after what must have seemed an eternity, Allan took his place in the history books after clinching the 500 British Championship at the penultimate round at the Lancashire GN. Vic Eastwood did the winning out on the track, with a fine double, whilst the 'man of the hour' scored a brace of 2nd places, which netted him the title. The meeting was also notable for the performance of 17 year-old Graham Noyce from Eastleigh, Hampshire, who led race one before trapping his right foot under the footrest. Showing all the determination and sheer guts that would come to be hallmarks of his future career, Noyce rode on in considerable pain to register 6th place and his first ever 500 British Championship point. But the day belonged to Allan, who celebrated in style with a glass of champagne and a huge Cuban cigar!

A week later the championship was wound up at Tirley, where Allan had a quiet day by his standards, finishing 5th in the opening race, as local hero Davis, edged him out of fourth on the final lap and only managing 3rd next time out, as John Banks took his turn to record a double. Allan eventually finished a massive 32 points clear of Eastwood, Banks and Roberton, who finished in a three-way tie on 26 points.

A long time coming

Vic feels that the British Championship wins were something that were due to him. *I went a long time before I won and I began to wonder if I'd ever win it. Up till then it felt like I'd done all the hard work. Looking back on all that had happened to me, the win at St. Anthonis on the Greeves, doing*

Cecil Bailey captures the double British Champion at the final round of the 500 British Championship at Tirley in August.

the GPs on the 380, getting the works BSA ride and then battling back from the injuries, that was some apprenticeship!

Allan was head and shoulders above the others in 1974 and whilst few would dispute that he deserved his victories, it could be argued that they came at a time when the sport in Britain had reached a new low. Following the European and World titles that Bickers and Smith had won, John Banks had come very close to being World Champion in 1968 and '69, but since then there had been no serious attempts at a world title mounted by British riders. Relative 'veterans' Banks and Eastwood, whilst still competitive in the UK, were no longer the riders they had been and by that time Malcolm Davis and Bryan Wade had already reached the peak of their careers. That left Allan, Andy Roberton and younger riders such as Stuart Nunn, Vaughan Semmens, Roger Harvey and Rob Hooper who were coming through the ranks at that time, to fly the flag.

However, Vic firmly believes that Britain was still producing enough talent. *Though we weren't winning that didn't mean we weren't world class riders. I always looked on myself, be it rightly or wrongly, as being world class. To me it was a transition period from being full factory riders to riding for importers whose emphasis was on winning in Britain. In '75 when we changed the championship, all the top riders were there and although we weren't winning GPs and producing world champions, we beat all the top 10 riders in the world at some stage of the season.*

New British Champion

Having bagged the 250/500 double at the last possible attempt in 1974, Allan added his name to the history books the following year when he won the inaugural single class British Championship, though in contrast to the previous year when he dominated the racing, it was Vic's consistency over the course of the six-round championship with its 40 minutes

1975/6

In the new look British Championship in 1975, Allan rode consistently well all season. Here he is pictured at the opening round at Matchams Park in March, where he won the first race on his 250 Bultaco. (CB)

plus two laps race format that won him the title. He hit the front after finishing 2nd overall to teenaged sensation, Graham Noyce, at the Maybug Scramble in mid-May and tenaciously defended his lead in the face of stiff challenges from Vic Eastwood and Noyce, eventually clinching the title in the very last race of the championship at West Stow Heath, in late September.

When the dust had settled over the sandy Suffolk circuit, Allan was the Champion, two points clear of his great friend and rival Eastwood, whilst Noyce, who finished 3rd, would have to wait a little longer before he would experience British Championship glory, having crashed out in the final race breaking a collarbone in the process.

Back on a four-stroke

In 1976 Alan Clews persuaded the 30 year-old to make the switch to CCM, where he joined Eastwood and Banks. However, although he turned in some strong performances over the season and was the only rider to actually beat Noyce in a British Championship round all season, at Bootle in Cumbria in mid April, he was no match for the teenager, who ran away with the title. Indeed he was having more than his share of teenage problems, as he only wrested the runner-up spot away from Neil Hudson at the final round at Chalton, Hampshire in October.

However, he put all his experience to good use in a GP campaign which saw him match his 1970 performance, as he finished the season 12th overall. The highlights were a storming 3rd place in race two at the British GP at Dodington Park in July and a podium place for 3rd overall at the final round at Ettelbruck, Luxembourg in August.

Disappointing season on Husqvarna

In 1977 Allan joined Husqvarna racing for UK importer Brian Leask, but despite a promising start to his championship campaign that saw him lying 2nd overall to Noyce after the opening two rounds, sadly

1977-80

the Husky's reliability was found wanting and he would fade away to eventually finish the season in 8th place, which was a huge disappointment for the Scot.

As a result, he returned to Comerfords in 1978 to race Bultacos and he was soon at home again on the Spanish bike, taking 3rd overall in the opening round of the British Championship and improving to runner-up spot at Hawkstone Park, where he twice finished 2nd to the now dominant Noyce. Though not a vintage year by his standards, the 33 year-old performed well enough to finish a creditable 4th in the championship, behind Noyce, Hudson and Roberton .

1979 would prove to be his last season on a Bultaco, as sponsors, Comerfords, were keen to promote the Austrian KTM machines they were then importing. Vic had an up and down season, opening well at the Patchquick Trophy scramble at Higher Rocombe near Torquay, in March, where he raced the Spanish bike to 5th in race one and improved to 4th next time out. 4th place proved to be his best finish in the championship that season, a position he matched in the final race of the series at Cuerden Park, Lancashire in late September, by which time he was racing the KTM.

As he entered his third decade of racing in 1980, Vic was finding it difficult to remain competitive at championship level, despite picking up points on the KTM. Highlights of his championship season were 5th overall in round four at Pickwick Lodge Farm, Wiltshire, in May, a 4th place in race one at Howe Hills, Northallerton, behind Roberton, Paul Hunt and Dave Watson and 4th overall at Cureden Park in July, to finish the season in 11th place.

British Champion again!

The 1980 season pretty much marked the end of Allan's professional motocross days, as his career took a new path when he accepted a job in social services working with young offenders. However, he never lost his love for racing motorcycles and he soon turned his hand to classic road racing. Then in 1988 he was

Rolling Thunder! Allan raced the Bolton-built CCM in 1976, finishing second in the British Championship and enjoying some success in the GPs. Here Nick Haskell catches him in fine style at the Luxembourg GP.

Back on a Bultaco in 1978, and Allan, centre, is in the thick of it at the start of a British Championship race at Nantwich in June. Bryan Wade (8), John Banks (6), Rob Hooper (12), Neil Hudson (3) and Graham Noyce (1) provide the company! (RD)

persuaded to come out of retirement to compete in the inaugural British Four-Stroke Championship racing a KTM provided by an old friend, Peter Pearce. Vic pitted his vast experience against the youthful exuberance of his adversaries, coming out on top to be crowned British Champion once more at 43 years old.

Vic Allan MBE

In 2004, in recognition of his 23 years working with under privileged youngsters in Camden, North London, he was awarded an MBE. Today he is still heavily involved with off-road riding, providing training for youngsters and adults alike, in the business that he runs with his wife Ann, in Kingston upon Thames. Vic still enjoys a canter on a motocrosser, occasionally competing on the Classic scene racing a potent Cheney BSA and when I last spoke to him he was planning a bike riding trip 'down under' in the Antipodes.

Vic was a great Champion, who has dedicated his life to motocross and has served as a wonderful example to many young people, showing them how it is possible to win in the face of adversity. He followed a long, rocky road in his career, but today he can look back on his trail blazing days with pride, knowing that his grit, determination and belief carried him to a unique place in the history of British motocross.

Pictured in his last full season in the British Championship in 1980, Allan on a Comerfords KTM battles with CCM stalwart Bob Wright at Howe Hills, Northallerton in July. (RD)

The End of an Era

For me the introduction of the revamped British Championship in 1975 marked the end of an era in British motocross. However, that does not mean that I look back on it negatively, far from it. The new championship ushered in 45 minute races in keeping with the GPs and served as a test bed for our future World Champions, Graham Noyce, Neil Hudson and Dave Thorpe, not to mention a host of top GP runners who emerged in the late '70s and '80s.

Things changed. The bikes changed, with long travel suspension (culminating with mono shock rear ends), water cooling and disc brakes all becoming the norm. Attitudes changed, as top riders became part of a huge team with amazing resources. They began to arrive at meetings in their motorhomes, whilst their bikes were transported there in big 'team' trucks; helpers were on hand to prepare bikes and equipment, leaving riders free to focus on the racing (remember Bryan Wade back in the late '60s!). And tracks changed, as with the technical advances, especially to suspension, circuits featured more corners and jumps linked by short straights, which afforded more vantage points for spectators and cameramen. And finally, the demographics changed. US riders, with their thoroughly professional approach, 'raised the bar', dominating the sport as the century drew to a close and forcing those in Europe to re-evaluate the way they did things in order to be competitive.

But having said all of that, things had been constantly changing since that first Southern Scott Scramble in 1924, with advances such as OHV engines, off-road specific tyres, telescopic front forks and swinging arm rear suspensions. By its nature the sport will continue to evolve, as we've seen in the last 10 years, as the once dominant two-strokes have disappeared to be replaced by a new generation of lightweight four-strokes hastened by the introduction of stringent exhaust emission laws in California.

Sadly, despite so many advances, the sport today doesn't seem to have the same draw that it did back in the 1950s and '60s, when crowds ran into tens of thousands for scrambles meetings. Today it's the real die-hards who turn up to watch motocross as even the GPs struggle to match the gate a humble national meeting would have attracted back then. However an afternoon tuned to Eurosport or Sky Sports will go a long way to explaining this, as there are now so many mainstream and radical sports being practised that sports fans are spoilt for choice. We should also remember that satellite and cable TV transmit motocross to audiences in their millions, worldwide.

The facts are simple; things were different back then. For me, the '60s and '70s were a real 'Golden Era' in the sport, but that can simply be explained by the fact that I identify it with my youth and a time when life was much simpler. I loved standing in the middle of a muddy field and being thrilled by the whole spectacle of the racing, eating hamburgers and simply enjoying being in the company of my dad, my family or my friends. Mind you, the endless queuing to get out of the car park at the day's close is something I don't get nostalgic for!

Things move on, things change. For me the scene today is neither better, nor worse, it is simply different and for many young fans watching the sport today, this will undoubtedly be another 'Golden Era' in days to come. However, scrambling and motocross in the 1960s and '70s was, as Jeff Smith and Bryan Goss so aptly put it, 'Wonderful' and though it can never come again, I hope this book has helped to rekindle a few precious memories.

⚑ Principal circuits used for the British Championship rounds 1960-74

1. Brownrigg Fell, near Penrith, Cumberland (Now Cumbria). Home of the Cumberland Grand National
2. Carlton Bank, near Redcar, Yorkshire. Home of the Cleveland Grand National
3. Cuerden Park, near Preston, Lancashire. Home of the Lancashire Grand National
4. Hatherton Hall, Nantwich, Cheshire. Home of the Cheshire Grand National
5. Hawkstone Park, Shropshire. Home of the 500 British GP 1954 – 1965, the Midland Championship and Brian Stonebridge Trophy
6. Tilton on the Hill, Leicestershire. Home of the Tilton Moto Cross
7. Builth Wells, Powys. Home of the Kidston Grand National
8. Corse Hill, Tirley, near Gloucester. Home of the Gloucester Grand National and Tirley Championship
9. Shrubland Park, near Ipswich, Suffolk. Home of the Shrubland Grand National and 250 British GP 1960 and '61
10. Little Loveney Hall, Wakes Colne, near Halstead, Essex. Home of the Essex GN and 1967 250 British GP
11. Nympsfield, near Stroud, Gloucestershire. Home of the Cotswold Scramble
12. Hadleigh, near Southend, Essex. Home of the traditional Spring Bank Holiday Monday Scramble
13. Beenham Park, near Reading, Berkshire. Home of the Jackpot Scramble and 250 British GP 1958 and '59
14. Farleigh Castle, near Trowbridge, Wiltshire. Home of the Maybug Scramble until 1973 and 500 British GP 1966 – 1972
15. Higher Wick Farm, Glastonbury, Somerset. Home of the Wessex Scramble and 250 British GP 1962, 1963 and 1965
16. Leighton, near Frome, Somerset. Home of the Rob Walker Scramble
17. Matchams Park, Ringwood, Hampshire. Home of the Hants Grand National and latterly Hants Grand International

● Other circuits used

18. Belmont, near Durham. Home of the Belmont Grand National
19. Halton, near Morecombe, Lancashire. Home of the 1962 Lancashire Grand National
20. Nether Silton, near Thirsk, Yorkshire. Home of the Cleveland Grand National from 1972
21. Boltby, near Thirsk, Yorkshire Home of the North v South team race and the Thirsk International
22. Cadwell Park near Louth, Lincolnshire. Home of the Lincolnshire Grand National and the 1964 250 British GP
23. West Stow Heath near Bury St, Edmunds, Suffolk. Home of the St. Edmund's Grand National
24. Elsworth near Cambridge. Home of the Cambridge Grand National
25. Larkstone, near Ilmington, Warwickshire. Home of the Experts Grand National 1963–'65
26. Hintlesham Park, near Ipswich. Home of the Shrubland Trophy 1966 and 67
27. Stepaside, near Saundersfoot, Pembrokeshire. Home of the Pembrokeshire Grand National
28. Dodington Park, Old Sodbury, Gloucestershire. Home of the 250 British GP 1968–1972
29. Pickwick Lodge, Corsham, Wiltshire Home of the Maybug Scramble from 1974
30. Padworth Park, near Reading, Berkshire. Home of the Bargepole Scramble
31. North Radworthy, Exmoor, Devon
32. Chard, Somerset.